AA

ORDNANCE SURVEY
LEISURE GUIDE

LAKE DISTRICT

Produced jointly by the Publications Division of the
Automobile Association and the Ordnance Survey

Cover: Harrison Stickle by E.A. Bowness
Title page: the placid surface of Derwent Water with the reflected
silhouette of Friar's Crag
Opposite: Taylor Gill Force, high up Borrowdale below the slopes of
Great Gable
Introductory page: Lingmoor Tarn with Harrison Stickle in the
background

Editors: Richard Powell, Donna Wood

Art editor: Dave Austin

Editorial contributors: Harry Griffin (Traditional
Sports), Dr William Rollinson (Man in the Landscape),
Ronald Sands (Literary Lakeland), Andrew and Isabel
Wilson (A to Z Gazetteer), John Parker (Lakeland
Wildlife, Fell Walking and Walks in the Lake District)

Picture researcher: Wyn Voysey

Original photography: Sarah King

Printed and bound in Great Britain by Purnell and Sons
(Book Production) Ltd., Paulton, Bristol

Maps extracted from the Ordnance Survey's 1:63,360
Tourist Series, 1:25,000 Outdoor Leisure Series, and
1:250,000 Routemaster Series, with the permission of
Her Majesty's Stationery Office. Crown Copyright
reserved.

Additions to the maps by the Cartographic Unit of the
Automobile Association and the Ordnance Survey.

Produced by the Publications Division of the
Automobile Association.

Distributed in the United Kingdom by the Ordnance
Survey, Southampton, and the Publications Division of
the Automobile Association, Fanum House,
Basingstoke, Hampshire RG21 2EA.

ISBN 0 86145 192 9 (softback) AA ref 56863
ISBN 0 86145 226 7 (hardback) AA ref 58117

Published by the Automobile Association and the
Ordnance Survey.

LAKE DISTRICT

Contents

"Using this Book"

The entries in the Gazetteer have been carefully selected to reflect the interest and variety of the Lake District. For reasons of space, it has not been possible to include every community in the region. Certain towns, like Carlisle for example, which are not usually considered to be within the Lake District, have been included because of their outstanding importance to the cultural and social life of the area as a whole.

Each entry in the A to Z Gazetteer has the atlas page number on which the place can be found and its National Grid reference included under the heading. An explanation of how to use the National Grid is given on page 66. This system of reference is also given for each place name in the index.

Beneath many of the entries in the Gazetteer are listed AA recommended hotels, restaurants, garages, camping sites and self-catering accommodation in the immediate vicinity of the place described. Hotels, restaurants and camping sites are also given an AA classification.

HOTELS

1-star	Good hotels and inns generally of small scale and with acceptable facilities and furnishing.
2-star	Hotels offering a higher standard of accommodation, with some private bathrooms/shower; lavatories on all floors; wider choice of food.
3-star	Well-appointed hotels; a good proportion of bedrooms with private bathrooms/showers.
4-star	Exceptionally well-appointed hotels offering a high standard of comfort and service, the majority of bedrooms having private bathrooms/showers.
5-star	Luxury hotels offering the highest international standards.

Hotels often satisfy *some* of the requirements for higher classifications than that awarded.

Red-star	Red stars denote hotels which are considered to be of outstanding merit within their classification.
Country House Hotel	A hotel where a relaxed informal atmosphere prevails. Some of the facilities may differ from those at urban hotels of the same classification.

RESTAURANTS

1-fork	Modest but good restaurant.
2-fork	Restaurant offering a higher standard of comfort than above.
3-fork	Well-appointed restaurant.
4-fork	Exceptionally well-appointed restaurant.
5-fork	Luxury restaurant.
1-rosette	Hotel or restaurant where the cuisine is considered to be of a higher standard than is expected in an establishment within its classification.
2-rosette	Hotel or restaurant offering very much above average food irrespective of the classification.
3-rosette	Hotel or restaurant offering outstanding food, irrespective of classification.

CAMPING SITES

1-pennant	Site licence; 10% of pitches for touring units; site density not more than 30 per acre; 2 separate toilets for each sex per 30 pitches; good quality tapwater; efficient waste disposal; regular cleaning of ablutions block; fire precautions; well-drained ground.
2-pennant	All one-pennant facilities plus: 2 washbasins with hot and cold water for each sex per 30 pitches in separate washrooms; warden available at certain times of the day.
3-pennant	All two-pennant facilities plus: one shower or bath for each sex per 30 pitches, with hot and cold water; electric shaver points and mirrors; all-night lighting of toilet blocks; deep sinks for washing clothes; facilities for buying milk, bread and gas; warden in attendance by day, on call by night.
4-pennant	All three-pennant facilities plus: a higher degree of organisation than one–three-pennant sites; attention to landscaping; reception office; late-arrivals enclosure; first aid hut; shop; routes to essential facilities lit after dark; play area; bad weather shelter; hard standing for touring vans.
5-pennant	A comprehensive range of services and equipment; careful landscaping; automatic laundry; public telephone; indoor play facilities for children; extra facilities for recreation; warden in attendance 24 hours per day.

LAKE DISTRICT
Introduction

*The Lake District has spellbound the adventurous traveller
since the earliest days of tourism two hundred years ago.
Thousands of people escape to the freedom and beauty of the
dales and fells each year. Whatever the weather, at any
time of the year, the Lake District exerts a special fascination.
Whether you are in search of the solitude Wordsworth treasured,
or bustling market towns, this guide will provide the key.
It explores the history, traditions and wildlife of the
Lake District. It lists and describes the towns, villages
and hamlets. Walks and motor tours seek out the hidden
corners and the finest scenery.
Written entirely by people who live and work in the
Lake District, backed by the AA's research expertise and
the Ordnance Survey's mapping, this guide is equally
useful to the faithful who return to the Lakes year after year
and to the first-time visitor.*

Man in the Landscape

For many people, the fells of the Lake District represent the epitome of the 'natural' landscape – the eternal hills, the wild, cloud-catching mountain summits, the lonely, barren upland tarns, the brawling, racing, tumbling becks, the silent, sombre forests – a seemingly timeless, unchanging landscape, fundamentally the same today as it was 4–5,000 years ago. Yet nothing could be further from the truth, for the present landscape of the Lake District is essentially 'man-made', the product of the interaction of Man with his environment, and everywhere it is possible to see evidence of the way in which Man has moulded and modified his environment over the centuries rather as if an artist has used, re-used, and re-used again a single canvas – look carefully and it is often possible to detect the outlines of an earlier picture.

Without the presence of Man, the landscape would look entirely different from the one we know; mixed oak forest would colonise the lower fells and above that, to a height of about 2,000 ft, pine and birch woodland would blanket the upper fells so that only the highest mountain peaks projected above the forest cover. It is difficult to appreciate that familiar and much-loved summits such as Cat Bells, Wansfell Pike, and Helm Crag were once submerged in a sea of green forest. Similarly, without Man, the valleys of Great Langdale, Borrowdale, Wasdale Head and Newlands would be choked with sedges and alder swamp; indeed, it takes all the power of imagination to conjure up such a scene for this is not the landscape which is known and cherished by millions of people today. So when did the transformation begin? The answer, quite simply, is about 5,000 years ago when, for the first time, Man met the challenge of the environment and began to control it – almost imperceptibly at first, but with an inexorability which ultimately led to the present landscape.

Stone axe factories
Although Mesolithic family groups, the first nomadic hunting and collecting communities, had inhabited the coastal areas since about 5,500 BC, they made little impact on the environment for they were largely governed by it. However, the next groups to arrive in the area, Neolithic peoples, were far more ambitious; as well as developing the arts of crop-growing and the domestication of animals, they made a positive response to the ecological challenge of the forest by the mass production of sharp, polished, hafted stone axes which could effectively clear large areas for crops and animals. Moreover, the Neolithic Cumbrians were skilled field geologists; they were clearly aware that only certain types of fine-grained volcanic rocks would produce the sharpest axes. Therefore they actively sought these outcrops and the evidence of 'factory workings' has been found on the Langdale Pikes and the Scafells as well as on other fellsides. Here axes were roughly chipped out before being carried along forest tracks to the coast where they were finely sharpened and honed using the sharp quartz sand of the sea-shore. When they were hafted in a wooden handle Man possessed a tool with which he could shape his destiny, for in some respects the development of the polished stone axe marks one of the revolutions in human history as great as the Industrial Revolution of the 19th century and the Social Revolution of our own day.

But it was not merely the stone axe which began the process of modification of the landscape; the domestication of animals meant that sheep, pigs, goats and cattle ranged widely in the newly-created clearings, grubbing, nibbling and browsing any new green shoots and therefore reducing the rate of natural regeneration of the forest cover, a process which continued almost unhindered until the re-afforestation of the 18th, 19th and 20th centuries.

Stone circles
If the felling of the primeval forest was an early expression of Man's impact on his environment, then the building in the early Bronze Age of the huge stone circles is arguably more tangible. Demanding, as they did, a high degree of social cooperation, they also mark a significant change in Man's awareness of himself, for now for the first time he was building something which would outlast his own life-span. The arguments about their purpose continue to rage – religious centres, market places, prehistoric computers – perhaps we will never know, but these massive stone monuments seldom fail to exert a fascination for the visitor. The largest is Long Meg and her

Castlerigg, near Keswick, a prehistoric henge monument in a superb setting. The functions of this, and similar structures, may never be clearly understood

Hardknott Fort – built by the Romans to command the whole of Eskdale

Daughters near Salkeld, but the best known and most visited is at Castlerigg near Keswick.

Few Bronze Age settlement sites have so far been identified, though the characteristic burial cairns dot the landscape. From about 500 BC the technology of the Iron Age accelerated the process of forest clearance, and settlements penetrated many of the inner valleys of the central fells, and in particular concentrated on the limestones which surround the uplands. Here, the distinctive enclosing walls within which are animal pens and the foundations of circular huts, can be seen in such locations as Ewe Close, near Crosby Ravensworth, High Borrans, near Windermere, Aughertree, near Ireby, and in the Kentmere valley. But the Iron Age marks a more sinister landscape development – the construction of hill forts; the largest is on the summit of Carrock Fell (2,174ft) dominating Mungrisdale, but more spectacular are those on Castle Crag, Borrowdale, and Castle Crag, overlooking Haweswater. Whether or not such fortifications were constructed as a response to inter-tribal strife or the fear of Roman invasion is unknown.

The Romans

It has been said that the Lake District was almost at vanishing point on the scale of Romanisation and, indeed, the civilising effect of Rome was minimal, but the impact of military might on the landscape is very apparent. Arriving in the fells at the end of the first century AD, the Romans subjugated the troublesome native Brigantes by a method as ingenious as it was effective; from a fort at Watercrook near Kendal, they drove a road through the high fells over Wrynose and Hardknott passes, to the sea at Ravenglass, thereby neatly dividing and dominating the native heartland. Along this road, like beads on a string, cohort forts, housing 500 men, were established. At Waterhead, near Ambleside, the remains of the fort with its turrets, granary, HQ and commandant's house, can still be traced, but to savour to the full the power of Rome, a visit should be made to Hardknott Fort, perched eyrie-like above the Esk valley, commanding unsurpassed views of Eskdale and the Scafells. Here it requires but little imagination to reconstruct the stone-

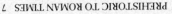

built granary and headquarters, the bath-house outside the walls and the wooden barrack blocks once inhabited by troops from Dalmatia, modern Yugoslavia. From Hardknott the military road ran along Eskdale to Ravenglass; sadly the fort there was largely destroyed by the railway in 1850, but the bath-house remains; known as Walls Castle, it is one of the most complete, upstanding Roman buildings in the north of England.

Probably the most spectacular of all the Roman roads in Lakeland is that which crosses the 2,000ft summit of High Street. Although intended only for foot soldiers, it probably connected the fort at Waterhead with the one at Brougham near Penrith and even today, suitably shod fell-walkers can literally follow in the steps of the Romans.

The Dark Ages

Roman rule in the Lake District seems to have ended in the late 4th century and from then until the 7th century the so-called Dark Ages are centuries of uncertainty, peopled by the *Cymry*, the Celtic descendants of the Brigantes, and by shadowy, legendary figures such as Urien, Vortigern, and Arthur. Although several Celtic river and mountain names still exist, the impact of the Celts on the landscape remains unclear. In the 7th century, however, people of Anglian farming stock moved from Northumbria into the Eden valley, the Cumbrian coastal plain and Furness and Cartmel, seeking the best and most fertile soils. Their settlements can be identified today by place-name elements such as *-ton*, *-ham*, and *-ington*, but in addition these Anglian farmers have left beautiful carved stone crosses; the finest in the north of England is at Bewcastle in northern Cumbria, but there are splendid examples at Irton, Dacre, Kendal, and Urswick.

The Norse settlers

If the Anglian settlers farmed the good quality lands surrounding the uplands, then the Viking peoples who followed them in the 9th and 10th centuries sought out an environment with which they and their ancestors were familiar – the fells and dales. Often synonymous with looting, rape, and pillage, the Vikings have had a bad press, mainly because their history was written by their enemies, but here in the Lake District the story is different. The Scandinavians who settled here were not the stereotyped horned-helmeted warriors of the sagas – they were, in fact, peaceful third or fourth generation Vikings who came not directly from the *viks* of Norway, but from Ireland and the Isle of Man. Nevertheless, they brought with them a characteristic settlement pattern of valley farms and summer pastures, or *saeters*, at the head of the valley or on the fellsides. That their ancestors came from western Norway rather than Denmark is revealed by place-name elements such as *-fell*, *-booth*, *-gill*, *-slack*, and *-beck* and the most common of all, *-thwaite*. The present map bristles with *-thwaites* which, significantly, means a clearing, usually in the forest, and the concentration is most marked within the uplands.

As well as place-names and, indeed, thousands of dialect words, the Scandinavians, like the Anglians, left carved stone crosses. Erected at a time when the Vikings were nominally Christian, many of the crosses bear a fusion of Christian and pagan symbols. Such crosses can be seen at Muncaster, Penrith, Kirkby Stephen, Brigham, but the finest of all is at Gosforth, near the coast,

St Bees – the intricate doorway of the Norman monastery church. This is the finest decoration of its kind in Cumbria. There is further Norman work inside the church

where a slender sandstone column tells the story of Ragnarok and the crucifixion.

Behind Fell Foot Farm in Little Langdale is a terraced mound bearing remarkable similarities to Tynwald Hill in the Isle of Man. Many authorities interpret this as a 'thingmount' or Norse parliament field. If they are correct, this is a unique monument to the Viking age in Lakeland.

The Normans

For most of England, 1066 meant the Norman conquest – but not for the Lake District, which remained under Scottish domination until 1092 when William II captured Carlisle and settled the region with his Norman followers. The Normans, of course, feared for their souls and consequently gave grants of land to the Church to ensure immortality; almost all the major Cumbrian monasteries were founded in the 12th century – Wetheral, Carlisle, Lanercost, St Bees, Furness, Holm Cultram – and although they were on the periphery of the Lake District, most owned land within the fells, many created granges or home farms, as well as clearing the waste and creating huge sheep-runs. None was more diligent in this process of land development than the great Cistercian abbey of Furness; already possessing much of the Furness peninsula, by the 13th century the abbey had acquired thousands of acres of fell land including all the area between Coniston Water and Windermere, part of Borrowdale (Fountains Abbey owned the other half), and upper Eskdale.

Scottish raids

But all was not sweetness and light; the 14th century was a period of fierce border warfare and, following the battle of Bannockburn, the Lake District soon felt the scourge of the Scots. Penrith, Appleby, and Carlisle were repeatedly besieged and destroyed, in 1316 Copeland and Furness were attacked, and in 1322 Robert Bruce again raided Furness, crossed the sands of Morecambe Bay and devastated Lancaster. The response was predictable; scores of stoutly-built pele towers were constructed as a defence against further raids. Several, such as Sizergh, Hutton and Muncaster became part of stately homes, while others such as Kentmere and Wraysholme became farm outbuildings; their presence in the landscape a constant reminder of border conflict. The dissolution of the monasteries – 'the Great Northern Tragedy' – undoubtedly had an effect on the landscape, yet sheep continued to be tended, the charcoal-burner still worked his pitsteads, and the woodland was depleted for fuel and for ships. Around Kendal, Hawkshead and Ambleside the woollen cloth industry flourished, while at the end of the 16th century, the Company of the Mines Royal, a Crown monopoly, began to open silver, lead and, later, copper mines.

The winds of change

In the late 17th and early 18th centuries the winds of change swept through Cumbria. This was the period, rather later than in other areas of England, when the old timber-framed farmhouses were demolished and built again in stone; although there are earlier examples, most of the dated lintel stones fall between 1640 and 1750, indicating the 'Great Rebuilding in Stone'.

From 1750 until about 1850 there occurred one of the last great major landscape changes – the enclosure of the open fells into a stone network of fields and intakes. During the Napoleonic Wars when the price of food was high, it paid the farmers to improve and reclaim the fellsides and gangs of itinerant craftsmen enmeshed the hills with a web of drystone walls.

The 18th century brought the turnpike roads and the early tourists in search of the mock perils of the 'picturesque'; the 19th century brought the railways and the nouveaux riches settlers to the shores of Windermere, able to travel to Manchester for a day's work in the Cotton Exchange but enjoy a late evening meal overlooking the placid surface of Windermere. In the 20th century the pressures on the landscape have increased a hundredfold; the need for great forestry estates, the demand for reservoirs to supply distant towns and cities with water, the expansion of great slate-quarries on the hillsides, the pressure of tourism which often destroys what it seeks to enjoy, the erosion of footpaths by sheer weight of numbers, the 'second home syndrome' – yet despite all that the Lake District remains a unique place, a landscape made by Man but no less beautiful for that. Long may it remain what Wordsworth envisaged:

. . . a sort of national property, in which every man has a right and an interest who has an eye to perceive and a heart to enjoy.

Above and right: Lakeland views. Both show the impact of man's hand on the landscape. Even mighty Scafell (above) has drystone walls marching across it. The majority of such walls were built in the 18th and 19th centuries, when the fells were being enclosed

Townend, Troutbeck – one of the best examples of a 17th-century stone-built farmhouse

Lakeland Wildlife

Seen from an aeroplane, the Lake District's complicated landscape is much fretted, pierced, buckled and scored, with a jagged jumble of crags and ridges, and a shining labyrinth of lakes and watercourses. It is as if stupendous forces had plucked and folded and crushed the land together to compress much into little. And so they did. In that great crushing of the earth millions of years ago there was unimaginable heat, rocks melted and burst, were slaked by the sea, smothered in dust storms and sculpted by deluge and ice. All these forces eventually created the Lake District landforms that we know today. There are three principal scenic types – in the north the angular landscape formed from shales of the ancient sedimentary Skiddaw Slates; in the centre the craggy heights of the Borrowdale Volcanic series; and in the south the softer tree-clad landscape of the Silurian Slates. Within these large themes are many intricate details, and each detail is inhabited by a complex tangle of wildlife.

The scourge of the axe

When Mesolithic man settled on the west coast of the Lake District some 6,000 years ago the forest stretched as far as the eye could see. High on some fells where soil has become exposed by erosion, it is still possible today to recover fragments of birch and pine root remaining from that ancient forest, for the tree cover reached the highest peaks. On the same fells it is possible to find one of the first causes of the forest's undoing, for at several places where a certain very hard rock occurs on the surface, you can walk on the chipping floors of stone-age man's axe factories. When polished and sharpened these prehistoric stone axes were very efficient tools.

For 4,000 years men hacked away at the forest cover, clearing even larger areas. Domestic animals like cattle and sheep prevented any natural regeneration by eating seedling trees. The result is a landscape largely cloaked in grass and short herbage. Is there any of the old forest left? Most naturalists would say not, though there is a possibility that the Keskadale woods in Newlands valley are a remnant of the primeval oak wood.

Lower down the fell sides a remarkable feature of the Lake District is the juniper scrubland. Juniper is our only native cypress. The berries were once valuable in medicine but are now mainly used for flavouring gin. Juniper charcoal was the best, and was much favoured by local mills making gunpowder. What is fascinating is the enormous variety of shapes the shrubs assume: some as flat as plates, some with tall spires, some twisted like bonsais. In similar situations, but on the crags, is often a profusion of bilberry, offering a rare feast of fruit if the birds don't get there first. Heather and ling favour the deeper soils of the Skiddaw Slate and Silurians.

Using the woodlands

It is the valley broadleaved woodlands of the southern Silurian soils, the northern Skiddaw Slates, and the perimeter limestones that are the richest habitats for wildlife. Through history these woodlands made an important contribution to the economy of the Lake District. For centuries they

were harvested and coppiced. An example of the prosperity which such woodlands could bring, and of the variety of uses to which they could be put, can be found in the records of Furness Abbey. Cutting rights were let here, and rights to feed swine on the acorns. Bark was sold for tanning. Charcoal was made, as were cartwheels, cups, dishes, and barrels.

Coppice wood was cut every 12–15 years in each wood. Its all-important use was to make charcoal, increasingly so as new sources of iron ore were found in the district, since charcoal was an essential ingredient of the smelting process until coal replaced it in the 19th century. The furnaces with their water-powered bellows were greedy and sometimes the woods were devastated. It is possible to find the flat platforms or 'pitsteads' where the wood was carefully stacked for the slow controlled burn which was necessary to produce the best charcoal. The commonest broadleaved trees are as they were always, sessile oak, birch, holly, alder, cherry, crabapple, rowan and wych elm. The conifers were Scots pine, juniper and yew. A lot of what is now seen has been planted in past centuries, and some of the best mixtures – often at their most colourful in autumn – were planted by new landowners who were not all the 'tasteless' philistines whom Wordsworth condemned.

The extent of the managed broadleaved woodlands has diminished in an age when woods, and traditional craftsmanship, have come increasingly to be regarded as disposable. Sometimes they have been replaced by alien regimented conifer plantations which produce a quick crop of straight timber. However, many of the remaining deciduous woodlands are now in caring ownership, including that of the National Trust and the National Park Authority. The Forestry Commission is now actively concerned and there are good hopes for their survival. These woods are one of the few remaining habitats of the red squirrel. Fortunately, the alien grey squirrels have never crossed the natural barriers of Morecambe Bay and the eastern moorlands to oust our less harmful and more handsome animal. The red's ideal habitat is pine wood with hazel undercover. They are extremely shy, but occasionally appear at winter bird tables.

Lakeland deer
The small roe deer inhabit nearly every wood. This, surely the most beautiful of our native animals, so delicately formed and graceful, has an uneasy existence. They are often road casualties. They are persecuted because of the damage they do to unfenced gardens. Their fawns are picked up under the mistaken impression that they have been 'abandoned', and without their mother's attention can soon die. Roe often move about in small family groups, while the largest of our mammals, the red deer, are herd animals. They have lived in the southern Lake District since long before human settlement. A stag here can stand about four feet six inches high with the antler spread another two feet high and three feet wide. The better-fed woodland stag is heavier than the stag adapted to the eastern fells. Red deer herds are sometimes seen on the woodland fringes where they emerge to graze. The nightly roaring of the challenging stags at the rut, and sometimes the clash of antlers as they fight, are the most exciting sounds of the woods.

A red deer stag with his harem of hinds. The stag barks to pronounce his superiority and to ward off rivals. The mating season lasts from mid September to October; for the rest of the year stags and hinds live apart

Masters of the air

The monarchs of the fell skies are undoubtedly the ravens. Sometimes their 'cronk' is the only sound to break the intense silence of the high places, and their acrobatics in spring, perhaps casting a twig away and then recatching it, are joys that can be shared. Claimants to the throne are golden eagles, which have returned to the Lake District after an absence of 200 years. Go purposely to see them and they will sit still for hours, merged into the background of a crag

Above and below left: a golden eagle, carrying prey, being mobbed by ravens. There are only a few pairs of golden eagles in the Lake District, but the honking call of the raven is commonly heard

Above: a buzzard. These handsome birds are common throughout the Lake District. They are most often seen gliding high in the sky on outstretched, motionless, wings

ledge. But it is pure delight to see them unexpectedly soaring in the air currents on the mountain edges. In recent years we have seen the return of the peregrine falcons. The Lake District is one of Europe's major breeding grounds of this most beautiful of all the hawks.

So well do high peaks, low fells and valleys blend and harmonise that it is very difficult to define clear ecological zones. Where for instance could you place the buzzard? Buzzards are common everywhere and are often mistaken for eagles. Like eagles they are masters of the air current, hardly moving their broad wings. Buzzards are equally at home among the fells or over the valley tree tops, and their plaintive cry is an essential part of the Lake District's character.

Purple saxifrage. This is one of several species of alpine plant that can be found in rocky places where grazing sheep cannot reach

Wild flowers in the wilderness

In moist places on the fells, on steep crags, and in deep shady ravines – anywhere the hungry sheep cannot reach – in such places it is possible to find examples of Lakeland's living botanical history. The isolated fragments of the ancient forests' flora survive here: primrose, foxglove, dog's mercury, bluebell, wood sorrel, anemone, stitchwort, lady fern and male fern and polypody. Trees grow where they can, sometimes seemingly from the rock itself. There are plants in the Lake District whose story is very different from that of the forest-living flowers. Higher in the inaccessible wet areas, where seeping springs have gradually dissolved minerals from the hard rocks, are less common plants like the purple, golden, and starry saxifrages. In high places can be found rare alpines left from the Ice Age. These are plants that can survive on thin soils and withstand extremes of temperature and drought. Lichens, mosses and liverworts are the only plants which can survive on the bare rocks of the most exposed sites. Typical plants of the grassy, rock-strewn mountainsides are heath bedstraw, moss campion and tormentil. Ferns abound. The mountain parsley fern, almost a luminous green in spring, is found among crags everywhere and grows in no other place in Britain so profusely. In the deeper soils there are vast areas of bracken, the curse of the farmer as the stuff is inedible by stock. Yet lovers of fine scenery also love bracken for its changing colours – light green in spring; and in the autumn a magnificent display of yellow, orange and brown.

Beside the waters

The lake and river margins are often excellent habitats rich in vegetation. Such places are perhaps at their best in summer when the banks are glowing with purple loosestrife, yellow flag, cow parsley, ragged robin, valerian; and heavy with the scent of meadowsweet. Metal-bright dragon flies and damsel flies – red and blue and green – flash in the sunlight. That marvellous bird of our upland rivers, the dipper, with the lovely liquid song and its subaqua walk is often present. Otters? They come and go like ghosts. Once they were numerous and otter hunting was a popular sport. Now maybe there is too much human activity. But it could happen that in the beck just off the beaten track you might see the bubbles rising, the curve of the shining body, and glimpse that lively little whiskered face.

Only the shallower lakes such as Esthwaite Water, Rydal Water, and Loweswater are 'eutrophic' waters, that is rich in the nutrients which support an abundance of plant and animal

Plants like the yellow flag are found in watery places where there are plenty of nutrients

growth. Anglers may not be too enthusiastic about rich habitats unless they like coarse fishing, but the perch and pike can give good sport. Sea trout, brown trout, and salmon favour the clearer water of the deeper lakes and rivers. One fish peculiar to the district is the char, a deepwater trout. Windermere potted char was once a delicacy much sought after by the gentry of past times. Two rare relics of the Ice Age survive uniquely in Lakeland waters. In Ullswater there are shoals of schelly, sometimes described as 'freshwater herring' though not related. They used to be netted in large quantities. The vendace is another rare whitefish. It is found only in Bassenthwaite and Derwent Water.

Creatures great and small

Of large animals on the hills the common fox is the sole native if one discounts the seasonal movements of red deer. Pine martens once occupied the fells but they are now almost certainly absent. There are occasional rumours of sightings, but the first-hand observer is now an endangered species.

The predators, particularly of rabbits and hares, are the stoats and weasels. They often make their homes in drystone walls. In winter there are frequent sightings of 'ermine' stoats, the animals shedding their brown coat for a creamy white but still with the black end to the tail. Drystone walls too give shelter to reptiles such as the common lizard and the harmless slow-worm, which is often mistaken for a snake but is in fact a legless lizard prone to shedding its tail when attacked. Adders are common. They are shy reptiles and will rush for cover on approach. They are recognised by their zig-zag striped back and the V on their heads. Adder bites are rare and not usually serious. The bitten are invariably people who have foolishly cornered them and picked them up; or more rarely have stood on them as they bask in the spring sunshine still sluggish after hibernation.

Purists among naturalists after a superficial observation of the Lake District might suggest that the hills are too bleak, the lakes too pure, the soils too acid. However, it is impossible to generalise, for the district offers the explorer a great wealth of interest; from liverworts to oak trees; tiny goldcrests to golden eagles; pigmy shrews to twelve-pointer stags. The great shaping of the Lake District back in geological times produced an enormous range of habitats, the depth, height and breadth of which could never be wholly appreciated in a single lifetime.

Left: a vendace, one of Britain's rarest fishes

Below: a male and female char in their spawning colours

Dorothy and William Wordsworth

Literary Lakeland

The lives and works of Dorothy and William Wordsworth shine with such a dazzling light over the literary landscape of Lakeland that we are apt to ignore the other rich associations with fine writers – past and present. True, one of the most memorised poems in English – *Daffodils* (or, 'I wandered lonely as a cloud . . .') – was inspired by a scene on the shores of Ullswater, but the same hills and dales, lakes and tarns, which inspired the Wordsworths, have also nurtured and stimulated generations of poets, novelists and essayists. To the Wordsworths belongs the enviable distinction of having been born in Cumbria; most of their long lives were spent among the hills and dales of Lakeland, and their adjacent graves in the churchyard of Grasmere – the very heart of Lakeland – are among the most visited literary shrines in the world. Pay homage by all means to their memory, but be sure not to neglect the other fascinating associations the area has to offer.

Naturally Wordsworth's contemporaries in Lakeland spring first to mind – especially his fellow Lake Poets, Samuel Taylor Coleridge and Poet Laureate Robert Southey, as well as that poet in prose, Thomas De Quincey. All three spent a good deal of time in the company of the Wordsworths, and helped to establish the Lake District as a desirable place to live in or visit. Among the distinguished visitors were Walter Scott, John Keats, Charlotte Brontë, Charles Dickens, Nathaniel Hawthorne, and Lord Alfred Tennyson. Others were so enchanted with the area that they made their homes in the Lakes: Matthew Arnold, John Ruskin, Beatrix Potter, Arthur Ransome, and Hugh Walpole.

Modern writers

Today the literary tradition continues, with many modern writers having their main or second homes among the lakes and hills or at least drawing on their Lakeland experiences for much of their inspiration. Among modern writers Norman Nicholson reigns supreme as the most impressive voice of the region. Many of the novels of Melvyn Bragg are set in his home area of Wigton and that vast tract of land between the northern fringes of Lakeland and the Scottish border. Best-selling author Richard Adams set his *Plague Dogs* in the Duddon Valley, and the spell-binding autobiography *The Shining Levels*, by John Wyatt, is set in the peaceful woodlands south-east of Lake Windermere. Present or past or famous or neglected, all give the literary traveller a wealth of riches from which to arrange a reading itinerary.

A Wordsworth tour

There can be no doubt that the best introduction
to Literary Lakeland is to follow in the steps of
Wordsworth, for his life and work, directly or
indirectly, is the source and inspiration of most of
the finest writing about Lakeland. Both William
and his sister Dorothy were born in Cockermouth,
that half-forgotten market town on the far north-
western fringe of the National Park. Their father's
imposing Georgian house, still the most
impressive façade in the town, is open to the public
and protected by the National Trust.

William briefly attended the school in the town
before going to Dame Birkett's school in Penrith,
although most of his education was at the
Grammar School in Hawkshead, an Elizabethan
foundation which at that time enjoyed a high
reputation for scholarship. The poet's initials are
carved in one of the desks.

Grasmere and Rydal

The more mountainous scenery around
Grasmere and Rydal was the setting for most of
the Wordsworths' lives. For it was to Grasmere in
December 1799, just as the century turned, that
William and Dorothy settled at Dove Cottage,
later to be joined by their childhood companion,
Mary Hutchinson, who married William in 1802.
In these early years at Dove Cottage Samuel
Taylor Coleridge was a frequent visitor, having
settled at Greta Hall, Keswick with his brother-
in-law Robert Southey. De Quincey, too, was a
frequent visitor and eventually made his own
home at Dove Cottage after the increasing
Wordsworth family made the house overcrowded.
The first move to Allan Bank proved
unsatisfactory and they moved again, to the
Rectory opposite Grasmere Church. Here
tragedy struck the family, two of their small
children dying within a few months of each other
in 1812. The front windows of the Rectory look
directly onto the graves and the proximity of the
churchyard cast a gloom over the whole
household. A further move, their last, was vital and

Below: daffodils and spring light at Ullswater.
Right: Wordsworth's birthplace at
Cockermouth

they settled on Rydal Mount, a mile and a half to
the south on the road to Ambleside.

Allan Bank and the Rectory, though not open to
the public, can easily be viewed from public ways:
Dove Cottage is open six and a half days a week,
and the guided tour of the tiny rooms is an
essential experience for Wordsworth fans.

Rydal Mount, too, is open and as well as the
house containing furnishings, paintings, portraits
and such homely reminders of their daily lives as
ice skates and picnic boxes, the gardens which
William so patiently laid out have now been
restored to their former glory.

All around Rydal and Grasmere are tracks and
footpaths which the Wordsworths habitually
walked – William composed most of his verse out
of doors. A favourite summertime activity was to
take a boat onto Grasmere and row out to the
island for a picnic – still a highly recommended
jaunt for discriminating visitors keen to escape the
roads and traffic.

Dove Cottage – most famous of Wordsworth's homes

The famous daffodils

Two other spots should not be missed in order to complete a Wordsworth tour. On the shores of Ullswater at Gowbarrow is the woodland where the famous daffodils were sighted. William was not in fact wandering alone, he was with Dorothy, and it was she who recorded the scene in her journal. Only two years later did William write the poem, and he clearly drew heavily on his sister's fresh and vivid description of those hosts of golden daffodils. Today alas, though the scenery is superb, there are few daffodils to be seen here. Those in search of Wordsworth's images must content themselves with a stop at Dora's Field just below Rydal Mount next to the church. Here, in a field which William bought and planted himself, we can be certain of seeing in early spring an excellent show of flowers worthy of William's poem:

> Ten thousand saw I at a glance,
> Tossing their heads in sprightly dance.

This pretty scene is perhaps a more fitting climax to the Wordsworth tour than the more common pilgrimage to the graves in Grasmere churchyard, with the tiny headstones of young Catherine and Thomas, and the poignant memorial to brother John, drowned in a shipwreck on the Dorset coast.

Samuel Taylor Coleridge

Coleridge and Southey

When Samuel Taylor Coleridge was introduced to the Lakeland scenery by William and brother John on a walking tour, he immediately fell in love with the area, though he wrote little poetry relating specifically to the Lakes. His notebooks and letters, however, abound with excited descriptions of the scenery and his accounts of his walks are full of joy and exhilaration. Indeed his report of his ascent of Scafell is one of the recognised classics of mountaineering literature, and shows Coleridge as a pioneer fell-walker. He lived for a time at Greta Hall, Keswick, with his brother-in-law Robert Southey, a prolific poet in his day but now largely neglected. His fame today rests on being Poet Laureate before Wordsworth accepted the honour, and for writing the tale of *The Three Bears*. Southey's memorial at Crosthwaite Church has been restored by the Brazilian government, a testimony to the high esteem in which that country holds him as their nation's first historian.

Just south of Keswick is Castlerigg Stone Circle, impressive both as an ancient monument

Robert Southey (above) was a prolific poet, but today is most remembered for his lines about the Lodore Falls (below). They begin: 'How does the water/Come down at Lodore?'

and for its setting, with mountain views in all directions. The circle provided Keats with the inspiration for his description in *Hyperion*:

> . . . like a dismal cirque
> Of Druid stone, upon a forlorn moor,
> When the chill rain begins at shut of eve,
> In dull November . . .

But see the circle on a bright summer morning, or on a soft balmy evening, and you may regret that Keats did not also celebrate this spot in its more benignly mysterious mood.

A Tennyson connection

Further north, on the shores of Bassenthwaite Lake, Tennyson gained inspiration for the lake imagery in *Morte D'Arthur* during a stay with his friends the Speddings at their fine home at Mirehouse – one of the most recent literary houses to be opened to the public. The ancient church of St Bega is a short walk from the house, standing alone like a stranded ship in the lakeside fields. The building has recently been sensitively restored and visiting this quiet corner of Lakeland it is possible to feel the full power and force of Tennyson's extraordinary story:

> Then bold Sir Bedivere uplifted him,
> Sir Bedivere the last of all his knights,
> And bore him to a chapel in the fields
> A broken chancel with a broken cross,
> That stood on a dark straight of barren land
> On one side lay the Ocean, and on one
> Lay a great water, and the moon was full.

Inspiring mountains

Connections with other eminent 19th-century figures can be found in another half-forgotten corner of Lakeland, off the main road between Ambleside and Rydal in an area known as Under Loughrigg. Here, at Fox How, by the banks of the River Rothay, the poet and critic Matthew Arnold lived in this solid house. He is better known for his poetry of the Oxfordshire countryside, and for being the son of Dr Arnold of *Tom Brown's Schooldays* fame, but he was deeply attached to the Lake District, and it is fitting that after his death his friends should have erected a memorial stone close to the church at Wythburn, near Thirlmere, marking the spot where he began a favourite walk to Harrop Tarn. Carved into the stone are Arnold's lines which capture the atmosphere that all fell-walkers relish:

> And now, in front, behold outspread
> These upper regions we must tread,
> Mild hollows, and clear heathy swells,
> The cheerful silence of the fells.

Wythburn Church itself is well worth visiting not only for its obvious picturesque qualities but for the interesting exhibition it contains on the history of the immediate area, which includes extracts from various poems about the tiny church. From Wythburn begins a popular route onto Helvellyn which Wordsworth, Walter Scott and Humphry Davy once climbed together, resulting in the two poets each versifying the moving story of the young man who died on the mountain and was guarded by his faithful dog. Scott brings out the drama of the ascent:

> As I climbed the dark slopes of mighty Helvellyn
> The torrents were roaring, the eagles were yelling . . .

A few miles to the north is another association with Scott, for St John's-in-the-Vale is the setting for his *Bridal of Triermain*: a highly imaginative story involving all the elements of far-off legend, with King Arthur and Guinevere and a purely fictitious castle perched on the so-called Castle Rock of St John, so named because earlier, fanciful travellers imagined that the natural configuration of the crags was in fact a castle.

More recently written historical romances can be found in the novels of Hugh Walpole, enjoying a revival as the result of the television adaptations of the Herries Chronicles, realistically set in the valley of Borrowdale. Walpole's house at Manesty, on the south-west side of Derwent Water is not open to the public; however, the gardens are occasionally opened for charity. Walpole's stories are characterised by highly accurate descriptions of selected locations which his devoted admirers delight in tracking down – such as Judith Paris' house by Watendlath Tarn.

In search of Mrs Tiggywinkle and Captain Flint

On the north-west shore of Derwent Water the gardens of Lingholm are regularly opened by the present owners Lord and Lady Rochdale. Here Beatrix Potter stayed, and her children's stories often have authentic and recognisable backgrounds. The shores and islands of Derwent Water, for instance, clearly figure in *The Tale of Squirrel Nutkin*. Beatrix Potter's most famous house though, is Hill Top, at Sawrey, and close by, the Tower Bank Arms is clearly recognisable to readers of *The Tale of Jemima Puddleduck*. Nearby Esthwaitewater was the home of Jeremy Fisher, and children and adults alike can spend many hours tracking down the settings of these immortal tales.

To many older children the Lake District is not Potter Country but Ransomeland, for Arthur Ransome's *Swallows and Amazons* combines elements of Coniston Water and Windermere. Imaginatively convincing on his pages, but frustratingly difficult to locate on the ground, his readers have to accept that there is often no very precise location for the adventures of Titty, Nancy, Roger and Captain Flint. Wildcat Island is often thought to be Rampsholme on Windermere, but Peel Island on Coniston Water is more likely

The flags of the 'Swallows and Amazons'

to be the island Ransome had in mind.

Coniston Water is also where we can see the former home of John Ruskin. This is Brantwood, a truly fascinating house enjoying quite one of the most impressive views in the Lake District. Brantwood is open to the public, a fascinating and extraordinary testimony to the roving mind of one of Britain's most famous 19th-century art critics, who found time for social reform, poetry and painting.

Glance in any Lakeland bookshop – the area is well served by them – and you will find ample evidence that the long and honourable literary traditions of the Lake District continue: the thrilling and unputdownable *Bride of Lowther Fell*, Margaret Forster's yarn set in the northern fells; John Wyatt's inspired and uplifting *The Shining Levels*; and Norman Nicholson's unforgettable poems, drawing their strength not only from the hills but also from the life of the industrial area around his Millom home. All of these are part of a rolecall of names and works stretching back to the poems and person of Wordsworth.

Fell Walking

The countryside of the Lake District is undoubtedly among the finest in the British Isles. Drive through it and the beauty of the landscape cannot fail to impress. That, for many, is enough; and of course to explore the Lake District by car enables the holidaymaker with only a week or two at his disposal to see a great many of the Lakes' attractions. But to walk in the fresh Cumbrian air away from the crowds and the restrictions of metalled roads is considerably more rewarding.

There is no need to be an athlete or a mountaineer – there are paths to suit everyone. But there are a few ground rules which should be adhered to.

An essential requirement is an ability to read a map – not a hard skill to acquire, as every map carries a 'legend' which lists and interprets all the symbols on the map. Equally important is the need to be properly prepared. Comfortable footwear with a good-grip sole is the main essential. Some choose well-fitting wellingtons; but they can be uncomfortably hot after a time. Light waterproofs are the next need, then plenty of food, and of course a map and compass. Do not be too ambitious when planning the walk – 2½ miles (4 km) per hour is a good speed to plan for over more or less level ground.

Fell walking

Exploring the Lake District on foot may involve sampling the delights of fell walking, which is a quite different proposition from walking in the gentler lowlands. Too many who have ventured onto the heights ill-prepared have found the experience exhausting and worrying; and a few have found it painful. The Lake District mountain rescue teams, volunteers all, turn out to over 130 rescues each year. Here more people have to be searched for on the mountains, or carried down off them, than anywhere else in Britain. This does not by any means give the whole accident picture. Very many minor casualties find their own way down, or are helped by passers-by. Ninety-five per cent of these incidents could have been avoided. The accident rate is not high here because more walkers are careless in the Lake District than anywhere else. It is just that far, far more people are attracted by the open-to-all freedom of hundreds of square miles of superb mountain summits. The small minority who get it wrong are still too many. It is not the intention to dissuade people from walking on the fells if they want to. Nor it it intended to suggest that fell walking is the best and ultimate adventure for everyone. Many walkers will find everything they want in the lower hills and valleys, the rivers and lakesides.

The weather

Conditions on the high fells bear no resemblance to the conditions in the valley. The difference can be extreme. When it is mild spring weather at low levels at Easter, bleak mid-winter is still in possession of the summits. One of the worst possible conditions on the fells is gale-force driven rain. Without proper equipment it can be lethal and it happens very often in July and August. No one should be on the fells in those conditions, nor any other bad conditions. Seek the weather forecast first. It is taped on Windermere 5151, the National Park's service. Be prepared to modify your plans, no matter how frustrating, if the forecast is bad.

It should go without saying that winter fell walking is only for those with a lot of fell walking experience. When daylight hours are short a map-reading error can mean being benighted.

On footwear

It is quite possible for a lot of people to traverse the fells in wellies or sandals given the right conditions of dryness underfoot. These conditions are not normal on the fells. It is also true that heavy and expensive mountaineering boots are not needed except in winter snows. Light boots with well-cleated soles are recommended. Get used to the boots first on wet rock or loose gravel or steep grass, before trying them out on the fells.

Windproofs and waterproofs

Cold wind is a serious hazard on the fells. A windproof is essential and it can be carried in a rucksack until needed. If it is also the essential waterproof, that saves carrying two garments. Most people go for the dual-purpose, but condensation on the inside of 'non-breathing' material can be a problem. There are now garments made of magical materials claiming to solve this. You may need to take out a mortgage to buy them. Light waterproof overtrousers are also needed – cold wet knees are hard to cope with.

Warm clothing

Warm clothing such as a sweater, hat and gloves is needed. If it is cold enough to wear woollies at low level some extras should also be put in the sack to prepare for the inevitable big drop in temperature on the heights.

Equipment

Map and compass and the know-how to use them are the first essentials. The rucksack should be large enough. A small tightly-packed bag is a nasty lumpy burden. Take plenty of food including extras for emergencies. It is not necessary to carry water on the Lake District fells as the high-level becks are pure (but cold – and can cause stomach complaints if indulged in too often). A flask of tea or coffee is a good idea. A simple first aid kit should be in the sack; and a torch – just in case unavoidable delay means a descent in the dark. (Without it a descent might be impossible.) For emergencies most experienced walkers carry two light extras: a whistle (six blasts at intervals summons assistance), and a large polythene bag big enough to crawl into, or to slide an injured person into, for an emergency shelter.

The plan

The route plan is all-important. A poor one, or a too ambitious one, is a main cause of serious trouble. Plan to walk at 2½ miles (4 km) per hour; but examine the contours and add one hour for every 1,500 feet (450 metres) to be ascended. To this add refreshment and taking-photographs-time, or slow-walker-in-party time. Best to keep some time in hand too in case of problems. A 'B' plan is also necessary. This is the essential foul-weather route alternative. Leave details of the final plan with someone at base wherever that is. This is very essential for lone walkers. If you break an ankle someone needs to know where to look for you. If you are delayed or descend into the wrong valley a telephone call could save a possible unnecessary rescue call-out. The police, who initiate rescues, would like to know. There are too many times when rescue teams turn out on the cold night fell to look for someone who is snug by the fire in some dale bar, and has not bothered to tell anyone of a change of plan.

The walk

The best comment on safety I heard was from an Everest mountaineer: 'The difference between a mountaineer and a novice is that the mountaineer knows when to turn back.' Do not be hesitant at making the decision to modify or shorten routes for safety reasons. Group or family leaders have a responsibility. Groups should not be split up but should journey at the speed of the slowest member. Keep to sensible routes. Walking the fells should never be confused with rock climbing. Rock faces and gullies are for devotees of a different sport.

The emergency

The procedure if one locates an incident is to work out the position carefully on the map, write down the map reference, and either take it or send it with someone to the nearest telephone. A 999 call to the police with details of the incident will start the rescue.

In winter

If there is snow on the hills an ice axe and know-how to use it is essential. In extreme conditions crampons may be needed. The phone-in weather service gives details of winter fell-top conditions.

The above advice is sensible and its observance does not involve heavy expense. For more specific advice the National Park Ranger Service (Barclays Bank Chambers, Crescent Rd, Windermere) is available. Youth leaders can obtain help from the National Park Youth & Schools Service, Brockhole, Windermere.

Having digested this advice relax and enjoy the walk. The fell walker is mainly after two things: complete freedom of the open air, and adventure. The safety rules do not restrict freedom and there are no National Park rangers hiding behind rocks ready to jump out on those who are not strictly observing them. Adventure suggests an element of uncertainty. But the environment should provide those delights of surprise. The wise take ability and experience into account and should heed the advice of Edward Whymper, the 19th-century pioneer of mountaineering who learned by some grim mistakes: 'Climb if you will, but remember that courage and strength are nought without prudence and that a momentary negligence may destroy the happiness of a lifetime. Do nothing in haste, look well to each step and from the beginning, think what might be the end.'

If the right decisions were made on the walk the end should be a hot shower, a good meal, a satisfied feeling of achievement, and a happy memory.

Right: walking is the best way to explore the Lake District. This view is from Silverhow, looking down on Grasmere

Below: fell walking in winter is exhilarating, but the correct equipment is essential

Traditional Sports

Long before tourists came to the Lake District the dalesmen were chasing foxes across the fells and wrestling on the village greens. Fell racing and hound trailing came much later – although both these events were staged at the first recorded Grasmere Sports meeting in 1852 – and these four preoccupations of the dalesmen are still the principal traditional sports of the district, all born in the fell country and still rarely seen outside it. Note the mountain association in three of these four activities, and even the wrestling in the specialised Cumberland and Westmorland style, today held against the backcloth of the fells, at one time took place on the summit of High Street. You need strong legs and arms, good lungs and sure balance for all these pursuits – the men who lay the trails for the hounds cover the same rough mountain course that the animals have to follow – and the mountains breed such men. The traditional sports of Lakeland, then, are a heritage from the hills, for the dalesman has never been greatly attracted to the lakes and the lake sports. The Royal Windermere Yacht Club is more than 120 years old and today there are motorboating, water-skiing and swimming races, but these things are not bred in the dalesman. One can

imagine him looking on, with some wonder and amusement, at the regattas on Derwentwater and Windermere in the early 19th century, but probably begrudging the time spent away from the hunting or the wrestling.

Hunting and huntsmen

Fox hunting is the main interest, almost the obsession, of the dalesman during the winter months and, increasingly, an attraction for visitors who view the chase through binoculars from cars parked on mountain roads and join in the merriment at the inn later. There are six mountain packs covering the whole of Lakeland and well to the east of the Shap Fells road. The hunts, often two or three times a week, are advertised in the local newspapers. Hunting in the fells has little in common with the fashionable sport of the shires, for the dalesman hunts on foot and only the huntsman wears the red coat. Killing foxes is just another job like keeping down the crows or repairing fences, for foxes slink down from the heights to prey on the poultry and young lambs; but the farmers and shepherds are out for sport as well, and a kill before breakfast, before the sun has ruined the scent, is common enough. Fell hunting is a hard game and you need to know the ways of a fox and have a feeling for the lie of mountain country, besides sound limbs and good lungs, to be up with the kill. To some it seems a sickening business, chasing a beautiful animal to the death, but it is necessary to keep down the number of foxes and it is arguable that hunting is the most practical way. The fox is normally killed in an instant by a snap from the leading hound, and the Lakeland packs do not break up their victim, which is often hung in state on a farmhouse door – an honoured foe and perhaps an example to his fellows.

Above: a fell runner making the headlong descent of Wasdale Head

Right: traditional Lakeland wrestling at one of the region's many shows

Far left: hounds of the Coniston pack with their huntsman

Below: they're off! The start of a hound trail

Below right: fell runners clearing a wall at the famous Grasmere Sports

The legendary John Peel is mostly remembered in the song written by his old friend John Woodcock Graves. His hunting country was largely to the north of what is now the National Park. He often hunted the flatter land on horseback, and he was a flamboyant character rather than a particularly heroic figure. Several later, less-publicised fell huntsmen, notably Tommy Dobson of the Eskdale and Ennerdale hunt, Billy Porter of the same pack, the great Joe Bowman of the Ullswater, Joe Wear who succeeded him and Anthony Chapman of the Coniston, probably all exceeded Peel's records of kills and were, in some ways, more interesting men. But present-day hunting owes something to John Peel, for some of his hounds were used for breeding the forebears of the present Blencathra pack which hunts the Keswick country.

Hound trailing

When the hounds are resting from their hard work of the winter the dalesman turns to his summer absorption with dogs – the Lake District sport of hound trailing. Trail hounds are basically fox hounds but specially bred and trained into sleeker, lighter animals capable of considerable speed and endurance over rough mountain ground. Hound trailing can provide some fine spectacles – the excitement of the 'slip', the yelping surge over the first stone wall, the wonderful sight of scurrying specks coursing along a distant shoulder of fell and the thrill of a close-fought finish – but undoubtedly the betting is the principal attraction. The hounds are groomed and cosseted like racehorses and although, doubtless, their owners show them affection, they are really the stock-in-trade of the itinerant bookie. Every sports meeting, agricultural show and sheepdog trial has its hound trail – generally two or three in an afternoon – and there are trails nearly every day in summer in one part of the district or another. The sport is highly organised with a ruling body founded as long ago as 1906, and the corruption that was formerly a feature of the sport – hounds substituted, drugged or even taken part of the way by car – has now been stamped out. But to some it may seem a pity that a potentially fascinating outdoor spectacle is really little more than a gamble.

Cumberland wrestling

But wrestling in the Cumberland and Westmorland style has little or no attraction for the betting man and although there are tales of faked contests in the past it is nowadays one of the cleanest of sports. The best man wins and the one who throws all his opponents becomes the champion of the meeting at his weight. And the best wrestlers, at specially selected competitions, become 'world champions' in this particular style – an honour that many an 18-year-old farm lad from the dales has been able to claim. It looks a simple sport but, in fact, is highly technical. The round ends when one man is down, and there is no need for both shoulders to be touching the ground; if both fall together the winner is the one on top. Most visitors understand little or nothing of the many types of attack and the curious jargon, but the secret of the game is to tempt your opponent into a position of apparent security and then quickly to get him off balance. Mere strength is by no means the whole of it.

The best wrestlers, however, seem well-built and sturdy, and the heavyweights are often very big men indeed. Perhaps the outstanding man in the long history of the sport – probably up to 300 years – was the great George Steadman, who died at Brough in 1904 – a powerful but paunchy man who measured $51\frac{1}{2}$ inches round the chest but probably even more round the waist. He won the heavyweight contest at Grasmere on 14 occasions, represented England at many international competitions, collected enough cups and trophies to stock a jeweller's shop and probably made more money out of the game than anybody else. One or two others have since equalled or exceeded his total of Grasmere wins but Steadman who looked, with his bald, smiling face and white side-whiskers, rather like a bishop, remains the personality of the sport.

The traditional wrestling costume must be mentioned – white vest and hose with gaily embroidered trunks – and there are usually competitions for the best costume, generally judged by ladies. Wrestling in the fell country is a fine, manly sport and the sight of sunburned dalesmen, dressed in white, struggling good-naturedly on a circle of green turf set among the hills remains a picture of the best of old England.

Fell racing

The beginnings of fell racing in the Lakes – or guides racing, as it is sometimes called – have long been forgotten but it was already an established sport at Grasmere in the 1850s. Here, for many visitors, is the main attraction of the dales sports, for this is sheer spectacle throughout – the long climb up through the bracken and over the rocks to the flag on the summit of the nearest fell and then the breakneck dash down the fellside, over walls, across slippery slopes and into the arena, while the band strikes up 'See the conquering hero comes'. Most of the outstanding fell runners, with many wins at the main sports meetings at Grasmere and Ambleside to their credit, have been young farmers, farm hands or shepherds to whom this peak of physical fitness has presented a worthwhile challenge. Here is another traditional sport where the bookmaker has intruded but the game is clean enough, with the race in full view through binoculars, and the honour of winning at an important meeting highly prized. Some champions are better on the climb, others on the wild descent, and the first man to the summit is not always the first to breast the tape. Even youngsters of ten or twelve have their own races and they often become the great champions of later years.

These, then, are the main traditional sports of Lakeland – most of them to be seen at a score of summer sports meetings but, notably, at Grasmere on the nearest Thursday to 20 August and at Ambleside on the last Thursday in July. But there is one more traditional 'sport' of the fell country – the ancient gurning, or grinning, competitions most often associated with the old Crab Fair at Egremont. You simply place your head through a horse-collar and the winner is the man who pulls the ugliest face. It has been reported of one former champion gurner that the first time he won the prize he had not really entered the competition at all but had been merely 'following the efforts of the others with interest and sympathy'. But perhaps this 'sport' should be placed in the same category as the competitions at Wasdale Head and elsewhere to find the best liar in the district.

LAKE DISTRICT
Gazetteer

Each entry in this Gazetteer has the atlas page number on which the place can be found and its National Grid reference included under the heading. An explanation of how to use the National Grid is given on page 66.

Above: judging sheep at Wasdale Show

Ambleside

Map Ref: 85NY3704

Ambleside is a major Lake District centre, lying in a strategic position on the main north to south road (A591). It is a good base for a touring, walking or climbing holiday and has many facilities and shops.

The Romans showed their appreciation of Ambleside's strategic attractions in AD 79 when they built Galava Fort at Borrans. The site has been excavated and Roman artifacts can be seen in the Lake District History Centre on Lake Road, together with a model of the fort. It includes a permanent 'Man in Lakeland' exhibition designed to help visitors discover and appreciate the Lake District's distinctive heritage and the character, life-style, sports and pastimes of its people through 5,000 years.

Granted its charter as a market town in 1650, Ambleside has many remnants of the 17th century, such as the tiny Bridge House over the Stock Ghyll, built as a summer house for the former Ambleside Hall. It is now owned by the National Trust, who opened it as their first Information Centre in 1956.

St Mary's Church has a 180ft spire, unusual in the Lake District. It contains a mural depicting the ancient Rushbearing Ceremony painted by Gordon Ransome, a student of the Royal College of Art during World War II, when the college was evacuated to Ambleside. The annual ceremony is held on the first Saturday in July, when children carry rushes through the town. It dates from medieval times, when the rushes used as flooring in the church were renewed each year.

The area is rich in historical and literary associations. William Wordsworth and his sister used to walk into Ambleside from Grasmere (see page 41) to get their post and later, in 1813, when Wordsworth became Distributor of Stamps for Westmorland, he had his office here.

The writer Harriet Martineau lived at The Knoll from 1835–76. In 1912 the Armitt sisters, who also lived in the town, left their unique and valuable collection of local history books for the use of students (now housed in a special section of the Ambleside Library).

The historic centre of Ambleside is now a conservation area. Stock Ghyll Waterfall, well worth a visit, used to serve several mills. The Old Mill on North Road has a good reproduction waterwheel. Glass blowing may be watched at the Adrian Sankey workshop in Rothay Road during the holiday season.

There is a new Dolls House Museum in Kirkstone Road, with a large collection of beautifully dressed dolls. Traditional Lakeland sports are held at Ambleside on the Thursday before the first Monday in

Above: The Bridge House, Ambleside
Below: Mural of the rush-bearing ceremony St Mary's, Ambleside

August, and the traditionally renowned sheepdog trials take place in Rydal Park. Boat and steamer trips are available from Waterhead (see page 63). The main Information Centre in Church Street (tel. Ambleside 32582) has details of a two-and-a-half-mile Nature Trail around nearby Loughrigg Fell, and of guided walks through the town. Fishing permits are available from the cycle shop in The Slack.

AA recommends:
Hotels: Rothay Manor, Rothay Bridge, 1-rosette, 3-star, *tel.* Ambleside 33605
Kirkstone Foot Country House, Kirkstone Pass Road, 2-star, *tel.* Ambleside 32232
Riverside, Rothay Bridge, Upper Loughrigg, 2-star, *tel.* Ambleside 32395
Vale View, Lake Road, 2-star, *tel.* Ambleside 33192
Fisherbeck, Old Lake Road, 1-star, *tel.* Ambleside 33215
White Lion, 1-star, *tel.* Ambleside 33140
Campsites: Skelwith Fold Caravan Park, 3-pennants, *tel.* Ambleside 32277
Low Wray National Trust Campsite, 2-pennants, *tel.* Ambleside 32810
Self Catering: Badgers Rake, Fisherbeck Park, *tel.* Ambleside 32411
Eden Vale Holiday Flats, Lake Road, *tel.* Ambleside 32313
Kirkstone Foot Hotel, Kirkstone Pass Road, *tel.* Ambleside 32232
Guest Houses: Borrans Park Hotel, Borrans Road, *tel.* Ambleside 33454
Chapel House Hotel, Kirstone Road, *tel.* Ambleside 33143
Compston House, *tel.* Ambleside 32305
Gables, Compston Road, *tel.* Ambleside 33272
Gale Crescent, Lower Gale, *tel.* Ambleside 32284
Hilldale, Church Street, *tel.* Ambleside 33174
Horseshoe, Rothay Road, *tel.* Ambleside 32000
Oaklands Country House Hotel, Millans Park, *tel.* Ambleside 32525
Riverside Hotel, Gilbert Scar, *tel.* Ambleside 32395
Rothay Garth Hotel, Rothay Road, *tel.* Ambleside 32217
Rysdale Hotel, Kelsick Road, *tel.* Ambleside 32140
Smallwood Hotel, Compston Road, *tel.* Ambleside 32330
Garages: Pinfold, The Green, *tel.* Ambleside 32864
Young Motors, Knott Street, *tel.* Ambleside 32322
Bells Kelsick, Knott Street, *tel.* Ambleside 33273

Appleby-in-Westmorland

Map Ref: 68NY6820

The historic town of Appleby, nestling in a loop of the River Eden, was granted its charter in 1174. Until 1974 it was the county town of Westmorland (now incorporated into Cumbria), and has since had '-in-Westmorland' added to its name to commemorate the fact.

The castle dominates the town. The keep dates back to 1100; a 13th-century tower and the Great Hall still survive. The rest of the castle, destroyed by Cromwell, was restored in 1653 by Lady Anne Clifford, a remarkable woman whose chief passion in life was the restoration and improvement of her family's many houses and estates in the area. There are also many later additions. The grounds and all the floors of the keep have recently been opened to the public. The Great Hall contains the famous Triptych of Lady Anne Clifford and her family, painted in 1646 (a triptych is a painting on a set of three panels). The castle is now a centre for the Rare Breeds Survival Trust, with many rare birds and animals for the public to enjoy. There is a free car park, picnic area and tea room and castle visitors can follow a one-and-a-half-mile nature trail through neighbouring countryside. The Tudor Moot Hall houses the Information Centre.

The famous Gypsy and Horse Fair is held in Appleby on the second Tuesday and Wednesday in June. It is an extremely colourful occasion, where gypsies from all over Britain, travelling in vehicles ranging from horse-drawn caravans to glittering mobile homes, gather. There are pleasant riverside walks for those who wish to get away from the traffic, although the town is now by-passed by the A66. At nearby Little Asby visitors can watch craftsmen make leather goods onto which they burn intricate designs, a process known as pyrography.

AA recommends:
Hotels: Appleby Manor, Roman Road, 3-star, Country House Hotel, *tel.* Appleby 51571
Royal Oak Inn, Bongate, 2-star, *tel.* Appleby 51463
Tufton Arms, Market Square, 2-star, *tel.* Appleby 51593
Courtfield, Bongate, 1-star, *tel.* Appleby 51394
White Hart, Boroughgate, 1-star, *tel.* Appleby 51598
Campsites: Wild Rose Park, Ormside, 4-pennants, *tel.* Appleby 51077
Guest Houses and Farm
Houses: Bongate House, *tel.* Appleby 51245
Howgill House, *tel.* Appleby 51574
Gale House, *tel.* Appleby 51380
Garages: Appleby Motor Co, The Sands, *tel.* Appleby 51133
Cumbria Jeep Centre, The Sands, *tel.* Appleby 51664 or 51678

Applethwaite (nr Keswick)

Map Ref: 72NY2625

This little village is perched on a terrace made when the flanks of Skiddaw were ploughed in the 13th century. Halfway along the terrace from Applethwaite to Millbeck is the beautiful vista which the poet Robert Southey regarded as the best view of Derwent Water.

Applethwaite's most historic house is The Ghyll, built in 1867 on property given to poet William Wordsworth in 1802 by Sir George Beaumont, a founder of the National Gallery, to enable him to be near Coleridge, who lived in Keswick.

Although Wordsworth chose not to build there, he had already immortalised the hamlet in a sonnet *At Applethwaite, near Keswick*. In it he wrote that, whether he lived at Applethwaite or not:
'Old Skiddaw will look down upon the Spot
With pride, the Muses love it evermore.'

AA recommends:
Hotels: Underscar, 2-star, Country House Hotel, *tel.* Keswick 72469

Ponies and their riders in the River Eden at Appleby's horse fair

Arnside

Map Ref: 68SD4578

This seaside village is on the south-east side of the Kent Estuary on the opposite shore to Grange-over-Sands (see page 40). At the end of the promenade a slipway leads down to the beach. A long, low stone viaduct carries the Carnforth-Barrow railway line over the estuary and links Arnside with Grange.

Arnside is outside the Lake District National Park, but, together with Silverdale it is now an Area of Outstanding Natural Beauty. It is a popular holiday area with a variety of scenery, including limestone pavement, saltmarsh, foreshore fen, parkland and woodland. Facilities include fishing, sailing, horse riding, wildfowling, ornithology, picnic spots and a nature walk. Guided walks across the sands to Grange can be arranged through the Guide to the Kent Sands, Cedric Robinson (Grange 2165).

There is a Nature Trail around Arnside Knott (521ft), belonging to the National Trust, and from the summit on a fine day a wide panorama is visible from the Pennines to the Lake District fells.

AA recommends:
Self Catering: Hampsfell, The Promenade, *tel.* Arnside 761285
The Moorings, The Promenade, *tel.* Arnside 761340
Guest Houses: Grosvenor Private Hotel, The Promenade, *tel.* Arnside 761666
Garages: Arnside, Station Road, *tel.* Arnside 761206

Askham

Map Ref: 81NY5123

In a district abounding in stone circles, earthworks and ancient settlements, Askham is of great historical interest. The records of St Peter's Church go back to the 13th century; but it was rebuilt in Neo-Norman style in 1832 by Robert Smirke, designer of the British Museum. It is one of 12 buildings in the village on the government's list of Buildings of Architectural or Historic Interest. Another one (listed Grade I) is Askham Hall, which dates from the 14th century and is now the residence of the Earl of Lonsdale.

Most of the dwellings and barns were built in the 18th century. They line the

main street with a succession of village greens which lead up from the River Lowther. This reinforces the village's linear shape, characteristic of settlements situated on limestone. Good examples of the old agricultural strip pattern of fields can be seen running north and south of the main street. Many of the old barns have recently been converted into houses.

A new Lakeland Country Base and Museum in the village contains a fine display on life in the countryside.

AA recommends:
Hotels: Queen's Head, 2-star, *tel.* Hackthorpe 225

Aspatria

Map Ref: 68NY1442

Aspatria is situated a few miles north of the National Park on the north bank of the River Ellen where the A596 Maryport to Carlisle road crosses the B5301.

It has a beautiful, spacious church, dedicated to St Kentigern, built in 1848 on an earlier religious site. Many original architectural features are preserved; there is a Norman arch over a doorway and a medieval font.

Buried in a simple grave outside the church is Sir Wilfrid Lawson (1829–1906), a great teetotaller and Parliamentarian, who lived at Brayton Hall. In 1864 he introduced a local veto bill which proposed that the pubs in any district should close when two-thirds of the inhabitants wished. It was thrown out by a big majority, but he continued to urge his temperance views both in the House and on the platform in a simple style, tinged with humour, that always brought him respect. New leisure facilities have recently been provided in the 40 acres of parkland in front of ruined Brayton Hall. They include a nine-hole golf course with the third hole called The Whisky Pond, as it marks the spot where Sir Wilfrid is said to have poured all the whisky from Brayton Hall when he 'went religious'.

Angling permits for fishing in the Ellen can be obtained from the Colour Shop in Aspatria and 'Inglenook' at Plumbland south of Aspatria. There is a cinema.

AA recommends:
Guest Houses: Scales Demesne (farmhouse), *tel.* Aspatria 20847
Garages: Ellenvale (Tinnian Bros Ltd), Arkleby Road, *tel.* Aspatria 20538

The red sandstone ruins of Furness Abbey, near Barrow-in-Furness

Backbarrow

Map Ref: 91SD3584

Backbarrow was once the centre of a thriving industrial valley, drawing its water from the River Leven.

Much of the charcoal produced in the Furness fells was used by the Backbarrow Iron Furnace, and boats transported charcoal from the fells across Windermere to Newby Bridge. The coppice wood from which charcoal was made was also used for basket-making.

The last of the old industries was the Blue Works, established in 1890 by the Lancashire Ultramarine Company at a former cotton mill, (which itself succeeded a corn mill that existed there from the 16th century). Reckitts took over the company in 1929, continuing to produce ultramarine or blue for industrial purposes – including the famous 'Dolly Blue' for laundering – until it closed in 1981. The tall chimney, which never succeeded in taking all the blue away from the area, was demolished in 1983.

By then, however, the site was under new ownership and a major time-share leisure complex called 'The Lakeland Village' was being developed on it. This has served both to save it from dereliction and to provide an abundance of new leisure facilities, not only for time-share clients but for local people and visitors too. Seventeen time-share units are already open; there will eventually be 76. The five-storey mill has been converted into a hotel, together with a restaurant, two bars, a shop and conference rooms.

From January 1985 the leisure provision will include a pool, squash courts, sauna, jacuzzi and exercise rooms – all open to the public.

For horse riding contact the Bigland Hall Riding Centre south of the village.

Bampton (Haweswater)

Map Ref: 81NY5118

Bampton is just within the National Park at the confluence of the River Lowther and the Haweswater Beck. The area has been settled for thousands of years and there are remains of an ancient British settlement nearby.

The Children's Sports, held on the first Saturday in September, dates from the old traditional Bampton Sports, which in turn stemmed from a centuries-old festival of sport that used to be held on top of the High Street ridge.

Another historic event in Bampton is the Mardale Hunt, which used to meet at the Dun Bull Inn at Mardale before that village was demolished in 1937, when Manchester Corporation flooded the Mardale valley to form the Haweswater reservoir. Also transferred from Mardale to Bampton at that time was the Shepherds Meet, which had been held at the Dun Bull for over a century. Now both the Hunt and the Meet gather at the St Patrick's Well Inn in Bampton on the Saturday nearest 20 November, and the sheep are penned in Bampton Hall yard.

Until recently, the lake and lake shore were closed to the public. Now, however, although the intention of the North West Water Authority and the Lake District Special Planning Board is to keep Haweswater a 'near wilderness' area, more public access is allowed. Visitors can get on to the lake shore from the car park at the valley head (about two and a quarter miles past the hotel) and walk along the north shore and along a short section of the south shore. No boating is allowed, but fishing permits can be obtained from the Supply Manager, the North West Water Authority, Mintsfeet Road South, Kendal, LA9 6BY.

Barrow-in-Furness

Map Ref: 68SD1969

Regular visitors will notice that the A590 to Barrow from the M6/A6 has recently been much improved. On the left hand side approaching Barrow is the town's most famous historic monument, Furness Abbey, built in 1147 in red sandstone. It looks magnificent even as a ruin. The dormitory alone is 200ft long. Furness Abbey became the second richest Cistercian establishment in the country after Fountains Abbey. The east end, transepts and tower together with parts of the infirmary and Abbot's House can all still be seen.

The main road into Barrow, called Abbey Road, is long, wide, tree-lined and almost straight through to the central Ramsden Square, with its fine library and museum.

Not far from Ramsden Square, in Duke Street, is the superb Victorian town hall. The newer civic hall, where concerts and other activities take place and where the Tourist Information Centre (tel. Barrow 25795) is situated, is opposite the town hall. Leaflets describing walks around the town can be obtained here.

Over a bridge from Barrow is Walney Island where there is a Nature Reserve run by the Cumbria Trust for Nature Conservation. The Gullery is worth a visit and eider ducks breed here. The island's west coast is one vast beach 12 miles long, backed by dunes for much of its length. The sandy shore is scattered with smooth boulders and low tide pools.

Fishing permits are available from Hannays in Crellin Street, and from the Angling and Hiking Centre, Forshaw Street.

AA recommends:
Hotels: Victoria Park, Victoria Road, 3-star, *tel.* Barrow-in-Furness 21159
White House, Abbey Road, 2-star, *tel.* Barrow-in-Furness 27303
Campsites: South End Caravan Site, 3-pennants, *tel.* Barrow-in-Furness 42823
Garages: Holkerford Motor Co Ltd, Holker Street, *tel.* Barrow-in-Furness 23310
Crellin Street Autos, 88 Crellin Street, *tel.* Barrow-in-Furness 21715

Bassenthwaite

Map Ref: 71NY2332

Bassenthwaite village is near the north-east corner of Bassenthwaite Lake, on the old coaching route from Keswick to Carlisle. The A591 to Carlisle now passes between the village and the lake. Many of the houses are grouped around the picturesque village green, but there are some important outlying properties such as the Castle Inn, a mile west on the A591, and Armathwaite Hall, another half mile further west at the north end of the lake.

Bassenthwaite Church is three miles south of the village between the main road and the lake. There is a sign to it from the A591, but it stands in the middle of a field near the lake shore and the final stretch of the way is along a country track. This unique church was founded in the 12th or 13th century and was dedicated to the saints Bridget and Bega. Restored in the 19th century, it retains its Norman chancel arch and many of its early English features.

Wordsworth and the lake poets knew this church and also Mirehouse, the nearby property owned by the Spedding family. James Spedding, the biographer of Francis Bacon, was visited at Mirehouse by Tennyson, Carlyle and Edward Fitz-gerald. The house, grounds, nature trail and forest walks in Dodd Wood are now open to the public from April to October.

Bassenthwaite Lake, four miles long, is the fourth largest area of water in the National Park. Since 1979 it has been owned by the Lake District Special Planning Board, to whom the freehold was transferred from the Egremont Estates (along with other land at Barf to the west and at Caldbeck and Uldale) in settlement of estate duties. The Board's policy is to give priority to the protection and enhancement of the nature conservation interests of the lake and surrounding area.

Nevertheless, areas of the shore are open to the public (at Ouse Bridge, Beck Wythop and Woodend) and there is a public footpath running the length of the west shore. Canoeing is now possible from Peel Wyke harbour (north end), although permits must be obtained (information from the Lake District Special Planning Board). Members of clubs affiliated to the RYA may be permitted to use the Bassenthwaite Sailing Club facilities at Dubwath but there is no public launching point. Motor boating is prohibited by law, except for safety craft. Rowing boats for fishing can be launched from Peel Wyke, but licences and permits must be obtained (from Temple Sports, 9 Station Street or Field and Stream, Keswick; from the Gun Shop, Jubilee Bridge, Lorton Road, or D W Lothian, 35 Main Street, Cockermouth).

AA recommends:

Hotels: Armathwaite Hall, 4-star, Country House Hotel, *tel.* Bassenthwaite Lake 551
Castle Inn, 3-star, *tel.* Bassenthwaite Lake 401
Overwater Hall, 2-star, Country House Hotel, *tel.* Bassenthwaite Lake 566
Pheasant Inn, 2-star, *tel.* Bassenthwaite Lake 234
Self Catering: Bassenthwaite Hall Farm, *tel.* Bassenthwaite Lake 393
Guest Houses and Farm
Houses: Bassenthwaite Hall (West), *tel.* Bassenthwaite Lake 279.
Bassenthwaite Hall (East), *tel.* Bassenthwaite Lake 393
Link House Hotel, *tel.* Bassenthwaite Lake 291
Ravenstone Hotel, *tel.* Bassenthwaite Lake 240

Bassenthwaite Lake, often visited by migrating birds, from the vantage point of Dodd Wood

Blawith

Map Ref: 90SD2888

Blawith lies between Torver and Greenodd on the A5084, half a mile south of the southern end of Coniston Water.

The church of St John the Baptist, built in 1863, replaced a 16th-century church, the ruins of which can be seen on the other side of the road.

A beacon once stood one and a half miles north-west of Blawith, on the highest part of the Blawith Fells, hence the name of Beacon Tarn which lies just below.

The tarn is now part of the 1,600 acres of Blawith Common purchased by the Lake District Special Planning Board in 1971; earlier (1967) it had negotiated a 99-year lease on the adjoining Torver Commons (2,114 acres). The Board is now preparing a management plan for the whole of both commons, which are important wildlife havens, so that they are retained for walking and picnicking – and a happy relationship is achieved between nature conservation and public access.

There is now a beautiful designated walk from Blawith along the shore of Coniston, past the two commons and Coniston Hall, right through to the centre of Coniston. At Brown Howe, on the shore north of Blawith, the Board has developed a car park and picnic area where canoes and sailing dinghies may be launched.

Blindcrake and Isel

Map Ref: 70NY1434

Blindcrake is an unspoilt village, with some 18th-century houses and farms and a neat little green. With a name meaning 'top rock' it lies half a mile inside the north-west boundary of the National Park.

Two miles from the village, but in the same parish, is Isel Church, which stands almost alone beside the Derwent.

Dedicated to St Michael, this church was erected by the Normans in 1130 on the site of an earlier church, and restored in 1878 through voluntary subscriptions, with all the best features of the former church scrupulously preserved. Its carved stones show that the earlier church dated back at least to the Vikings. Among them is the strange Triskele Stone, with its three-linked knot, which is believed to be unique. The symbols on it – a swastika, a three-armed triskele, a triskele with one arm turned backward, and Thor's thunderbolt – are among the earliest used by man. They date from the time when these age-old signs were just starting to be given a Christian interpretation.

One of the chief delights of the church is the chancel arch, which has not been altered since 1130. Over the arch are the Royal Arms, dated 1721, showing the white Horse of Hanover. These are believed to have been provided by Sir Wilfred Lawson, Groom of the Bedchamber to King George I. Lawsons have lived at nearby Isel Hall, which was the seat of the lords of the manor, since the time of Elizabeth I.

The intriguing Triskele Stone in Isel Church is one of the rare remnants left by Viking settlers

Boot

Map Ref: 82NY1701

Boot is half way along Eskdale on the west side of the central fells. Eskdale was already settled in neolithic times, as witness the stone circles on Burnmoor. Bronze Age cairns abound on the surrounding fells.

The Romans arrived in the valley about AD 100, building a fort at Hardknott that accommodated 500 men three miles up the dale from Boot, at an elevation of 800ft. Covering three acres, the fort is on the north side of the road first built by the Romans over the Wrynose and Hardknott passes to facilitate troop movements between Galava Fort at Ambleside (see page 24) and Ravenglass (see page 54). The remains of the bath houses and parade ground have been excavated and the wall and gateway reconstructed in original, fallen, stone. It is believed that the fort was a back-up for a Roman invasion of Ireland through Ravenglass which never happened.

One of the features of Boot village is the Eskdale corn mill, restored by Cumbria County Council in 1975. A corn mill had been operating in the area since the 13th century, when it was established to serve the tenants of the Manor of Eskdale. A Manor Court was held in Eskdale annually to deal with local matters. The earliest documentary evidence for the present mill is 1578 and it remained in use for milling corn until the 1920s. The mill is now open to the public from Easter to September and an exhibition there explains the

method of milling as well as the agricultural techniques used in the area.

Another traditional activity of the area was mining, including iron and copper. Up to 1875, iron ore was transported along rough tracks to the coast for shipment. But then the mining company built the 3ft gauge Ravenglass & Eskdale Railway from Ravenglass to the Nab Gill mines at Boot to speed up the traffic. A year later it was opened up to the public. The iron traffic ceased in the 1880s, but it continued to carry granite and an increasing number of tourists until 1913. In June 1915 a new company opened it up, converting it to a 15 inch gauge, but the last climb to Boot was too much for the new locomotives and Dalegarth became the terminus.

Granite and tourists continued to be carried on the railway, off and on, until 1960 when, following a public auction, the railway was acquired by its present company. With the help of a Preservation Society, it now operates purely for passenger traffic, with a daily service from the end of March to the end of October and some trains at other times. The journey from Boot to Ravenglass takes 40 minutes. The railway is now affectionately known as 'La'al Ratty'. (For other details see Ravenglass, page 54.) From Dalegarth station there is a nature trail to spectacular Stanley Force. The two mile walk takes in a glaciated valley, mixed woodland and a gorge. Leaflets are available from National Park Information Centres.

AA recommends:
Guest Houses: Brook House, *tel.* Eskdale 288

The ruins of Hardknott Roman Fort, built by Emperor Hadrian in about AD 120.

Bootle

Map Ref: 88SD1088

This is a village within the National Park on the western coast road between Ravenglass (see page 54) and Millom (see page 50). It is about one and a half miles from the sea, but the road to the shore comes out at a pleasant beach.

To the south-east of the village is Black Combe (1,969ft), an isolated outcrop of Skiddaw slate that is believed to be one of the oldest hills in the world. Its base covers a greater area of ground than any other peak in the area and from its summit there is said to be a more extensive view than from any other point in Britain, taking in four kingdoms. On a clear day can be seen not only a wide panorama of Lake District fells, but also views of hills in Wales, Scotland and the Isle of Man.

Immediately to the east of the village and north of Black Combe there is evidence of Bronze Age settlement. On the fells between Black Combe, Dunnerdale and Eskdale there are about 10,000 cairns, making the area what an archaeologist recently described as 'one of the most remarkably preserved prehistoric landscapes in England'.

As a village, Bootle is nearly 1,000 years old, with an entry in the Domesday Book. The church of St Michael is of Norman origin, although only the chancel bears any trace of its original Norman style. In it, however, is an interesting memorial to Sir Hugh Askew, Henry VIII's cellarer, to whom was given the site of nearby Seaton Nunnery (revenue valued at £12 12s 6d) when it was dissolved in 1541. The remains of the Nunnery can still be seen one mile north of Bootle along the A595.

Bouth

Map Ref: 91SD3285

Bouth is a small village on the southern edge of the Furness fells.

It has become well known in recent years for the Hay Bridge Deer Museum, established in 1971 in the woods to the north of the village.

Hay Bridge was declared a nature reserve in that year by the owner, Helen Fooks, as a memorial to her husband, Major Herbert Fooks, who spent a lifetime working in the game management and conservation field. In 1956 he was appointed Game Warden to the Forestry Commission at nearby Grizedale Forest (see page 42) where he set up a deer museum. The Hay Bridge Deer Museum is a continuation of his work, its prime task being to educate young people in some of the main aspects of deer conservation.

The function of the Nature Reserve is to provide red and roe deer with an area containing all their needs, without pressures. It displays, say its operators, 'a fascinating remnant of the old Lake District countryside in a largely unspoilt setting'. Both species were plentiful on the Furness fells until timber-felling in the 17th and 18th centuries. With the lost woodlands the roe vanished and the red deer only just survived. Since then Austrian roe have been introduced into the Lake District and have multiplied, and native deer are now returning.

AA recommends:
Campsites: Black Beck Caravan Park, I-pennant, *tel.* Greenodd 274

Bowness-on-Windermere

Map Ref: 92SD4096

Bowness is the older of the two towns of Windermere and Bowness, and dates from the 10th or 11th century, when the area was colonised by Vikings. A Nordic chief called Vinand named the lake after himself 'Vinand's Mere'.

St Martin's Church, Bowness, is the parish church of Windermere. The Bowness rectory, the oldest inhabited house in the area, was built in the 15th century. In 1480 the church was destroyed by fire and a new one built. Its outstanding feature is the 15th-century stained glass in the east window, thought to have come from Cartmel Priory (see page 32).

In the churchyard is the common grave of 47 people who were drowned in 1635 when the cross-Windermere ferry capsized as they were returning from a wedding at Hawkshead. The first mention of a ferry was in 1454; the present diesel boat *Drake* takes 10 cars and operates a frequent service daily (weather permitting) from Ferry Nab south of Bowness.

The famous round house on Belle Isle in the middle of the lake, opposite Bowness, was built in 1774. It is now open to the public and a boat plies to it by request from the end of the Bowness promenade.

The first public steamer on Windermere was launched in 1845. Two years later the railway reached Windermere and Windermere village itself then began to develop (see page 64). Bowness expanded rapidly to cater for the influx of tourists, and several of the older hotels were established. In 1869 H W Schneider settled at 'Belsfield' and initiated many improvements. Among them was the pier just below his house. He used to walk down each morning preceded by his butler carrying his breakfast on a silver tray; he then had breakfast on his steam launch *Esperance* while it took him to Lakeside, where a special train (he owned the railway) took him to his office in Barrow.

His pier is now used by the Bowness Bay Boating Company for their public launch service. *Esperance* is now one of the fine working collection of historic Lake District craft in the Windermere Steamboat Museum (opened in 1977).

Sealink steamers operate daily to Lakeside and Ambleside and there are minibuses for touring the area. Boats of all sorts may be hired.

The whole of the Bowness area is geared to the visitor trade during the season, and most leisure activities are represented.

One new attraction is the Windermere Lake Festival, started in 1982 to revive the tradition of earlier regattas and festivals on the lake. Another new annual event, also started in 1982, is the Windermere Marathon which starts and finishes on the Bowness promenade. Held on the last Sunday in October, this is regarded as one of the most scenic marathons in the world.

Various other sporting events take place on the lake every year, including water skiing, long distance swimming, and power boat record attempts.

A new attraction in Bowness is the Windermere Railrama in Fallbarrow Road. Here two large computer controlled model railways plus video and film shows offer live action for railway buffs of all ages.

Details of the attractions and facilities of Bowness can be obtained from the Tourist Information Centre at Bowness Bay (tel. Windermere 2895).

The northern reaches of Lake Windermere from Bowness-on-Windermere

AA recommends:
Hotels: Old England, 4-star, tel. Windermere 2444
Beech Hill, Cartmel Fell, 3-star, tel. Windermere 2137
Belsfield, 3-star, tel. Windermere 2448
Burn How Motel, Back Belsfield Road, 3-star, tel. Windermere 6226
Hydro, Helm Road, 3-star, tel. Windermere 4455
Wild Boar, Crook, 3-star, tel. Windermere 5225
Bordriggs, Longtail Hill, 2-star, tel. Windermere 3567
Burnside, 2-star, tel. Windermere 2211
Lindeth Fell, 2-star, Country House Hotel, tel. Windermere 3286
Linthwaite, 2-star, Country House Hotel, tel. Windermere 3688
Royal, 2-star, tel. Windermere 3045
St Martins, Lake Road, 2-star, tel. Windermere 3731
Knoll, 1-star, tel. Windermere 3756
White Lodge, Lake Road, 1-star, tel. Windermere 3624
Restaurants: Porthole Eating House, 3 Ash Street, 1-fork, 1-rosette, tel. Windermere 2793
La Silhouette, Ash Street, tel. Windermere 5663
Campsites: Braithwaite Fold Touring Caravan Park, Glebe Road, 2-pennants, apply to South Lakeland District Council, Ashleigh, Windermere
Park Cliffe Farm Caravan and Camping Site, Tower Wood, 3-pennants, tel. Newby Bridge 31344
Self Catering: Deloraine, Helm Road, tel. Windermere 5557
Fair Rigg, Ferry View, tel. Windermere 3555
Howe Foot Holiday and Tourist Flats, tel. Windermere 2792
Linthwaite Hotel (bungalow), tel. Windermere 3688
Spinnery Cottage Holiday Flats, Brantfell Road, tel. Windermere 4884
Guest Houses: Biskey Howe Villa Hotel, Craig Walk, tel. Windermere 3988
Brooklands, Ferry View, tel. Windermere 2344
Craig Brow Cottage Private Hotel, Helm Road, tel. Windermere 4080
Craig Foot Hotel, Lake Road, tel. Windermere 3902
Eastbourne Hotel, Biskey Howe Road, tel. Windermere 3525
Elim Bank Hotel, Lake Road, tel. Windermere 4810
Fairfield Country House Hotel, Brantfell Road, tel. Windermere 3772

Victorian pleasure craft at the Windermere Steamboat Museum, Bowness

Braithwaite

Map Ref: 77NY2323

Braithwaite is a secluded village two miles west of Keswick just off the A66.

The church was built in 1900 on the site of a former mission room. It is dedicated to St Herbert, the local saint, who was a hermit on the island of Derwent Water and a close friend of St Cuthbert (see page 46).

Braithwaite is at the foot of the Whinlatter Pass. There is a scenic road over the Pass to Lorton and the western lakes, Loweswater, Crummock and Buttermere (B5292). One mile up the road to the Whinlatter Pass is Noble Knott, where a layby and picnic area have been provided so that people can enjoy superb views over Bassenthwaite to Skiddaw.

Another mile further up the Pass is the Whinlatter Forest Centre, where the Forestry Commission has an exhibition with working models showing the story of the forest. There is also a lecture room where films are shown connected with forestry, nature and the Lake District. The centre is the starting point for a forest walk. It is open daily from Easter to October.

AA recommends:
Hotels: Ivy House, 2-star, tel. Braithwaite 338
Middle Ruddings, 2-star, tel. Braithwaite 436
Campsites: Scotgate Caravan Site, 1-pennant, tel. Braithwaite 343

Bridekirk

Map Ref: 70NY1133

Bridekirk is just half a mile outside the National Park. It is in the triangle between the A595 Cockermouth to Carlisle road and the A594 Cockermouth to Maryport road and can be reached from either.

The church, dedicated to St Bridget, or Bride, has given the village its name. The original Saxon church was a wooden one. Then came a Norman stone church, which was gutted in the 19th century, only some of the wall now remaining. This was followed by the beautiful Neo-Norman church of today, built in 1870 with a brick interior most unusual for its time.

An even more unusual feature of the church is the 12th-century font – a survivor from the original church – which is so profusely ornamented with sculpture that it is regarded as an outstanding piece of workmanship from that period.

It was designed by a sculptor known as Richard, the Carver of Durham. On three sides of the font he carved the baptism of Jesus; Adam and Eve being expelled from

Exquisite carving on the 12th-century font in Bridekirk Church

the Garden of Eden; and a sculptor with chisel and mallet. On the fourth side he carved in runic letters an inscription deciphered as: 'Rikarth he me iwrokt and to dis merhr gernr me brokte' ('Richard has wrought me and to this glory brought me').

Brigsteer

Map Ref: 93SD4889

Brigsteer is four miles south-west of Kendal, just half a mile outside the National Park, on the Levens to Underbarrow road. There is also a road to it from Kendal over Helsington Barrows.

The village lies below the limestone escarpments of Scout Scar and the Barrows on the eastern slopes of the Lyth Valley. It is a long village lying on two lanes, one of which is the Levens to Underbarrow road. From St John's Church, which is on the higher side of the village, there are lovely views over the vale.

Brigsteer Wood to the south, which is owned by the National Trust, is notable for its flora and fauna. The Cumbria Trust for Nature Conservation look after two areas of old woodland within it and sees that unwanted new growth is cut away every 15 years or so in order to maintain the delicate ecological balance.

AA recommends:
Guest Houses: Barrowfield (farmhouse), *tel.* Crosthwaite 336

Autumn tints on the lakeside at Buttermere

Broughton-in-Furness

Map Ref: 89SD2187

Broughton is an interesting little market town lying close to where the beautiful River Duddon joins the sea. It is on the southern edge of the National Park at the crossroads of the A593/595.

It was first mentioned as 'Brocton', meaning 'settlement by the brook', in 1196. The present church dates from the 11th century with Saxon walls and a Norman archway. The splendid Broughton Tower and its dungeons – to the north end of the town – are all that remain of the old castle of the Broughtons who settled in the area in Anglo-Saxon times and continued to flourish under the Normans and Plantagenets. Easily accessible, there are several public footpaths that traverse the old castle grounds.

Broughton retains its character as a compact 18th-century market town. Fine chestnut trees shade the square, where fish slabs and a set of old stocks remain from former times.

A new visitor attraction is the Jack Hadwin Motorcycle Collection. Opened in 1981 as the Lakeland Motorcycle Museum, this attractive display includes a variety of classical machines surrounded by many other items of motoring interest.

Cycle spares and repairs can be obtained from the Mountain Centre, Market Street. Fishing licences are available at the post office.

Burneside

Map Ref: 93SD5095

Burneside can be reached from Kendal on the B5284 (turn right past County Hall) or from the A591.

This large village is famous for its paper mills. There have been mills on the River Kent at Burneside at least since 1283, where there is known to have been a corn mill. Traces of the mill dam and race can still be seen. The oldest of the existing mills dates to 1750. This mill was bought in 1854 by James Cropper, who later built the Bowston mill (1874) and whose family still own the paper business.

Tolson Hall was built in 1638 by Thomas Tolson, an early tobacco merchant. The gateway to the south of the

Hall – which a road to the village from the A591 passes – was built in 1750 by the then owner, John Bateman, who also erected opposite the western entrance an eccentric field gateway spanned by the jaw bones of a whale, but these have now disintegrated. Another of the Bateman family's eye-catching constructions was the William Pitt Monument on the hill opposite the hall (visible from the Plumgarths roundabout). It was put up in 1814 to commemorate William Pitt and the British victory at Waterloo; however, when Napoleon escaped from Elba, the Batemans were so disgusted that they never added the plaque.

AA recommends:
Guest Houses: Garnett House (farmhouse), *tel.* Kendal 24542

Buttermere

Map Ref: 76NY1716

Buttermere village lies between Buttermere and Crummock Water. It can be reached over the Honister Pass (B5289) from Keswick or from Cockermouth.

The village made national news in 1802 when Mary Robinson (daughter of the landlord of the Fish Hotel, and known as the 'Beauty of Buttermere', was married to a 'gentleman' calling himself the Hon. Alexander Hope MP, brother of the Earl of Hopetoun. The *Sun* newspaper described her as having 'long attracted the notice of every visitor by her exquisite elegance and the becoming manner in which she is used to fillet her beautiful long hair'. (Courtesy Cumbria County Record Office, Carlisle.)

Later, however, the 'gentleman' was found to be an impostor named John Hatfield, a bankrupt wanted for forgery, and he was hanged a year later in Carlisle. The 'Beauty' later married a local farmer, had a large family, and was buried at Caldbeck (see page 31).

Today Buttermere is a centre for exploring some of the wildest and grandest scenery in the Lake District. The Buttermere fells soar up from the north-east shore of the lake to Robinson and from the south-west shore to Red Pike, High Stile and High Crag to Scarf Gap.

At the south end of the lake the Haystacks and Fleetwith are prominent. Here there are tough walks and climbs or easy strolls along the lake shore. The lake and most of the shore are now owned by the National Trust. A guided walk starts at the car park (details from National Park Information Centres).

Just half a mile to the north-west of the village of Buttermere and sharing the same valley, is two-and-a-half-mile long Crummock Water. The B5289 from Buttermere to Cockermouth runs along much of its eastern shore amid very beautiful scenery. Brackenthwaite Fell rises steeply from the east shore and Mellbreak rises from the west. Also here is Scale Force, the highest waterfall in the Lake District. The stream leaps, in one clear fall of 120ft, between rock walls.

AA recommends:
Hotels: Bridge, 2-star, *tel.* Buttermere 252

Legendary huntsman John Peel is buried in Caldbeck churchyard

Caldbeck

Map Ref: 73NY3239

Caldbeck is on the northern boundary of the National Park.

It was made famous by John Peel, the renowned huntsman, who was born at Park End, Caldbeck, in 1776, and buried in Caldbeck churchyard on 13 November 1854, after a hunting accident at Ruthwaite. His gravestone is decorated with hunting symbols.

The words of the song *D'ye Ken John Peel* by which he is immortalised, were written by his friend John Woodcock Graves at his home in Caldbeck after a day's hunting in 1832. After the poem was first sung to its original tune at the Rising Sun Inn, such was the applause that Graves is reported to have said: 'By Jove, Peel, you'll be sung when we're both run to earth!'

However, it was not until William Metcalfe, the choirmaster of Carlisle Cathedral, put new music to it in 1869 that it became a national song.

There is a plaque now outside the house where Graves composed the song, and in 1939 a shelter was erected opposite the church as a memorial to Peel and Graves.

AA recommends:
Restaurants: Parkend, 1 fork, *tel.* Caldbeck 442
Guest Houses: High Greenrigg House, *tel.* Caldbeck 430
Friar Hall (farmhouse), *tel.* Caldbeck 633

Calder Bridge

Map Ref: 68NY0405

Calder Bridge is on the western boundary of the National Park, south-west of Egremont on the A595. As its name suggests, it was built where the route crosses the Calder.

Calder Abbey, three-quarters of a mile higher up the Calder, was founded in 1134, but dissolved in 1536. There are still some interesting parts remaining, including a west doorway, five bays of the north aisle, some transept arches and part of the chancel. It is in private hands and there is no public access to it, but it can be clearly seen from the road.

To the south-west is the world's first industrial-sized nuclear power station at Calder Hall, opened in 1956, and the Sellafield nuclear fuel re-processing plant, opened in 1951.

Cark-in-Cartmel

Map Ref: 68SD3676

This little village is handy for both Cartmel Sands and Grange-over-Sands.

In the 18th and 19th centuries this village contained a number of mills, and its industrial history is reflected in the name of a village pub, 'The Engine Inn'.

Nearby is Holker Hall, on the road from Cark to Haverthwaite which joins the A590 Newby Bridge to Ulverston road. The Hall was one of the favourite homes of the Duke of Devonshire; and it has remained in Cavendish hands ever since. Dating from the 16th century, it features unique woodcarving and stonework, and also a fine collection of paintings and

Rambling Holker Hall near Cark-in-Cartmel

furniture. Surrounded by 122 acres of parkland with two herds of deer, the formal and woodland gardens are famous for a year-long flower display.

Cark-in-Cartmel's other attractions include the Lakeland Motor Museum and the many events held at Holker Hall such as horse-driving championships and the internationally famous Lakeland Rose Show (held in July).

AA recommends:
Campsites: Old Park Wood Caravan Site, 2-pennants, *tel.* Flookburgh 266
Garages: Central, *tel.* Flookburgh 330

Carlisle

Map Ref: 68NY3955

Carlisle, the county town of the old Cumberland and now of Cumbria, first began to develop as a Roman frontier town when Hadrian's Wall was built east to Newcastle and west to Bowness-on-Solway.

Norman invaders reached Carlisle in 1092, when William Rufus set about building Carlisle Castle. The massive Norman keep was finished in the 12th century. That and the 14th-century main gate are the most impressive surviving buildings of the castle today. In the keep can be seen the 15ft thick walls and the condemned cell decorated with graffiti scratched by desperate prisoners.

There is also in the keep an exhibition which brings to life the history of the castle and the Border wars in which it played a part for 600 years. The Border Regiment Museum contains uniforms, medals, weapons, documents and trophies dating from 1702.

The cathedral was built in 1124. Although small by cathedral standards, it is the third oldest in the north. The decorated choir has many notable features; and the painted ceiling and the stalls with painted backs are of especial interest.

The city's half-timbered guildhall was built in the 15th century and is now open as a museum of guild, civic and local history.

One of the most important museums in Cumbria is based at Tullie House, Castle Street, with collections featuring Roman and prehistoric archaeology. There is also an art gallery with British paintings, porcelain, costume and natural history.

There is a small theatre in West Walls, called The Green Room Club. Also of note is the Stanwix Arts Theatre, with its professional productions by noted players.

The recently-developed Animals' Refuge at Oak Tree Farm, Wetheral Shields, is well worth a visit.

Details of other visitor attractions in and around the city can be obtained from the Tourist Information Centre in the Old Town Hall (tel. Carlisle 25517)

AA recommends:
Hotels: Crest, Kingstown, 3-star, *tel.* Carlisle 31201
Crown and Mitre, English Street, 3-star, *tel.* Carlisle 25491
Cumbrian Thistle, Court Square, 3-star, *tel.* Carlisle 31951
Swallow Hilltop, London Road, 3-star, *tel.* Carlisle 29255
Central, Victoria Viaduct, 2-star, *tel.* Carlisle 20256
Cumbria Park, 32 Scotland Road, 2-star, *tel.* Carlisle 22887
Pinegrove, London Road, 2-star, *tel.* Carlisle 24828
Vallum House, Burgh Road, 1-star, *tel.* Carlisle 21860
Campsites: Orton Grange Caravan Park, Wigton Road, 3-pennants, *tel.* Carlisle 710252
Self Catering: Millstone Cottage, Blackhall Wood, *tel.* Worcester 830899
Guest Houses: Angus Hotel, 14 Scotland Road, *tel.* Carlisle 23546
East View, 110 Warwick Road, *tel.* Carlisle 22112
Kenilworth Hotel, Lazonby Terrace, *tel.* Carlisle 26179
Garages: Grahams Motor Engineers, London Road, *tel.* Carlisle 21739
Carleton Service Station, Carleton, *tel.* Carlisle 27287
Robert Street Motor Engineers, Robert Street, *tel.* Carlisle 33823

Cartmel

Map Ref: 68NY3778

Cartmel is a very attractive village half a mile outside the National Park.

The village is well-known for its priory, built in 1188, of which only the gatehouse and church remains. The rest was destroyed when the priory was dissolved in 1536–37. The church was restored in 1620 by George Preston of Holker Hall (see page 31) and became the parish church. As a result, Cartmel now has one of only four monastic churches in Cumbria (apart from the cathedral) that remained in use as parish churches after the Dissolution; and it is the only one in the county – and one of very few in England – where the whole church was preserved.

One of the features of this church is the

Towering above the Great Langdale Valley are the dramatic Langdale Pikes

Harrington family tomb, with its effigies of Sir John Harrington (who died in 1347) and his wife, both literally 'lifting up their hearts'.

The beautiful 14th-century monastic gatehouse in the village square was used from 1624–1790 as a grammar school. It was acquired by the National Trust in 1946 and is now an art gallery and folk museum.

Cartmel is a natural place for artists and craftspeople and there are a number of places in the village where their work is being either created, displayed or sold. At Michael Gibbons Carved Art Gallery in Grammar School Road the artist's own wood sculptures are displayed in a 17th-century barn.

Cartmel Races are set in beautiful parkland and attract the top jockeys. A fairground atmosphere with stalls and refreshments transforms the park on race days.

AA recommends:
Hotels: Aynsome Manor, 2-star, *tel.* Cartmel 276
Grammar, 2-star, *tel.* Cartmel 367
Priory, The Square, 1-star, *tel.* Cartmel 267
Self Catering: Aynsome Manor Park, *tel.* Cartmel 433
Church Town House, Market Square, *tel.* Lytham St Annes 734736

Cartmel Fell

Map Ref: 92SD4188

Cartmel Fell parish now includes much of the residential area on the south-eastern shore of Windermere. But the unique parish church, built in 1504, is on its own, two miles up on the fells to the east.

The church can be reached via the Fell road that leaves the A592 Newby Bridge to Bowness road at Fell Foot one mile north of Newby Bridge. Dedicated to St Anthony, the church was built by local farmers to save the walk of seven miles to Cartmel Priory (see this page). There is a 17th-century three-decker pulpit and beautifully carved 16th- and 17th-century box pews. The 16th-century east window is worthy of note, being a good example of a seven-sacrament window.

Its most precious possession is the best of only three pre-Reformation carved wooden figures of Christ that have survived to the present, but that is now on display at the Borough Museum in Kendal.

The writer, Arthur Ransome, lived at Low Ludderburn, Cartmel Fell, from 1925–35, and the present owners are happy to have people call to see where he worked. It was there that he wrote *Swallows and Amazons*, the first of his popular children's books set in the Lake District. He also lived at The Heald on Coniston (1940–45); Lowick Hall (1947–50); and Hill Top, Haverthwaite (1963–65).

Chapel Stile (Great Langdale)

Map Ref: 85NY3205

Chapel Stile is at the foot of Great Langdale. It can be reached on the Langdale road (B5343) from Skelwith Bridge, which is on the Coniston road (A593) out of Ambleside.

Slate quarrying was once the mainstay of the area. Stone and slate houses were built for quarrymen and for the employees of the gunpowder works at Elter Water (see page 37).

In the valley itself are many old farmhouses, mostly 17th century. Many of these have been acquired by the National Trust – who now own 88 farms throughout the Lake District – in order to ensure that their traditional construction and appearance are maintained, while keeping them as working farms. In some cases purchase by the National Trust has prevented large scale farms being split up and disappearing as workable farming units.

The dale is the centre for exploring many of the Lake District's most beautiful and popular fells, as well as other attractions such as the Dungeon Ghyll waterfalls. The Langdale Pikes are perhaps the most familiar of the mountains, and their distinctive shapes have been much painted and photographed.

At the head of the dale is Bow Fell. Whimsically-named Crinkle Crags and Pike o' Blisco further enclose it. The only way out at the head of the valley for motorists – who only have one narrow, wall-lined road to use in the valley floor itself – is up a steep and even narrower road over to Little Langdale (see page 48).

On the heights of Pike o' Stickle is a 4,000-year-old 'axe factory' where rock for axe heads was quarried and taken down to the valley for finishing. Axe heads were exported all over Britain. Pike o' Stickle is today a favourite area for antiquarians and archaeologists.

Clappersgate and Brathay

Map Ref: 86NY3603

Clappersgate is an old residential village adjoining Ambleside to the west of the Rothay River Bridge. It is mainly strung out along the river and along the A593 to Coniston.

The dominant property of the village is the 18th-century former Croft Hotel. This was at one time being considered for demolition as it had been disused for some years. But thankfully this listed building has been saved through a scheme to convert it into flats, now completed. It therefore still retains its prominent position at the head of Lake Windermere.

On the south side of the road and just over another bridge on the Hawkshead road (B5286) is the associated area of Brathay. This contains Brathay Hall, an 18th-century mansion, which is now the focus of the Brathay Education Centre.

The River Brathay is a popular training ground for canoeists and a number of local canoeists have reached national standard. Fishing permits for the river are available from the Windermere and District Anglers Association, c/o The Cycle Shop, The Slack, Ambleside.

AA recommends:
Hotels: Nanny Brow Country House, 2-star, Country House Hotel, *tel.* Ambleside 32036

Clifton (nr Penrith)

Map Ref: 75NY5326

Clifton, on the A6 two miles south of Penrith, was the scene of the last pitched battle fought on English soil. It is not difficult to imagine the scenes of chaos and destruction on the night of 18 December 1745, when the Duke of Cumberland caught up with Bonnie Prince Charlie and his retreating Scottish Jacobites at Town End, Clifton. You can even see the 'Rebel Tree' (an ancient oak) at Town End Farm, at the south end of the village. Under it five slaughtered Highlanders were buried. A plaque there reads: 'Here is buried the men of the Army of Prince Charles who fell at Clifton Moor 18 December 1745.' In the churchyard there is a stone to the memory of the six troopers of Bland's regiment who were killed; five other English dragoons also fell, and are buried there.

The battle of Clifton ended with the Scots abandoning their position, although afterwards both sides said they were satisfied with the result. It certainly did little to improve the Prince's position, for his retreat continued until the Battle of Culloden in Scotland where his hopes were dashed for good.

To the west of Clifton at Clifton Dykes is the Wetheriggs Pottery, which started making bricks, tiles and pottery in 1855. Although modern methods are now used, all the processes of the old country pottery can be seen in the museum. Weaving is also demonstrated, and there is a gallery with displays of work by local artists and craftsmen.

Horse riding is available from the White Horse stables in Clifton.

AA recommends:
Hotels: Clifton Hill, 2-star, *tel.* Penrith 62717

Cockermouth

Map Ref: 70NY1230

Cockermouth is an ancient market town now bypassed by the A66 cross-Cumbria trunk road. It stands in attractive countryside on the fringe of the National Park, at a point where the River Cocker joins the River Derwent.

The Romans recognised its strategic importance and controlled its warlike Brigante tribes from here. The castle was built in the 12th century so that the English could protect the area from the marauding Scots – but Robert the Bruce destroyed part of it in 1315. In the Civil War it was held for Parliament despite a siege in 1648. The building then fell into decay and just one wing, rebuilt last century, is now used as a residence by the Wyndham family; another is an estate office.

After being granted its market charter in 1221, Cockermouth gradually developed in importance as a market town. In 1568 Mary Queen of Scots stayed here after her flight from the Battle of Langside. In the 17th century it was the chief commercial centre in the old county of Cumberland. Although considerably developed since then, it has retained much of its original character. A typical Cumbrian agricultural show is held here each summer, with classes for livestock, produce and crafts; also hound trails and Cumberland and Westmorland wrestling.

Many famous people have been born in Cockermouth or the surrounding villages. These include Fletcher Christian, the *Bounty* mutineer, who was born at Moorland Close and baptised at Brigham in 1764 (see page 36); John Dalton, the discoverer of the Atomic Theory, who was born in 1766 in Eaglesfield (see page 36); and, of course, poet William Wordsworth, who was born in Cockermouth's Main Street in 1770. The Georgian mansion he was born in became the home of Wordsworth's father in 1766 when he was appointed to the position of steward to Sir James Lowther. The house overlooks the Derwent and has a delightful garden and terraced walk. William and his sister Dorothy refer to it many times in their writing even though they lived most of their lives in Grasmere (see page 41) and Rydal (see page 55). The house is now in the possession of the National Trust and open to the public from April to October.

All Saints Church, the oldest of the four Parish churches, is beside the Market Square. The present building was completed in 1854. It has a 180ft spire with a peal of eight bells and a memorial window to Wordsworth.

The town now serves a wide rural area in general business and industry and has facilities for tourists with car parks, shops and accommodation. The Cockermouth Festival is held during the third week in August; it includes talks by well-known authors, concerts, art and craft exhibitions. Popular cattle auctions, sheep fairs and auctions are also held. A walk round Cockermouth will reveal many interesting viewpoints and examples of domestic Georgian architecture and industrial archaeology.

The Tourist Information Centre (tel. Cockermouth 822634) is in the market place and riverside car park at the eastern end of the shopping area.

AA recommends:
Hotels: Broughton Craggs, Great Broughton, 3-star, *tel.* Cockermouth 824400
Trout, Crown Street, 3-star, *tel.* Cockermouth 823591
Globe, Main Street, 2-star, *tel.* Cockermouth 822126
Wordsworth, Main Street, 2-star, *tel.* Cockermouth 822757
Restaurants: Old Court House, Main Street, 1-fork, *tel.* Cockermouth 823871
Campsites: Violet Bank Caravan Site, off Lorton Road, 3-pennants, *tel.* Cockermouth 822169

Wordsworth House in Cockermouth, faithfully restored as the poet's childhood home

Colton

Map Ref: 90SD3186

This is a small, scattered village two miles north of Greenodd (see page 41). But the parish of Colton is a large one, extending from the southern shores of Windermere, four miles to the east, and to the River Crake over a mile to the west.

An amazing feature is the Holy Trinity Church, perched near the top of a hill, reached by a winding track above the village. Built in the 15th century, it was enlarged in the 16th century and consecrated in 1578 by Bishop Sandys, Archbishop of York, who was born near Hawkshead (see page 42). The present church was rebuilt in the 17th century. It is in a splendid setting with superb views across the River Crake to the southern Lake District fells.

There are some beautiful walks over moors and through the valleys. Two of these start from Bandrake Head, three-quarters of a mile north of Colton, and go through Abbot Park to Stock Wood on Bethecar Moor, from which there are magnificent views of both Morecambe Bay (to the south) and Coniston Old Man (to the north-west). Footpaths then lead west to Low Nibthwaite on the River Crake or east to Ickenthwaite and the Rusland Pool, or back through Oxen Park to Bandrake Head.

Coniston

Map Ref: 90SD3097

Coniston village is at the northern end of five-and-a-half-mile long Coniston

Water. It used to be a railway terminus, with trains joining the Barrow-Grange line at Foxfield, but the line is now closed.

The best-known resident of Coniston was the Victorian writer John Ruskin, who lived at Brantwood, on the east side of the lake, from 1871 to 1900. The house, now administered by an Educational Trust, is open to the public. It contains many items associated with Ruskin, including paintings by his protégé William Turner. There are plans to bring more Ruskin paintings, manuscripts and diaries to Brantwood for display and to hold regular art exhibitions. A three-and-a-half-mile nature trail starts from the house.

Ruskin's ideas on education inspired people in many countries and the local secondary school is named after him. There is also a Ruskin museum in the village where one of the main exhibits is a linen pall worked with Ruskin Lace, made by the women of the area to cover his body for his burial in Coniston churchyard. Ruskin Lace was derived from a Greek lace pattern which the writer brought back from the Continent; he encouraged his housekeeper to ornament the household linen with it. Other women took up the idea and then the Lakeland linen industry adopted it. Ruskin Lace survived as a cottage industry until the mid-1970s, but now it is just kept alive by enthusiastic needlewomen sewing for pleasure in their own homes.

Other famous people associated with Coniston include (later Sir) Malcolm

Main picture: the charming Victorian steam yacht, Gondola, operated by the National Trust. Inset: Coniston Water from Brantwood

Campbell and his son Donald. In August 1939 at Coniston, Donald christened the first 'Bluebird' powerboat for his father, who, a few days later, set up a new world record of 141.74mph. After the war, Donald returned to Coniston many times and between 1956–59 broke the world record five times (the last time reaching 276.33mph). Then, on 4 January, 1967, he was killed on the lake when trying to raise the world record to 300mph. His body was never recovered. It was out of deference to Campbell and his efforts that the Home Secretary gave authority for world waterspeed record attempts to continue on the lake (with the permission of the Lake District Special Planning Board) despite the 10mph limit he imposed on other lake users.

An historic vessel on the lake is the *Gondola*, an 1859 steam launch which the National Trust restored after it had lain rotting in the reeds for many years. This beautiful, stately vessel now takes passengers on regular scheduled trips around the lake. Sailing, motor and rowing boats can be hired from the Coniston Boating Centre, where private boats can also be launched. Horse riding is available at Spoon Hall and fishing information from the Coniston Gifts and Sports Shop.

To the west of Coniston is The Old Man of Coniston, a well known peak, which can be reached from the village on foot. There are several other mountains over 2,500ft in the Coniston group.

The beauty spot Tarn Hows is two miles to the north-east, approachable along the road to Hawkshead.

For other attractions and interests around Coniston Water see entries for Torver (page 60) and Blawith (page 27).

AA recommends:
Hotels: Sun, 2-star, *tel.* Coniston 248
Black Bull, 1-star, *tel.* Coniston 335
Guest Houses and Inns: Crown Inn, *tel.* Coniston 243
Garages: Hellens, Broughton Road, *tel.* Coniston 253

Crook

Map Ref: 92SD4695

Crook is on the B5284 Kendal to Bowness road. It is mainly a community of scattered farms, but there is a concentration of dwellings along the road around the inn and the post office.

Crook Hall, now a farmhouse, used to be the home of the Philipsons. Robert Philipson, a Royalist officer – known locally as 'Robin the Devil' – was once besieged on Belle Isle, Windermere, by some of Cromwell's Roundheads under Colonel Briggs. After being rescued by his brother, Robert decided to take his revenge on Colonel Briggs by riding right into Kendal Church (see page 44), where he was at worship, and capturing him there. But when the congregation saw Robert and his brother on horseback inside the church with swords drawn, they were so angry that they chased them out. In his enforced haste Robert left his sword and helmet behind in the church, where they are displayed today.

The Crook area is full of history, and industrial archaeology. Recently, staff at the Wild Boar Hotel (even further west along the road) in conjunction with a local historian, have developed an easy two-mile history trail from the hotel. Greenhills Stables offers horse riding.

AA recommends:
Hotels: Wild Boar, Crook, 3-star, *tel.* Windermere 5225
Guest Houses: Greenbank (farmhouse), *tel.* Staveley 821216

Crooklands

Map Ref: 93SD5383

Crooklands is a busy little village just north of the No. 36 Interchange on the M6, where the A65 to Skipton and the A591 to the Lakes meet the motorway.

Much of the business of Crooklands is based on passing traffic and its hotel is well known. Its church, officially the church of St Patrick, Preston Patrick, is a landmark for travellers at Christmas time, for the large cross on top is lit up and can be seen from the M6 motorway.

About half a mile north-west of Crooklands church is Preston Patrick Hall, a 14th-century manor house, and one of the oldest houses in the area. This is now a farm house, but free admission is available throughout the year by appointment. The court room and west wing have excellent traceried windows.

A canal bank nature trail runs along a short length of the Lancaster–Kendal Canal between Crooklands and Stainton. Leaflets describing the trail, which starts at Field End, one mile south of Stainton, are available from the Cumbria Trust for Nature Conservation, Ambleside (tel. Ambleside 32476).

AA recommends:
Hotels: Crooklands, 3-star, *tel.* Crooklands 432
Campsites: Millness Hill Camping Site, Preston Patrick, 2-pennants, *tel.* Crooklands 306
Garages: Canal, Exit 36 off M6, *tel.* Crooklands 401
Crooklands Motor Co., Adjacent M6, Junction 36, *tel.* Crooklands 414
Crooklands Mill, *tel.* Crooklands 216

Crosthwaite (Lyth Valley)

Map Ref: 92SD4491

Crosthwaite lies on the north side of the Lyth Valley, about half a mile off the A5074.

The Church of St Mary is a large one built on the site of former churches going back to the time when a preaching cross – hence Cross-thwaite – was put up there.

Most of the large parish is between the Lyth and Winster valleys (see page 65), an area which is one of the best damson-growing regions in the country. Damsons are native here and the clouds of white damson blossom in spring are one of the attractions of the area. It is worth choosing the Lyth Valley route to the Lakes from the south – already one of the approach roads – just to see the damson blossom in bloom.

Lyth Valley Damsons are one of the special 'Tastes of Cumbria' promoted by the Cumbria Tourist Board. They have a distinctive nutty flavour, and are used for making desserts, jam, wine, punch and damson gin.

AA recommends:
Hotels: Damson Dene Country, Lyth Valley, 3-star, *tel.* Crosthwaite 227
Campsites: Lambhowe Caravan Park, 1-pennant, *tel.* Crosthwaite 483

Dacre

Map Ref: 74NY4526

Dacre village is steeped in history. It lies just inside the National Park in the triangle between the A66 road west from Penrith and the A592 Penrith to Ullswater road, about a mile from each. Ullswater is two miles to the south.

Dacre Castle, a massive 14th-century pele tower, was one of a line of fortified towers erected in the Eden valley to keep out the Scots during the Middle Ages. The battlements are remarkably well preserved and still look very impressive. The castle is open to the public by written appointment. It was restored in 1675 and in 1723 became the property of Edward Hassell, owner of Dalemain, a stately home which exists to this day about a mile to the east of Dacre on the A592. This fine-looking house is of medieval and Elizabethan origin, with an imposing early Georgian façade, set in elegant parkland where deer roam freely. Dalemain is open to the public and contains interesting pictures and furniture, the Westmorland and Cumberland Yeomanry Museum, agricultural bygones and portraits. Tea is served in the banqueting hall and there is an adventure playground.

Much of Dacre Church has survived from the Norman period. But one of its main treasures is a big 17th-century lock (now on the south door) with the initials and date 'AP 1671' carved on it. These stand for 'Anne of Pembroke' (Lady Anne Clifford, Countess of Pembroke), who gave the lock and key in that year.

Also unique to the church are four stone bears at the corners of the graveyard. They are carved in different positions and tell a story anti-clockwise of a sleeping bear waking up and eating a cat or lynx that jumped on its back. Their origin is still a mystery, although it is believed they might have stood originally on top of the castle.

It is thought that the Church stands on the site of a monastery referred to by the Venerable Bede as having existed in the

One of the four stone bears in the churchyard at Dacre

720s. Archaeologists have been excavating there to see if that is true. If it is confirmed, this will be only the third pre-Viking monastery found in the north of England.

Dalton-in-Furness

Map Ref: 68SD2374

Dalton, between Ulverston and Barrow, was once the main town of Furness. A tower-like fortress was built here in the 14th century by the Abbots of Furness to protect the area. They held their courts there until the dissolution of Furness Abbey in the 16th century (see page 26). The castle still exists today and contains a small but interesting collection of armour and local records. It is open daily, and the key can be obtained from 18 Market Place.

Gradually Ulverston (see page 61) replaced Dalton as the main market centre for Furness. But its former importance is reflected in the number of 17th-century cottages that remain around the Market Square. There are also many good examples of both Georgian and Victorian architecture to be seen. Dalton Town Trail has been established so that visitors can enjoy some of the historic buildings of the town on a leisurely walk, and details of the one-and-a-half-mile trail can be obtained from the Tourist Information Centre in Barrow.

Dalton's most famous son was the artist George Romney, who was born here in 1734. He was employed by his father as a cabinet maker in Dalton before being apprenticed as an artist to Christopher Steele of Kendal. He married a Kendal girl in 1756 and then went to London, where he became one of the leading portrait painters of his day. His portraits are found in the National Gallery, in Abbot Hall Art Gallery, Kendal (see page 44) and in many stately homes, including Sizergh Castle (see page 57). Romney returned to Kendal in 1799 and died there in 1802. He is buried in Dalton churchyard.

Tytup Hall, a 17th- and 18th-century house north of Dalton containing period panelling, may be visited by appointment (tel. Dalton 62929).

AA recommends:
Garages: Abbey Road, *tel.* Dalton-in-Furness 62336

Drigg

Map Ref: 68SD0698

Drigg is a mile off the A595, between the main road and the coast, just north of Ravenglass.

Drigg's main attraction is sand dunes. West and south of the village, on the dunes, is the Ravenglass Gullery and Nature Reserve, owned by Muncaster Castle but managed by Cumbria County Council. It has a large black-headed gull colony. Other breeding birds include sandwich, common, arctic and little terns, shelduck, red-breasted merganser and ringed plover. Natterjack toads – Britain's rarest amphibians – are among other species that breed here.

Access can be obtained by permit from the County Estate Surveyor and Valuer, Arroyo Block, The Castle, Carlisle (Phone: Carlisle 23456).

For other attractions and interests in the area see entries under Holmrook (page 44), Muncaster (see page 51) and Ravenglass (page 54).

Duddon Bridge (and Valley)

Map Ref: 89SD1988

Although there are only a few houses around Duddon Bridge, it has great strategic importance. This is the point where the A595 Barrow to Whitehaven road crosses the River Duddon just before it flows out over the Duddon sands. Here the river completes its 12-mile journey from Wrynose Pass before it merges with the sea.

Wordsworth wrote a series of 35 poems on the theme of the Duddon. Where it reaches Duddon Bridge he describes the river as 'majestic Duddon' making 'radiant progress towards the deep'.

From Duddon Bridge, there is a choice of two routes northwards up the valley, one on either side. Each has its own scenic merits, and they join at Whistling Green, just south of Ulpha (see page 61).

Swinside Stone Circle, a 90ft prehistoric circle, can be seen on the fells two miles west of Duddon Bridge.

Eaglesfield

Map Ref: 70NY0928

In this village, two miles south-west of Cockermouth and one mile west of the A5086, is John Dalton's House.

This is where, on 6 September 1766, John Dalton, the Discoverer of the Atomic Theory, was born. In addition to the house name there is also a plaque to him above another door. He published the famous theory in 1804.

Fletcher Christian, the *Bounty* mutineer, was born at Moorland Close, near Eaglesfield, as a plaque on the house commemorates. He was baptised in Brigham Church on 25 September, 1764.

After entering the Navy, Fletcher Christian became first mate to Captain Bligh on HMS *Bounty*. On 28 April 1789, when they were in the middle of the Pacific, Fletcher organised a mutiny and put Captain Bligh in a longboat. Fletcher scuttled the *Bounty* on the Pitcairns, where he remained for the rest of his life, and where the population is still mainly descended from him and other mutineers.

Robert Eaglesfield, founder of Queen's College, Oxford, was also born in the village which shares his name. He was buried at Oxford in 1349.

Brougham Castle, near Eamont Bridge, on a site fortified since Roman times

Eamont Bridge

Map Ref: 75NY5228

Eamont Bridge, which is on the A6, three-quarters of a mile south of Penrith, is noteworthy for its two prehistoric henge monuments.

In the field on the corner of the A6 and the B5320 to Ullswater is Arthur's Round Table, which has a bank outside and two entrances, probably of early Bronze Age date (about 1800 BC). It was used for religious purposes.

Two hundred yards up the road on the right is a turning off to the Mayburgh monument. This formerly contained two concentric circles of standing stones, and two pairs flanking the entrance. Only one stone, about 15ft high, now remains – in the centre. Probably of late Neolithic date (about 2000 BC), this, too, had a religious origin.

One mile along the B6262 on the other side of the A6 is Brougham Castle. This was one of the castles restored by Lady Anne Clifford in the 17th century and it is regarded as one of the most interesting castle ruins in northern England.

The 'greasy pole' competition in progress at Egremont's annual Crab Fair

Egremont

Map Ref: 68NY0110

This old market town, with a wide tree-lined main street, developed where the west coast route (A595) crosses the Ehen river flowing from Ennerdale.

One of its attractions is the 12th-century Norman castle, built of red sandstone. It was destroyed in the 16th century and is now a ruin, but the gatehouse is still very impressive

Also open to the public is the Lowes Court Gallery, a 16th-century building restored by local enthusiasts to promote appreciation of the arts. All work exhibited

Wild and naked Ennerdale, one of Lakeland's most remote valleys

is by artists living in Cumbria or with strong local connections; there are regular exhibitions. The Tourist Information Centre (tel. Egremont 820693) is at the Gallery, 12/13 Main Street. There is a street market every Friday.

Egremont is famous for its Crab Fair. Held since 1267, this old-fashioned country fair is connected with fruit not fish, and held in celebration of the crab apple. The parade of the Apple Cart takes place in the main street at 12.30pm on the third Saturday in September, when about £40 worth of apples are thrown to the public.

The main street then also becomes the site of the 'greasy pole' competition, with the pole itself being erected at dawn on the day of the fair. This originally had a sheep fastened to the top; the prize for anyone able to scale the 30ft pole without artificial aids. These days a £1 note is stuck on top instead. If that doesn't seem like much of a prize in these days of inflation, remember it's the glory not the reward that counts.

In the evening the World Gurning Championships are held. The person who can pull the most grotesque face through a horse collar is the winner.

There are also track and field events, shows and hound trails during the day.

Elterwater

Map Ref: 85NY3204

Elterwater is a small village at the entrance to the Langdale valley where the Langdale Beck meets the River Brathay.

Elter Water is one of the smallest lakes and it is privately owned. Its name is derived from the Norse meaning 'Swan Lake'. It is still visited sometimes in winter by Whooper swans.

Elterwater Common to the east of the village is managed by the

National Trust, who have provided a convenient car park. The village itself has a small green and a new car park.

Elterwater quarries nearby are still working, providing attractive green slate that is exported as well as used for buildings in this country.

AA recommends:

Hotels: Britannia Inn, 1-star, *tel.* Langdale 210

Eltermere, 1-star, *tel.* Langdale 207

Embleton

Map Ref: 70NY1730

This is a mainly linear village strung out for about two miles along the line of the old Keswick to Cockermouth road.

Higham Hall is to the north of the road through the village, about one mile west of Bassenthwaite Lake. This is a Cumbria County Council establishment where weekend summer schools study such topics as the natural history of the Lake District, creative writing and painting.

Between the Hall and the lake is Dubwath, home of the Bassenthwaite Sailing Club (see page 27).

To the west of the village is the Cockermouth Golf Club.

On opposite (south) side of the A66 is Wythop Mill, where centuries of history are gathered under one roof. It is a beautifully-restored mill where the visitor can see vintage water-powered woodworking machinery and a display of hand tools used by craftsmen centuries ago. Delicious home-made fare is available in the coffee shop.

Ennerdale

Map Ref: NY0615

The village of Ennerdale Bridge developed at the first crossing point over the River Ehen after leaving Ennerdale Water.

Now on the boundary of the National Park, Ennerdale Bridge is a quiet village surrounded by fine scenery. The original chapel was built in 1543. After a visit to a later chapel on the site, Wordsworth was inspired to write his poem *The Brothers* (1799). The present church succeeded

that one in 1857.

One mile to the east of the village is two-and-a-half-mile long Ennerdale Water, one of the most remote and unspoiled lakes. Great efforts have been made to preserve it and to prevent any more water being taken from it for coastal industries.

Measures to preserve the beauty of Ennerdale Water are now being undertaken by the Forestry Commission. The straight line planting of the Ennerdale Forest in the 1930s aroused so much criticism that in 1936 the Forestry Commission agreed with the Council for the Protection of Rural England that they would not plant any more trees in the central 300 square miles of the Lake District. Since 1981 the Forestry Commission themselves have been trying to soften the lines of the Ennerdale Forest pattern to follow the contours, and also to introduce different species. Signs of the improvements can now be clearly seen at various points in the valley.

There is now a marked trail (Nine Beck Walk) along cleared forest roads giving magnificent views. The nine mile walk starts from Bowness Knott along the north shore, where a leaflet gives details of a shorter two to three mile walk (Smithy Beck Nature Trail) along the edge of Ennerdale Water; this has eight stops along the way including a visit to the site of a small medieval settlement and bloomery (iron furnace).

There is no road round the lake. Cars can be taken as far as Bowness Knott where there is a car park and picnic area. The view of the lake and fells from Bowness Knott is one of the best.

All private craft are prohibited on Ennerdale Water, but anglers are allowed to fish from the shore. Fishing permits are obtainable from Phyllis Humphreys, High Bridge Farm, in the village.

Trekking and hacking facilties are offered by Low Cock How at Kinniside one mile from the village.

The Ennerdale Show is held at Bowness Knott on the last Wednesday in August. Started as a flower show in 1895, it is now a major agricultural and horticultural show with local crafts, cooking competitions, hound trails, foxhounds, terrier and sheepdog shows, a gymkhana and fell racing. Proceeds go to provide a Christmas party for local children.

Eskdale Green (and Devoke Water)

Map Ref: 82NY1400

Eskdale Green is a village that you will pass through travelling from the A595 at Gosforth to Santon Bridge and Eskdale; or, from the central Lakes, over Wrynose and Hardknott passes via Boot (see page 28). The road over the passes is very steep (up to 1 in 3 gradient) and winding, but offers superb views of the surrounding fells. The Ravenglass & Eskdale Railway stops at Eskdale Green and at Irton Road just west of the village.

Eskdale Green is a good centre for exploring the valley and fells on which there are many prehistoric cairns.

Two miles south of Eskdale Green on the fells is Devoke Water, a remote and isolated tarn which can be reached by taking the Ulpha road from Eskdale Green up onto Birker Fell. At a point near the summit of the road there are splendid views of Scafell (3,162ft) and Scafell Pike (3,210ft) – England's highest mountain – as well as many other peaks. A bridleway to the right is signposted to Waberthwaite. Leaving the car near this signpost, follow the bridleway towards Waberthwaite for about half a mile. Devoke Water will appear, a beautiful, quiet unspoilt stretch of water, surrounded by moorland and less familiar crags. From the roadway there is also a footpath to Stanley Force waterfall where there is a nature trail.

Details of the Eskdale Show, the Eskdale Corn Mill and other attractions can be found under Boot (see page 28).

AA recommends:
Hotels: Bower House Inn, 2-star, *tel.* Eskdale 244

Far Sawrey

Map Ref: 91SD3795

Far Sawrey lies midway between Esthwaite Water (see page 43) and Windermere lake. One mile to the east is the Windermere ferry crossing, down a sometimes steep and winding road.

The Claife Crier Bar in Far Sawrey is a reminder of eerie happenings many years ago. The name derives from a local ghost story about a troublesome night walker who uttered weird, pleading cries for the Windermere ferry from the Claife shore on stormy nights over 400 years ago. One of the ferrymen who rowed across to answer the urgent call from the Crier of Claife 'returned horror-stricken and dumb, continuing speechless for some days, and then dying'. After that – so the story goes – travellers began to avoid the ferry until the monks of Furness laid the ghost in a desolate quarry on Claife Heights.

These days you do not have to call for a ferry, but you may have to wait your turn in the queue. There are signs to indicate how long you can expect to wait (eg '15 minutes' or '30 minutes', according to where you are in the queue. This also applies to the Bowness side (see page 29).

At Ash Landing, Far Sawrey, the Cumbria Trust for Nature Conservation is developing a nursery garden, with woodland and grassland, as a butterfly reserve. Visitors are welcome but they should make arrangements with the Trust on Ambleside 2476.

There is now a one-and-a-half-mile Trail around the Claife Shore of

Longsleddale – a peaceful valley on the eastern edge of the National Park

Windermere, and a guide for this can be obtained from National Trust and National Park Information Centres. Many paths lead through the woodlands and on top of Claife Heights where there are a number of small tarns.

The wooded heights can also be reached from Near Sawrey, the village made famous by Beatrix Potter, which is the subject of a separate entry (see page 52).

Horse riding is available from Sawrey Knotts Hotel in Far Sawrey.

AA recommends:
Guest Houses: West Vale, *tel.* Windermere 2817

Finsthwaite

Map Ref: 91SD3687

The small village of Finsthwaite, one mile north-west of Lakeside at the southern end of Windermere lake, is host to a major attraction.

The Stott Park Bobbin Mill, which appears on the right as the road from Lakeside forks to Finsthwaite, was built in 1836, and recently restored by the Department of the Environment. It looks just as it did in the 19th century, complete with wood for bobbins. The lathe shop and coppice wood sheds are typical features of an industry that was widespread in the area.

The mill is now open to the public from April to October (but party bookings should be made through the Department of the Environment, The Castle, Carlisle. (tel. Carlisle 31777).

The mill was powered by water from the High Dam tarn on Finsthwaite Heights. This tarn was included in 70 acres of woodland bought by the Lake District Special Planning Board in 1973 in order to provide public access to this beautiful spot. There is a free car park, well screened. The entrance is just a hundred yards up the road from the mill towards Finsthwaite village. A footpath climbs up to the tarn through unspoilt woodland. There is a footpath round the tarn. This area has become very popular for walking, picnicking and swimming. Fishing is also allowed.

Also of interest in Finsthwaite is St Peter's Church, a large edifice built in 1873, with some good stained glass. In the churchyard is a white marble cross set up in 1913 to mark the grave of 'The Finsthwaite Princess'. It is inscribed to

Clementina Johannes Sobiesky Douglas, of Waterside, who some say was the illegitimate daughter of Bonnie Prince Charlie by Clementina Walkinshaw. Many romantic stories have been told about her in the belief that she was sent to Finsthwaite to live in seclusion. About that there is some doubt, but what is certain is that a woman of that name did live at Waterside, Finsthwaite, and was buried in the churchyard on 16 May 1771, as the cross indicates.

Flookburgh

Map Ref: 68SD3675

Flookburgh is literally 'fluke-town', the place where the flat fish called flukes are caught and sold.

Flookburgh was first granted its charter as a market town by Edward I in 1278. The charter was renewed in 1412 and 1675. Although it is no longer really a town an annual charter fair is still held annually on the Saturday nearest 24 June.

The sword, staff and halberd given to Flookburgh with its charter are housed in the church. The importance of fluke fishing to the area is shown by the large fluke in the church's weathervane, which can be clearly seen from the road.

Fluke fishing is still a major industry here. Flukes are caught with stake nets on sands around the village and are available from local fishmongers during the fluking season which is from October–December and again from April–May. They have a flavour similar to plaice.

Flookburgh is also famous for its Morecambe Bay shrimps, which are fished by tractors in the shallow waters when the tide is right. They are available from fishmongers or direct from fishermen in the area from October–November and from March–May. They are 'considered to be among the finest of all' shrimps – and are widely sought after.

Cockles are harvested on the sandbanks at low tide from October–April. They are brought to the surface by rocking a wooden board (called a 'jumbo') on the sand and then they are flicked into a basket by a 'cramb', a long wooden tool with three metal prongs.

AA recommends:
Campsites: Lakeland Caravan Park, Moor Lane, 3-pennants, *tel.* Flookburgh 235

Garnett Bridge (Longsleddale)

Map Ref: 87SD5299

Garnett Bridge is a pretty little village at the foot of Longsleddale, where the River Sprint cuts down through the rock on its way to meet the Kent. There is a mini-gorge where the river flows beneath the bridge and it makes a delightful picture.

From Garnett Bridge to Sadgill, a cluster of farms at the head of the dale, it is exactly five miles by way of a single-track road. For sheer peace and quiet and the sense of achievement at reaching the end of the long dale, the drive is well worth it. But for motorists, there is no way out but back the same way. There are no shops at Sadgill, but half way along the road opposite the church is a modern, stone-built toilet and a phone box. There is a box containing mountain rescue kit at Sadgill (in memory of a local climber), a pack-horse bridge, and some spectacular views of the Sleddale fells. There are footpaths west to Kentmere and straight on to Haweswater, which was the old road to Mardale.

There are only 20 dwellings in the dale, which has a population of just 70. Most dwellings are farms, but there is also an outdoor pursuits centre.

Glenridding (and Ullswater)

Map Ref: 79NY3817

Glenridding lies on the A592 Windermere to Penrith road at the southern end of Ullswater. Although it was once a mining village concentrated around the nearby lead mines, it is now almost wholly geared to catering for tourists, who come for the fells and the lakes.

Seven-mile-long Ullswater is the second largest lake in the Lake District. Its main water source is the Goldrill Beck, flowing in from the south from Brothers Water past Patterdale.

The lake is a public highway, and anyone can launch boats on it, but as from 13 July 1983, a 10mph speed limit has been imposed.

The Ullswater steam service started in 1859. In 1954, when there were proposals to close it down, Lord Wakefield of Kendal stepped in to keep the company (Ullswater Navigation & Transit Co Ltd) going. His organisation refurbished *Lady of the Lake*, which had been operating since 1877, and put *Raven* on the lake again. There was a fire on *Lady* in 1966, but in 1979 this was put back into service at a ceremony conducted by the local MP the Rt Hon William Whitelaw (now Viscount Whitelaw).

Both steamers, based at Glenridding pier, operate a daily scheduled service in the season to Howtown on the eastern shore (see page 44) and Pooley Bridge at the north end (see page 53). They are both available for dances and parties.

Public launching is available for non-powered craft on National Trust land north of the steamer pier by the Willow Trees, or on the adjoining beach. Sailing craft, canoes and rowing boats may also be launched at Glencoyne Bay one mile north of Glenridding on the A592 near Glencoyne Bridge; small craft may be launched over a beach. Power boats are not allowed at this public site.

The Ullswater Sailing School at Glenridding (tel. Pooley Bridge 438) offers sailing tuition, dinghy hire, launching and parking facilities from April to September. No power boats.

Information on the possibility of hiring rowing boats for fishing can be obtained from fishing permit distributors in Pooley Bridge (see page 53). For other launching and hire facilities available on Ullswater see entries for Pooley Bridge, Howtown, and Watermillock.

In the centre of Glenridding village at the car park is a Tourist Information Centre (tel. Glenridding 414). A guided walk starts here. West from the car park, away from the A592, is the main street of the village, leading towards the disused Greenside Lead Mines (which closed in 1962). That eventually becomes a bridleway and then a footpath up to Helvellyn (3,118ft).

Glenridding Common (some 2,500 acres of fell land extending from the village to the summit) is very important both for nature conservation and for industrial archaeology. It includes some of the most popular fell paths in the Lake District and the only permanent ski tow for the Lake District Ski Club who have a hut 2,500ft up on The Raise. The Board is carrying out improvement schemes on the areas of dereliction of the mines and is ensuring that important relics of the industrial past are retained.

North from Glenridding village, the main road follows the lake shore. It is a beautiful drive, with woodlands and fells on one side and the lake with views of the mountains on the other. About one and a half miles along, the road passes through the area where Wordsworth's famous golden daffodil field is believed to be. It has never been accurately pinpointed, but Dorothy Wordsworth described it from the north as being 'in the fields beyond Gowbarrow Park', which is just the other side of the junction of the A592 with the A5091 to Dockray. It is therefore thought to lie somewhere beneath the half mile stretch of A592 lying south of the junction. Certainly there are many daffodils around here in April, and it is not difficult to see how Wordsworth was inspired to write his famous poem *Daffodils*.

Just past the junction is the Aira Force car park provided by the National Trust to allow people to visit the famous waterfall, about a quarter of a mile from the road. Bridges across the gorge enable visitors to get a good view of the 60ft fall, and the area is threaded by numerous footpaths. In all, the National Trust owns nearly 8,000 acres in this area.

AA recommends:
Hotels: Ullswater, 3-star, *tel.* Glenridding 444

Glenridding, 2-star, *tel.* Glenridding 228
Guest Houses: Bridge House, *tel.* Glenridding 236

A boat trip aboard the Lady of the Lake offers the most leisurely exploration of Ullswater

Gosforth

Map Ref: 68NY0603

This large village, now almost a small town, lies on the western boundary of the National Park.

It is notable for the ancient 10th-century cross in the churchyard, which is of national importance. Fourteen feet high, complete and remarkably slender, the cross has pagan and Norse devices on one side and Christian symbols on the other. Both tell the story of the triumph of good over evil. The Christian interpretation of a Norse legend is believed to be indicative of the transition from pagan beliefs to Christianity, although at the time the very survival of Christianity was in doubt.

Trekking and hacking are available from Fleming Hall Riding School one mile west of Gosforth.

The Gosforth Show is one of the major traditional shows in Cumbria, held on the third Wednesday in August. The different classes of sheep, cattle, horses and crafts are exhibited in a superb setting, whilst a gymkhana, hound and terrier racing and other contests provide plenty of excitement.

AA recommends:
Self Catering: The Cottage, Haverigg Moorside, *tel.* Gosforth 410
3 Hardinghill Cottage, High Boonwood Farm, *tel.* Gosforth 423

Grange-in-Borrowdale

Map Ref: 77NY2517

Grange-in-Borrowdale is one of the most attractive villages in the area. Borrowdale is a stunningly scenic Lake District valley, with wooded fell sides topped by towering crags.

About a mile from Grange on the north side are the famous Lodore Falls, reached by a path near the Lodore Swiss Hotel. Robert Southey describes these falls vividly in his poem *The Cataract of Lodore*. They are best experienced after

heavy rain. Lake launches can be caught nearby at the Lodore pier on Derwent Water where self-drive motor-boats or rowing boats may also be hired. Light craft may be launched onto Derwent Water from the car park at Kettlewell half a mile north of Lodore.

Grange itself was once the site of a grange or granary of the monks of Furness Abbey, who once owned this charming village, reached over an old narrow double bridge off the B5289.

Some three quarters of a mile south of Grange, on the east side of the main road, is the Bowder Stone, the largest boulder in the Lake District. It is 62ft long and stands 36ft high. A left-over from the Ice Age, it stands precariously on one point, so that two people lying under it can shake hands from opposite sides. There is a ladder up one side.

AA recommends:
Hotels: Lodore Swiss, 4-red-star, *tel.* Borrowdale 285
Mary Mount Hotel, 3-star, *tel.* Borrowdale 223
Borrowdale Hotel, 2-star, *tel.* Borrowdale 224
Gates Country House, 2-star, *tel.* Borrowdale 204
Guest Houses: Grange Guest House, *tel.* Borrowdale 251

Grange-over-Sands

Map Ref: 68SD4077

Grange-over-Sands, on the north shore of Morecambe Bay, has been called the Riviera of Cumbria. It lies on the B5277 which leaves the A590 midway between Levens and Newby Bridge.

Grange is a quiet, restful resort in a natural sun trap between the Lake District Fells and the sea. It is reputed to have a higher temperature in spring than any other place in the north of England.

The coming of the railway in 1857 made Grange one of the most popular holiday resorts for Lancashire folk at a time when the Furness area was part of Lancashire.

Now it is part of Cumbria, but the old connection between Furness and Lancashire is still evident in its 'over-Sands' title. For it was the route over the sands of Morecambe Bay that linked the two parts of Lancashire before the railway. Even the Romans used this route. Then it became the short cut for the monks of Furness Abbey to get to and from Lancaster, and later a stage coach route.

However, the sands were always tricky, and as far back as the 16th century the Duchy of Lancaster appointed an official guide to lead people across the sands and gave him rent-free use of a house in Grange. That house, known as Guide's Farm, is still the guide's residence today, occupied now by the present guide, Cedric Robinson, and his family. A local fisherman, he knows the sands and the channels better than anyone, and takes groups across them at low tide during the season. His planned walks are very popular (either to Arnside or, when the channels permit, to Hest Bank); if you wish to arrange to cross the sands, he can be contacted on Grange 2165.

The town has many attractions. There are two golf clubs, Grange-over-Sands in Meathop Road, and Grange Fell in Fell Road. There is a fine outdoor swimming pool open during the season at the west end of the promenade, and tennis and bowls near the pool.

Behind Grange is Hampsfell, the summit of which (where there is an old shelter for 'wanderers') offers marvellous views on a clear day of the Isle of Man, the Yorkshire hills and the Lake District Fells. There is a Nature Trail through deciduous woodlands and open limestone fells to the summit, and a leaflet about this is available at the Tourist Information Centre (tel. Grange 4126) in the Council Offices at the Victoria Hall. Fishing permits may also be obtained there.

Trekking and hacking is available from Guide's Farm and also from Kiln Croft Riding Centre at High Newton.

AA recommends:
Hotels: Cumbria Grand Hotel, 3-star, *tel.* Grange over Sands 2331
Grange Hotel, Lindale Road, 2-star, *tel.* Grange over Sands 3666
Graythwaite Manor Hotel, Fernhill Road, 2-star, Country House Hotel, *tel.* Grange over Sands 2001
Kents Bank Hotel, Kentsford Road, 2-star, *tel.* Grange over Sands 2054
Netherwood Hotel, Lindale Road, 2-star, *tel.* Grange over Sands 2552
Commodore Hotel, Main Street, 1-star, *tel.* Grange over Sands 2381
Hardcragg Hall Hotel, 1-star, *tel.* Grange over Sands 3353
Methven Hotel, Kents Bank Rd, 1-star, *tel.* Grange over Sands 2031
Self Catering: Berkeley, Kents Bank Road, *tel.* Grange over Sands 2065
Granville Holiday Flats, Granville, Methven Terrace, Kents Bank Road, *tel.* Grange over Sands 2509
Kentholme, Kents Bank Road, *tel.* Grange over Sands 3235
Guest Houses: Elton Private Hotel, Windermere Road, *tel.* Grange over Sands 2838
Grayrigge Private Hotel, Kents Bank Road, *tel.* Grange over Sands 2345
Thornfield House, Kents Bank Road, *tel.* Grange over Sands 2512

Grange-in-Borrowdale – a group of cottages in a setting of romantic grandeur

Grasmere

Map Ref: 85NY3307

Grasmere is the northernmost village in the southern Lake District, set in a valley surrounded by hills. It lies two and a half miles south of the watershed at Dunmail Raise. The main settlement is a quarter of a mile north of Grasmere Lake, where the public can hire rowing boats to view a small and solitary island. Canoeing and sailing are permitted at a small charge from Easter to October.

The church in the village centre is dedicated to St Oswald, the oldest part being said to date from the 13th century. Grasmere's most famous resident, the poet Wordsworth, who lived in the village from 1799–1813, described the church (in *The Excursion*) as a building of 'rude and antique majesty', with 'pillars crowded' and 'naked rafters intricately crossed'.

From 1799 to 1808 Wordsworth lived at Dove Cottage, about a quarter of a mile from the village, just off the main road (A591). He wrote most of his best-known poetry there during the period called his 'Golden Decade'. He then moved to Allan Bank, a house now owned by the National Trust on the north side of Grasmere, but not open to the public. Later (1811) the Wordsworth family moved to the Rectory. Then they went to live in Rydal (see page 55). William and his wife, as well as his sister Dorothy and other members of his family, are buried in Grasmere churchyard.

Wordsworth called Grasmere 'the loveliest spot that man hath ever found'. Dove Cottage, administered by a special Trust, is today the world centre for the study of the poet and for Wordsworthiana. There is a new Grasmere and Wordsworth Museum in a converted barn behind the cottage.

Wordsworth taught in a tiny schoolroom built by public subscription in 1687. This is now the famous Gingerbread shop, situated between the church and the four-star Wordsworth Hotel, converted recently from the old Rothay Hotel after years of disuse. For over a hundred years the celebrated Grasmere gingerbread has been made here and it is one of the local specialities included in the Cumbria Tourist Board's 'Taste of Cumbria' promotions. The recipe is such a closely-guarded secret it has to be kept in the vaults of a local bank!

The annual Rushbearing Festival is held on the Saturday nearest 5 August. Children carrying bearings of flowers and rushes in traditional patterns follow the band through the village; then the bearings are placed in the church to commemorate

Grasmere and Grasmere village, where Wordsworth composed his finest work

the time when rushes constituted the flooring of the church. The famous Grasmere Sports are held on the Thursday nearest 20 August and include local sports such as Cumberland and Westmorland wrestling, fell races, and hound trailing (see page 20).

Grasmere is a good centre for many fell walks and climbs and has a Tourist Information Centre (tel. Grasmere 245) in Bowers' Newsagents in Broadgate.

AA recommends:

Hotels: Wordsworth, 4-star, *tel.* Grasmere 592
Gold Rill Country House, 3-star, *tel.* Grasmere 486
Grasmere Red Lion, 3-star, *tel.* Grasmere 456.
Michael's Nook, 3-star, Country House Hotel, *tel.* Grasmere 496
Prince of Wales, 3-star, *tel.* Grasmere 666
Swan, 3-star, *tel.* Grasmere 551
Oak Bank, Broadgate, 2-star, *tel.* Grasmere 217
Grasmere, Broadgate, 2-star, *tel.* Grasmere 277
Rothay Bank, 2-star, *tel.* Grasmere 334
Moss Grove, 1-star, *tel.* Grasmere 251
Self Catering: Beck Allans Self Catering Apartments, *tel.* Grasmere 329
Wood Close, How Head Lane, *tel.* Hackthorpe 531
Guest Houses: Beck Steps, College Street, *tel.* Grasmere 348
Bridge House Hotel, Stock Lane, *tel.* Grasmere 425
Chestnut Villa Private Hotel, Keswick Road, *tel.* Grasmere 218
Dunmail, Keswick Road, *tel.* Grasmere 256
Lake View, Lake View Drive, *tel.* Grasmere 384
Titteringdales, Pye Lane, *tel.* Grasmere 439
Garages: Oak Bank, Broadgate, *tel.* Grasmere 423

Greenodd

Map Ref: 90SD3182

Greenodd is on the Leven Estuary where the River Leven from Windermere and the River Crake from Coniston flow out to Morecambe Bay. Greenodd used to be a port for the shipment of local ores and slates. Some of the old staithes – waterside depots for coaling vessels – can still be seen. In the 18th century the Ship Inn was once on the quay. Eventually, however, houses were built and the quay became part of the main route (later the A590) through to Barrow. In 1983 the quay road was turned into a pleasant cul-de-sac as a new bypass was built for the A590 on the seaward side of the village.

The new bypass has served to open up a wide expanse of the Leven Estuary to general view. The Greenodd Picnic Area has now been provided just half a mile past the village. There is an information board with map and points of interest. Bring your binoculars, for there is a great variety of birds to be seen. Morecambe Bay attracts tens of thousands – waders, wildfowl, gulls and terns, oystercatchers, dunlins, knots, curlews, mallard, teal, widgeon, goldeneye, merganser, and shelduck drawn to the food available and the sheltered shores.

Greystoke

Map Ref: 74NY4330

Greystoke is an attractive village of old grey stone houses, as well as some modern ones, two miles north of the A66 on the B5288. It lies on the line of the old Roman road from Voreda (Old Penrith) to Keswick.

One of its main attractions is the church, which is bigger and more spacious than most in the area. This is because in the 14th century it became a collegiate church, with a master and six chaplains.

A hundred yards outside the church gates is a medieval sanctuary stone, protected by a wrought-iron grille. It used to stand in the middle of the causeway leading to the church to mark the boundary beyond which fugitives could claim the sanctuary of the church.

Visitors are also welcome at the Old Smithy, Blencow, about a mile north-west of Greystoke, to watch craftsmen making copper and brass artifacts.

Grizedale

Map Ref: 91SD3394

Grizedale, a village three miles south of
Hawkshead (follow sign just south of
Hawkshead), is well known for its forest, its
deer, its wildlife museum and its unique
Theatre-in-the-Forest, which has an
international reputation.

The Forestry Commission acquired the
8,000-acre Grizedale Estate in 1937.

The Grizedale Forest was the first one in
which the Forestry Commission made
special efforts to develop interpretive and
recreational facilities for visitors. A deer
museum was opened in 1956. To that
facility were added in succession: deer
stalking on day permits; a nature trail; a
camp site; a forest handicrafts centre; a
tree-top observation tower for studying
and photographing wildlife (including red
and roe deer which abound in the forest);
an angling club for fishing in Grizedale
beck (permits now from the Camp shop);
photographic hides; a wildlife centre; and a
picnic site and waymarked walks at Bogle
south of Grizedale.

Then in 1970 came the Theatre-in-the-
Forest. Quality was the keynote from the
start, and since then an average of 120
performances have been given each year,
with many top artistes returning again and
again because they like the place so much.
On many evenings there are plays,
concerts, variety shows, and folk music for
visitors to enjoy. The theatre is also open
during the day for exhibitions of local
artists' work in the bar lounge.

In the meantime, the forest
interpretation side progressed. The
wildlife exhibition and deer museum were
reorganised and combined into the
Grizedale Forest Visitor Centre. An
information room and camp shop were
opened. More nature trails and forest
walks were developed, varying in distance
up to nine and a half miles. Each offers fine
panoramic views of the forest and ends at a
picturesque picnic site. A colour coded
map of the routes can be bought from the
camp shop, where details of all the
activities can be obtained.

There are numerous small car parks and
picnic areas in delightful surroundings on
the forest edge, but no vehicles are allowed
on forest roads.

In 1976 the Restaurant-in-the-Forest
was opened at the nearby Ormandy Hotel,
providing early dinners for theatregoers.

AA recommends:
Hotels: Ormandy Hotel, 2-star,
tel. Hawkshead 532

Hartsop (and Brothers Water)

Map Ref: 80NY4013

Hartsop – meaning valley of the deer – is
an interesting fellside village. It is the first
village north of the Kirkstone Pass.
Hartsop contains some 17th-century farm
buildings and a few cottages with spinning
galleries. There is a small car park just
beyond the village where the road stops.
Remains of an early 18th-century corn mill
can be seen to the east, and a drying kiln
stands in the village itself.

Brothers Water, under half a mile long
and just a quarter mile wide, lies at the foot
of Dovedale. Folklore suggests that it is so
called because two brothers were drowned
there. It is now owned by the National

A cottage in Hartsop, complete with spinning gallery.

Trust who do not permit any boating, but
fishing is allowed and no permits are
needed.

In winter, when the conditions are right,
there is some skiing on the slopes by the
Kirkstone Pass Inn, where there is a public
car park.

AA recommends:
Campsites: Skyeside Camping Site,
3-pennants, tel. Glenridding 239

Haverigg

Map Ref: 68SD1578

This small village on the coast between
Millom and Silecroft is now recovering
from the decline of the local iron industry
by capitalising on the holiday trade.

There are sand dunes and a beach, a
caravan site, a children's playground and a
few shops.

Some self-catering accommodation with
adjacent moorings has been developed and
near the Rugby Union Club there is public
access for small boats, which may be
launched from the beach within two and a
half hours of high water.

Between Haverigg and Millom, Port
Haverigg Holiday Village is being
developed. The total area of the complex is
500 acres, of which 200 acres are covered
by a fresh water lake. A major centre for
waterskiing is now in operation. Boating
and sailing facilities, picnic areas,
children's play areas, and caravan sites for
touring and static caravans are available.
There is a reception centre and a shop.

Haverthwaite

Map Ref: 91SD3483

Haverthwaite lies on the north bank of the
River Leven. The village is mainly
contained between the main road (A590)
and the river which flows out of
Windermere; but the Haverthwaite base of
the Lakeside and Haverthwaite Railway –
for which Haverthwaite is becoming
increasingly well-known and popular – is
on the north side of the main road.

The steam engines and carriages are
kept in sheds and sidings at Haverthwaite.
There are always engines to be seen, often
from the main road, and with steam up;
there is a big car park by the sheds. A daily
train service operates between
Haverthwaite, Newby Bridge and
Lakeside from 1 May to the end of
October, with some running at other times

(tel. Newby Bridge 31594).

Haverthwaite village itself consists of a
nucleus of old houses with scattered
developments and farms; there is also a
newer estate separated from the main
village. St Anne's Church stands away
from the village near the main road, but the
vicarage was demolished to make way for
the road. There is a new sports and
community centre with a children's
playground.

Near Haverthwaite is Roudsea Wood
National Nature Reserve. This is very
diverse, rich woodland developed on both
limestone (giving rise to ash trees) and slate
(mainly oak). Permits to visit it may be
obtained from the Nature Conservancy
Council, Blackwell, Bowness-on-
Windermere, Cumbria. It can be reached
by car from Haverthwaite on the farm road
which goes west of the B5278 immediately
south of the bridge over the Leven.

Hawkshead (and Esthwaite Water)

Map Ref: 85SD3598

Hawkshead is a picturesque village in the
vale of Esthwaite with white-washed
buildings, archways, stone steps and
squares. It was originally founded in the
10th century by a Norseman called Haakr
– hence the name.

There is now no through road for
vehicles through the village – which
enhances its character – but there is a
large, clearly signed car park near the
village centre, reached by the relief road
round Hawkshead. The Tourist
Information Centre (tel. Hawkshead 525)
is in the car park and open throughout the
season; a guided walk starts from here.

Among the interesting buildings is St
Michael's Church, which stands above the
village overlooking the Esthwaite valley. It
is a handsome 15th-century edifice with
some murals and Elizabethan transcripts
of parish registers. Musical evenings
especially for visitors are held there during
the summer.

The old Grammar School, founded in
1585, is open to the public from April to
October. William Wordsworth was
educated here from 1779–1787, and the
desk on which he carved his name can still
be seen. There are also an exhibition room
and a library.

Anne Tyson's cottage, where
Wordsworth lodged while he was at school,
still exists. It is not open to the public, but

there is a plaque outside. He is also thought to have lived at Colthouse for a while, a hamlet half a mile to the east. There is a Quaker Meeting House dating from 1690 here.

About half a mile north of Hawkshead at the junction of the roads to Ambleside and Coniston is Hawkshead Courthouse. Built in the 15th century, it is all that is left of the manorial buildings of Hawkshead which were once held by Furness Abbey. Now owned by the National Trust, the Courthouse is open to the public as a museum of local rural life, illustrating the history of Hawkshead. It includes displays on coppicing, charcoal burning, the local iron industry and char fishing.

One and a half miles south of Hawkshead on the west shore of Esthwaite Water is Esthwaite Hall, the birthplace of Archbishop Sandys, who became Archbishop of York in the 16th century and founded Hawkshead Grammar School. About 200 yards along that road out of Hawkshead is the signpost to the Theatre-in-the-Forest at Grizedale (see page 42).

Esthwaite Water, (about one and a half miles long), is owned by the Esthwaite Estates which belong to the Sandys family. The launching of rowing boats only (no sailing or powered craft) is possible from the south-western shore where the Lake District Special Planning Board has a public car park and access point. Permits are necessary, however, and can be obtained from Hawkshead Post Office or from Esthwaite Howe, Near Sawrey (see page 52) where rowing boats may also be hired (tel. Hawkshead 331). Fishing permits may be obtained from the post office, who will also advise on rowing boats for fishing.

Trekking facilities are available from the Tarn Hows Hotel, between the village and the famous Tarn Hows beauty spot two miles north-west (follow signs on B5285).

Hawkshead Show is held on the first Tuesday in September. It has become particularly well known for Herdwick sheep; there are also competitions for the best cows, horticultural produce and handicrafts as well as hound trailing and horse jumping.

AA recommends:
Hotels: Tarn Hows, Hawkshead Hill, 3-star, Country House Hotel, *tel.* Hawkshead 330
Red Lion, 1-star, *tel.* Hawkshead 213
Self Catering: Rogerground House, *tel.* Prestbury 828624
Ramsteads Coppice, Outgate, *tel.* Hawkshead 583
Guest Houses: Highfield House, Hawkshead Hill, *tel.* Hawkshead 344
Ivy House, *tel.* Hawkshead 204
Rough Close Country House, *tel.* Hawkshead 370
King's Arms Hotel (inn), *tel.* Hawkshead 372
Balla Wray Country, High Wray, *tel.* Ambleside 33308

Hesket Newmarket

Map Ref: 73NY3338

Before the 18th century Hesket (as it was then called) was probably only a small cluster of buildings, subsidiary to Caldbeck. Then, its most notable feature was Hesket Hall, built after 1630 for Sir Wilfred Lawson. This rather curious square building has gabled wings, a pyramid roof and big central chimney.

During the early 18th century Hesket was granted a market charter and by 1751 it lengthened its name to Hesket Newmarket. As with other planned market towns, tight rules controlled the shape of the market place and the building frontage, with traders' houses looking onto a market cross, a coaching house and an inn.

AA recommends:
Self Catering: Haltcliffe House, *tel.* Caldbeck 619

Heversham

Map Ref: 93SD4983

When the Duke of Windsor, then Prince of Wales, opened the A6 bypassing Heversham in 1927 he named it 'Prince's Way'. The bypass left the village relatively quiet and undisturbed.

Its three main points of interest are its church, its school, and surprisingly, its cockpit.

The ancient church was restored in the 1870s, but many of its earlier features survived, including the north chapel oak screen (dated 1605). All the old footpaths in the area make for the church, and from the field just above it are fine views.

Heversham Grammar School was founded in 1613. A new school was built in 1878 on the road through the village. It survived as a Grammar School, with some boarding pupils, until 1983.

The original Heversham Grammar School, founded in 1613, is on the hillside behind the church. It can be reached via a footpath through the churchyard. Looking like a cottage, the building stands on its own and has 'Old School' on the door.

Just past the 'Old School' in the next field is the cockpit. Cock-fighting used to be the most popular blood sport in Cumbria until it became illegal in 1835. The Heversham cockpit, the outline of which can be clearly seen, was 17ft in diameter, surrounded by a circular ditch and a bank from which the spectators watched the fight.

AA recommends:
Hotels: Blue Bell at Heversham, The Prince's Way, 3-star, *tel.* Milnthorpe 3159

*Left: The old square at Hawkshead
Below: Tarn Hows near Hawkshead, one of Lakeland's most famous and unspoilt beauty spots*

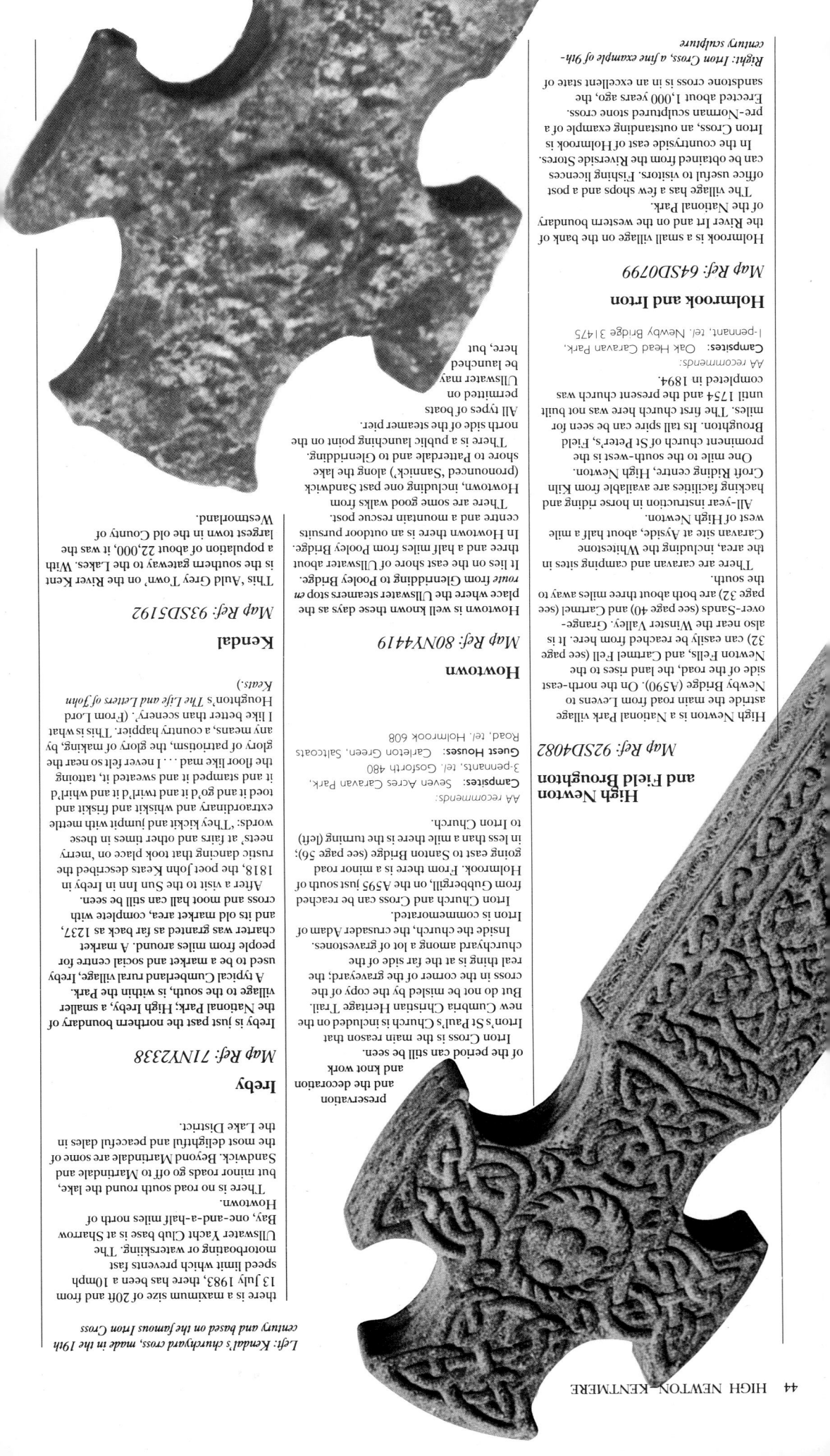

High Newton and Field Broughton

Map Ref: 92SD4082

High Newton is a National Park village astride the main road from Levens to Newby Bridge (A590). On the north-east side of the road, the land rises to the Newton Fells, and Cartmel Fell (see page 32) can easily be reached from here. It is also near the Winster Valley. Grange-over-Sands (see page 40) and Cartmel (see page 32) are both about three miles away to the south.

There are caravan and camping sites in the area, including the Whitestone Caravan site at Ayside, about half a mile west of High Newton.

All-year instruction in horse riding and hacking facilities are available from Kiln Croft Riding centre, High Newton.

One mile to the south-west is the prominent church of St Peter's, Field Broughton. Its tall spire can be seen for miles. The first church here was not built until 1754 and the present church was completed in 1894.

AA recommends:
Campsites: Oak Head Caravan Park, 1-pennant, tel: Newby Bridge 31475

Holmrook and Irton

Map Ref: 64SD0799

Holmrook is a small village on the bank of the River Irt and on the western boundary of the National Park.

The village has a few shops and a post office useful to visitors. Fishing licences can be obtained from the Riverside Stores.

In the countryside east of Holmrook is Irton Cross, an outstanding example of a pre-Norman sculptured stone cross. Erected about 1,000 years ago, the sandstone cross is in an excellent state of preservation and the decoration and knot work of the period can still be seen.

Irton Cross is the main reason that Irton's St Paul's Church is included on the new Cumbria Christian Heritage Trail. But do not be misled by the copy of the cross in the corner of the graveyard; the real thing is at the far side of the churchyard among a lot of gravestones.

Inside the church, the crusader Adam of Irton is commemorated.

Irton Church and Cross can be reached from Gubbergill, on the A595 just south of Holmrook. From there is a minor road going east to Santon Bridge (see page 56); in less than a mile there is the turning (left) to Irton Church.

AA recommends:
Guest Houses: Carleton Green, Saltcoats Road, tel: Holmrook 608

Howtown

Map Ref: 80NY4419

Howtown is well known these days as the place where the Ullswater steamers stop en route from Glenridding to Pooley Bridge. It lies on the east shore of Ullswater about three and a half miles from Pooley Bridge.

In Howtown there is an outdoor pursuits centre and a mountain rescue post. There are some good walks from Howtown, including one past Sandwick (pronounced 'Sannick'), along the lake shore to Patterdale and to Glenridding.

There is a public launching point on the north side of the steamer pier. All types of boats permitted on Ullswater may be launched here, but there is a maximum size of 20ft and from 13 July 1983, there has been a 10mph speed limit which prevents fast motorboating or waterskiing. The Ullswater Yacht Club base is at Sharrow Bay, one-and-a-half miles north of Howtown.

There is no road south round the lake, but minor roads go off to Martindale and Sandwick. Beyond Martindale are some of the most delightful and peaceful dales in the Lake District.

Ireby

Map Ref: 71NY2338

Ireby is just past the northern boundary of the National Park; High Ireby, a smaller village to the south, is within the Park.

A typical Cumberland rural village, Ireby used to be a market and social centre for people from miles around. A market charter was granted as far back as 1237, and its old market area, complete with cross and moot hall can still be seen.

After a visit to the Sun Inn in Ireby in 1818, the poet John Keats described the rustic dancing that took place on 'merry neets' at fairs and other times in these words: 'They kickit and jumpit with mettle extraordinary and whiskit and friskit and toed it and go'd it and twirl'd it and whirl'd it and stamped it and sweated it and tattoing the floor like mad . . . I never felt so near the glory of patriotism, the glory of making, by any means, a country happier. This is what I like better than scenery.' (From Lord Houghton's *The Life and Letters of John Keats*.)

Kendal

Map Ref: 93SD5192

This 'Auld Grey Town' on the River Kent is the southern gateway to the Lakes. With a population of about 22,000, it was the largest town in the old County of Westmorland.

Right: Iron Cross, a fine example of 9th-century sculpture

Left: Kendal's churchyard cross, made in the 19th century and based on the famous Irton Cross

After early settlement by ancient Britons, Romans and Saxons (a 9th-century cross shaft can be seen in the parish church) the Normans came and built a castle on a hill to the east of the town in the late 12th century.

Kendal was made a barony in about 1189, the same year that its market charter was granted. Later, the barony was split three ways, one portion (including the castle) going to Sir William Parr. It was in this castle in 1512 that Katherine Parr was born, later to become Henry VIII's sixth and surviving wife.

The parish church, built in the 13th century on the site of an earlier one, is one of the largest in England, with five aisles. It has an 80ft tower and a peal of ten bells. The sword and helmet left behind by 'Robin the Devil' of Crook (see page 35) are on display. The church stands at the southern end of the town, now known as Kirkland.

There is now a public park around the ruins of the castle accessible from Aynham Road along the east bank of the river and up Parr Street.

From the castle there is a marvellous panoramic view of the town.

The Castle Dairy in Wildman Street, as its name implies, once served the castle; at the time when Katherine Parr lived there. It is the oldest habitable stone-built house in the area and has many interesting period features, including carved oak beams and a hand-carved four-poster bed. The house is open to the public from Easter to September.

There was a thriving wool trade in the Kendal area by the 13th century. This was stimulated in 1331 when Edward III granted a special Letter of Protection to John Kempe of Flanders and Flemish weavers came to settle. They made Kendal England's pioneer wool town, and Kendal bowmen made 'Kendal Green' cloth famous throughout the land. Shakespeare refers to men wearing Kendal-green in *Henry IV* Part I. Kendal's motto is '*Pannus mihi Panis*' ('Wool is my bread').

Other trades and industries established themselves, many of them making use of the 'yards' off the main street for protection.

Much of the industrial and social life of the time is reflected in the Museum of Lakeland Life and Industry which is housed in part of the Abbot Hall complex. Here you can also enjoy the Abbot Hall Art Gallery with its splendid collection of furniture, objets d'art and paintings, including many by the local artist George Romney. There are often special displays. Abbot Hall, built in 1759, is found next to the parish church.

Another museum well worth visiting is Kendal Museum of Archaeology and Natural History near the station. 'A Walk Through South Lakeland' series of dioramas depicts the natural history and geology of the area, while a fascinating array of objects of many kinds traces the human story.

There are two Kendal Town Trails, details of which may be obtained from the tourist office in the Town Hall. There is also a leaflet about the Serpentine Woods Nature Trail.

Entertainment is offered at the Brewery Arts Centre, with car park, on the main road not far from Abbot Hall. The Centre is open throughout the year with a photographic gallery, small theatre, exhibitions and changing events (Tel. Kendal 25133).

Kendal is famous for its Kendal Mint Cake, a hard, mint-flavoured sugar slab used on expeditions (including Everest) and sold in large quantities to visitors as well as walkers and climbers.

Fishing permits can be obtained from T Atkinson & Sons in Stricklandgate and V Carlson in Kirkland. Horse riding is available at a number of places around Kendal. (See entries for Crook and Natland.)

The Westmorland County Show is held on the second Thursday in September. This features agricultural exhibitions of all kinds, crafts and farm produce as well as show jumping, Cumberland and Westmorland wrestling, carriage driving and dog shows.

The Kendal Gathering is held in late August. This is a 17-day festival of varied first class entertainment, outdoor and indoor, ending with a torchlight procession (Tel. Kendal 20040).

On the A65 (Lound Road) is the new South Lakeland Leisure Centre, opened in 1982 by the Duke of Gloucester. A wide variety of leisure and sports activities is available, including swimming, in the evening there are concerts and shows (Tel. 29777).

A pavement cafe in the Kirkland area of Kendal

AA recommends:

Hotels: County Thistle, Station Road, 3-star, tel. 22461
Woolpack Inn, Stricklandgate, 3-star, tel. Kendal 23852
Shenstone Country, 2-star, tel. Kendal 21023

Restaurants: Castle Dairy, 26 Wildman Street, 1-fork, 1-rosette, tel. Kendal 21170

Campsites: Millcrest Caravan Park, 2-pennants, tel. Kendal 21075

Self Catering: Garth Cottage, 36 Castle Garth, tel. Kendal 23400
Plumgarths Holiday Flats, Plumgarths, tel. Staveley 82325
The Flat, 56 Gillingate, tel. Kendal 22208

Guest Houses: Natland Mill Beck (farmhouse), tel. Kendal 21122

Garages: Lakeland-Ford, Minsteet Road South, tel. Kendal 23534
Dutton-Forshaw, 84/92 Highgate, tel. Kendal 28800

Kentmere

Map Ref: 86 NY4504

Kentmere is a small, scattered village at the head of Kentdale, four miles from Staveley, along a narrow winding road with pleasant views of meadows, woods and hills.

The church in Kentmere, St Cuthbert's, has 16th-century roof beams. Kentmere Hall, on the west side of the valley, has a 14th-century pele tower.

In the church is a bronze memorial to Bernard Gilpin, who was born at Kentmere Hall in 1517 and went on to become Archdeacon of Durham and a leader of the Reformation. He was known as 'The Apostle of the North', and for his attacks on the Roman Church was in danger of being burnt at the stake in 1558. He was on his way to face charges of heresy when he had the good fortune to break his leg. Catholic Queen Mary died before he recovered and the Protestant Queen Elizabeth I restored him to his position as Archdeacon.

Craftsman John Williams works in Lakeland stone in the village at Low Holme, and welcomes visitors by appointment (Staveley 821505).

The public road ends in the village, where there is a small car park. From there footpaths wind westward to Troutbeck, eastward to Longsleddale, southward to Ings and northward to Kentmere reservoir. This was created by damming the streams which formed the headwaters of the Kent immediately below Kentmere Common. The water was used to supply the valley mills.

At Millriggs, the major Kentmere Sheep Dog Trials are held on the last Thursday in September.

AA recommends:

Guest Houses: Grove, tel. Staveley 821548

Keswick

Map Ref: 78NY2623

Keswick is the capital of the northern Lake District. Once a market and mining centre, it is now almost solely geared to tourism. With mountains and lakes in close proximity, it is a natural 'honeypot' for climbers, walkers and holiday-makers.

The famous Castlerigg Stone Circle, built in 1400 BC, is strategically placed on a hill east of Keswick. The National Trust owns it and the Department of the Environment cares for it. There are about 60 rough hewn stones, the tallest about 7ft.

One of those who brought Christianity to the region was St Herbert, friend of St Cuthbert. He established a hermitage on the biggest island in Derwent Water in AD 685, and died on the same day as St Cuthbert. According to the Keswick Official Guide: 'The remains of the Monk's cell can still be discerned in the undergrowth. This island is rather a jungle, but if you follow the path to the middle, you will find a mysterious clearing.' Boats can be obtained for the trip from the landings. Friar's Crag on the east shore of the lake was where monks embarked to visit St Herbert.

When tourists were starting to discover the Lake District in the early 19th century, Keswick was given a boost by the residence at Greta Hall (now part of Keswick School) of poets Samuel Taylor Coleridge and then Robert Southey. Wordsworth often visited them, and he also lived for a while at Old Windebrowe, where he had nursed Raisley Calvert and which is now used by the Calvert Trust Adventure Centre for the Disabled as a riding school. The kitchen and parlour have been restored to their 19th-century condition and contain an exhibition illustrating the involvement with the house of these four men (and also of Shelley, who lived in Keswick for a while).

Near the now closed railway station, in which is housed the Keswick Railway Museum, is the Fitz Park museum – set in a large public park – which contains interesting manuscripts of the local poets and a good mineral collection, as well as a unique instrument made of Keswick's famous 'musical stones' in the form of a huge xylophone.

Entertainment is provided by the Century Theatre, a mobile theatre come to rest on the Lakeside car park. Plays can be seen nightly (except Sunday) during the season; at other times of the year there are often shows of various kinds. There is a cinema in Keswick.

Craft workshops such as Lakeland Stonecraft in High Hill welcomes visitors. The Guild of Lakeland Craftsmen hold their Annual Exhibition at Old Windebrowe in the summer.

Details of a historic town walk may be obtained from the Tourist Information Centre at the Moot Hall in the Market Square, as well as information about other guided walks. Friar's Crag Nature Walk runs for one and a half miles along the east shore of the lake (leaflets from the boat landing). Near the Crag is a stone memorial to Canon Rawnsley and one to his friend, the critic John Ruskin who said that the view from the Crag was one of the three most beautiful scenes in Europe.

Riding facilities are available at the Keswick Riding Centre, Swan Field

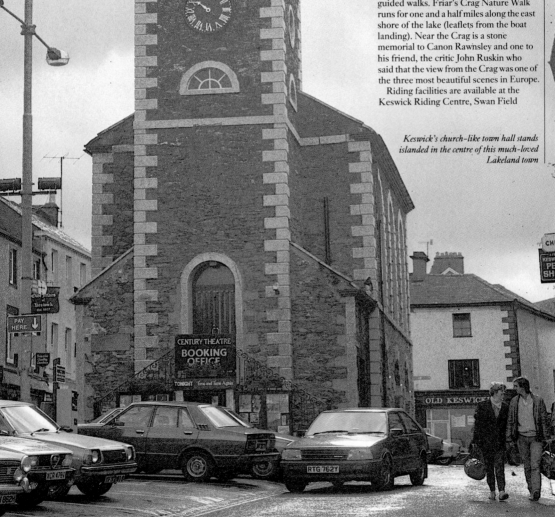

Keswick's church-like town hall stands islanded in the centre of this much-loved Lakeland town

Stables, near Crosthwaite Church.

The Keswick Agricultural Show is held on the late summer Bank Holiday Monday. The two-week religious Keswick Convention is held every July.

Rowing boats and self-drive motor boats can be hired at the Keswick Launch Company. A public launch service, with stops around the lake, is also operated from there. Boats may be launched from their base at Lakeside; and from National Trust land near the B5289 two miles south of Keswick (no power craft). There is a 10mph speed limit on the lake.

Derwent Water with Keswick at its head, nestling beneath mighty Skiddaw

AA recommends:

Hotels: Keswick, Station Road, 3-star, tel. Keswick 72020
Royal Oak, Station Street, 3-star, tel. Keswick 72965
Grange, Manor Brow, 2-star, tel. Keswick 72500
Lake, Lake Road, 2-star, tel. Keswick 72069
Millfield, Penrith Road, 2-star, tel. Keswick 71099
Queens, Main Street, 2-star, tel. Keswick 73333
Red House, Skiddaw, 2-star, Country House Hotel, tel. Keswick 72211
Skiddaw, Main Street, 2-star, tel. Keswick 72071
Walpole, Station Street, 2-star, tel. Keswick 72072
Chaucer House, Ambleside Road, 1-star, tel. Keswick 72318
Crow Park, The Heads, 1-star, tel. Keswick 72208
Larbeck, Vicarage Hill, 1-star, tel. Keswick 73373
Skiddaw Grove, Vicarage Hill, 1-star, tel. Keswick 73324

Guest Houses: Acorn House Private Hotel, Ambleside Road, tel. Keswick 72553
Allerdale House, 1 Eskin Street, tel. Keswick 73891
Bay Tree, 1 Wordsworth Street, tel. Keswick 73313
Clarence House, 14 Eskin Street, tel. Keswick 73186
Foye House, 23 Eskin Street, tel. Keswick 73288
Hazeldene Hotel, The Heads, tel. Keswick 72106
Highfields, The Heads, tel. Keswick 72508
Linnett Hill Hotel, 4 Penrith Road, tel. Keswick 73109
Lynwood Private Hotel, 12 Ambleside Road, tel. Keswick 72081
Melbreak House, 29 Church Street, tel. Keswick 72398
Parkfield, 4 Eskin Street, tel. Keswick 72324
Priorholm Hotel, Borrowdale Road, tel. Keswick 72745
Ravensworth Private Hotel, Station Street, tel. Keswick 72476
Richmond House, 37–39 Eskin Street, tel. Keswick 73965
Silverdale Hotel, Blencathra Street, tel. Keswick 72294
Squirrel Lodge, 43 Eskin Street, tel. Keswick 73091
Stonegarth, 2 Eskin Street, tel. Keswick 72436
Sunnyside, 25 Southey Street, tel. Keswick 72446
Woodlands, Brundholme Road, tel. Keswick 72399
George Hotel (inn), St Johns Street, tel. Keswick 72076
Kings Arms Hotel (inn), Main Street, tel. Keswick 72083

Garages: Crosthwaite, Carlisle Road, tel. Keswick 72606
High Hill, tel. Keswick 72768
Keswick Motor Co, Lake Road, tel. Keswick 72064
Millbank, Skiddaw Street, tel. Keswick 72955
Robert Furness & Son, Tithe Barn Street, tel. Keswick 72386

Kirkby Lonsdale

Map Ref: 68SD6178

This attractive market town lies on the River Lune 13 miles south-east of Kendal. Writer John Ruskin was enchanted with the view across the River Lune from the high river bank beyond Kirkby Lonsdale Church. After he had seen a painting of the view by his friend JMW Turner, he called there in 1875 and was so impressed by it that he wrote: 'The valley of the Lune at Kirkby Lonsdale is one of the loveliest scenes in England – therefore, in the world . . . I do not know in all my own country, still less in France or Italy, a place more naturally divine, or a more priceless possession of true "Holy Land".' The viewpoint has been called 'Ruskin's View' ever since, and can be reached through the churchyard.

Kirkby Lonsdale contains the best example of a Norman Church (St Mary's) in Cumbria. The church has been extended and altered, with major restoration in 1866. But there are many original features, including the massive pillars of the north nave and the Norman archway beneath the tower. From a fine gazebo in the grounds there are superb views of the Lune.

Spanning the Lune at Kirkby Lonsdale is Devil's Bridge, a beautiful three-arched structure that is one of the most famous and most photographed bridges in the north. The exact date of its construction is not clear, but it is known to have existed in the 14th century. In 1932, to protect the bridge, another bridge was opened for motor vehicles downstream.

AA recommends:

Hotels: Royal, Main Street, 3-star, tel. Kirkby Lonsdale 71217
Red Dragon Inn, Main Street, 1-star, tel. Kirkby Lonsdale 71205

Self Catering: 12 Durham Ox Cottages, Old Town, tel. Kirkby Lonsdale 71689

Garages: Kirkby Motors, Kendal Road, tel. Kirkby Lonsdale 71778

Lakeside

Map Ref: 91SD3787

Lakeside is the base for the Windermere steamers at the southern end of the lake. It is on the west side of the lake three quarters of a mile from Newby Bridge.

The pleasure boat Teal, nearly 50 years old, departing from the quay at Lakeside. The original Teal was the second steam yacht to be launched on Windermere.

The first steam yacht, *Lady of the Lake*, appeared on the lake in 1845. Then in 1866 the Furness Railway Company started to build a branch line from Plumpton Junction (near Ulverston) to Lakeside, where a new rail/boat terminus with three long platforms was constructed to cope with the expected tourist traffic. This was opened in June 1869. Two years later the company leased land from the owners of the bed of the lake to make piers at Bowness and Waterhead. Daytrippers arriving by train in the morning were then able to board the steamers for lunch in Bowness and tea in Waterhead before returning.

After the opening of their Lakeside branch, the railway launched its first screw steamer, the *Swan*. This was followed by the *Teal*. *Tern* was launched in 1891 and *Swift* in 1900. Other boats came and went, but the original *Tern* and *Swift* are still in the fleet, whilst the *Swan* and the *Teal* were replaced in the late 1930s by boats using the same names. Each of the four is registered to take over 600 passengers. The steamers carry from 650,000–750,000 passengers every year during a daily operation which lasts from April until the first Sunday in October.

Lamplugh

Map Ref: 7NY0820

This scattered village is on the north-west boundary of the National Park between Loweswater and Ennerdale. At one time the area was so thickly wooded that an old saying was coined:

'A squirrel could hop from tree to tree,

From Lamplugh Fells to Moresby.'

The Church of St Michael is noted for its three gargoyles and a double bell-cote. It was restored and enlarged in 1870. The village's main claim to fame however is as the home of Lamplugh Pudding, a speciality of the county now being promoted as a 'Taste of Cumbria' by the Cumbria Tourist Board.

Lamplugh Pudding consists of hot spiced ale poured over oats and/or crushed biscuits. Sometimes raisins and brown sugar are added. It is eaten very hot and was originally enjoyed by farmers after a long, cold day out in the fields.

Riding is available from Kerbeck Fell Ponies at North Fell Dyke, south of the village.

AA recommends:

Campsites: Inglenook Caravan Park, Fitzbridge, 3-pennants, tel: Lamplugh 240

Self Catering: Barn and Main House Apartments, Lowmillgillhead, tel: Oxford 57687 (after 6pm)

Levens

Map Ref: 93SD4886

This village has managed to maintain peace and quiet despite the A6 immediately to the east and the A590 to the south.

The small church of St John the Evangelist in the village overlooks the estuaries of the rivers Kent and Gilpin. An unusual feature is the three bells that hang outside the church.

The blooms of thousands of flowering plants at Levens Hall gardens strike a bold contrast to the formal topiary first established in 1690. The steam collection in the grounds includes this magnificent steam wagon

South of the A590, with its entrance on the A6, is Levens Hall. This is an Elizabethan mansion built in 1580 around a 14th-century pele tower; it illustrates well the evolution from a fortress to a home that took place at that time. Home of the Bagot family now, it contains beautiful Italian plasterwork, beautiful paintings, Cromwellian armour and Carolingian furniture. There are also items which belonged to Napoleon, Wellington and Nelson.

Outside there is a magnificent topiary garden, laid out by Monsieur Beaumont, the King's gardener, in 1692.

Adjacent to the house, by the car park, is a collection of steam engines with models under steam; on Sundays full-sized engines can be seen under steam also. A half-sized engine gives children rides. Opposite the Hall on the other side of the A6 is Levens Park – one of the oldest deer parks in England – to which the public has access at all times by way of a footpath.

Fishing permits are obtainable from Low Levens Farm in Levens.

AA recommends:

Hotels: Heaves, 2-star, Country House Hotel, tel: Sedgwick 60396

Campsites: Sampool Caravan Site, 2-pennants, tel: Witherslack 265

Lindale

Map Ref: 68SD4180

Lindale is on the southern boundary of the National Park, north of Grange-over-Sands. It lies just off the Levens to Newby Bridge road (A590) on the B5277. The improvement of the A590 which now bypasses the village has left it a much more tranquil place than before.

Near the crossroads in the village centre is the famous Wilkinson Monument. This 40ft cast iron obelisk is one of the country's most curious Ancient Monuments and is now preserved by the Department of the Environment.

Local ironmaster 'Iron Mad' John Wilkinson (1728–1808) asked that the 20 ton obelisk should be erected over his grave when he died. He had already had a cast-iron coffin made for the occasion and asked to be buried in his garden at Castle Head, south-east of the village. His instructions were carried out, but later owners of his house had the obelisk removed and laid beneath a hedge. His coffin was re-buried in the local graveyard. But in 1863 another resident, Edward Mucklow, had the monument erected where it is now.

Little Langdale

Map Ref: 84NY3103

The village of Little Langdale consists of a succession of farms and other properties strung out along the valley.

Although not having the grandeur of Great Langdale, Little Langdale is surrounded by lovely scenery. Among the amenities in the valley are a pub and a post office. Visitors come to the valley mainly for walking and climbing. There are two climbing huts.

Many of the farms are owned by the National Trust, who preserve them and maintain farming in an area where it is not very profitable. The Trust allow fishing by permit (obtainable from Blea Tarn Farmhouse) at Blea Tarn.

Some valley residents in the past supplemented their income by smuggling. Tales of smuggling are still told and the tricks of the arch smuggler Lanty Slee are legendary. At Fell Foot Farm at the end of the valley is the place where he kept his distilleries and the room where he stored illicit spirit.

Behind Fell Foot Farm is what is thought to be a Viking Thing Mount – a hillock with terraces – where the Vikings met to administer justice.

AA recommends:

Guest Houses: Three Shires (inn), tel: Langdale 215

Little Salkeld

Map Ref: 7SNY5636

A special attraction in this small village between Lazonby and Langwathby on the east bank of the River Eden is its working watermill.

It stands on a beck which flows into the Eden and is a distinctive building painted red, next to the bridge. This fine example of a small 18th-century country corn mill has been restored to working order. With two 12ft diameter cast-iron wheels, the mill produces stoneground 100% wholewheat flour the traditional way.

Freshly milled flour can be bought, as well as freshly made bread and confectionery. There is an exhibition about the mill and its operation. A tea room is also provided (tel. Langwathby 253 for opening times).

A short distance from Little Salkeld, to the north on high ground, stands a remarkable ancient monument called Long Meg and Her Daughters. This is a prehistoric stone circle dating from about 1500 BC. It stands on farmland but is open to the public; a farm road goes across it. The circle is about 80 yards in diameter and consists of more than 60 stones.

A picturesque village on the west bank of the River Eden, Great Salkeld consists mainly of red sandstone buildings. Not only the old houses but new ones too are made at least partly of local red sandstone. So is the church. The combination of the red buildings with the green lawns, flowers and trees, all neatly cared for, is delightful. It is easy to see why Great Salkeld is a frequent winner of the Best Kept Village competition.

Long Meg and Her Daughters, a prehistoric monument near Little Salkeld

The superb Norman doorway in St Cuthbert's, Great Salkeld

Lorton

Map Ref: 70NY1625

Lorton stands in the fertile vale between Crummock Water and Cockermouth.

The village is divided into two parts. Low Lorton lies in the bottom of the vale on the River Cocker and on the B5289 Buttermere to Cockermouth road. High Lorton stands higher up to the east where the B5292 comes down from the Whinlatter Pass.

Lorton Hall in Low Lorton has a 15th-century pele tower joined to a chapel by a 17th-century frontage and domestic building. It contains priest holes, oak panelling, Jacobean and Carolingian furniture. The public may view the house, which has many historical connections, by appointment (tel. Lorton 252).

The village hall, in High Lorton, is called Yew Tree Hall because of the famous Yew Tree beneath which George Fox, the Founder of Quakerism, preached to a large crowd while Cromwell's soldiers looked on. The great Yew Tree, which stands behind the hall, was immortalised by poet William Wordsworth in his poem *Yew-Trees*.

AA recommends:
Self Catering: Midtown Cottages, High Lorton, tel. Keswick 74392

Loweswater

Map Ref: 76NY1420

Loweswater is a scattered village in a beautiful setting about half a mile east of Loweswater lake and about three-quarters of a mile from the foot of Crummock Water (see page 31).

The church of St Kentigern was rebuilt by the villagers in 1884. A public appeal was launched in 1983 to enable urgent major repairs to be carried out so that it could survive for another 100 years. From this part of the village there are magnificent views of the mountains surrounding Crummock Water and of Mellbreak (1,676ft) which towers above the village.

Nearby is the school with its bell cote. The school field is used on the third Thursday in September for the Loweswater and Brackenthwaite Show. This includes all the attractions of a major Cumbrian Show.

The lake itself is about a mile long, with the road to Mockerkin and the A5086 running along the north shore. There is a lovely drive along here, with opportunities to picnic informally among the trees. Loweswater means 'leafy lake', and it is easy to see why. The lower fellside on the south shore is covered with woodland. The area is called Holme Wood and has a footpath running through it, and a waterfall. Both the lake and Holme Wood are owned by the National Trust, who do not allow private craft on the lake but do allow rowing boats and fishing with permits. Rowing boats may be hired and fishing permits obtained from the Scale Hill Hotel on the road from Loweswater to Lorton.

AA recommends:
Hotels: Grange, 1-star, tel. Lamplugh 211

Lowther

Map Ref: 81NY5323

Practically everything about Lowther, which is on the north-east boundary of the National Park, is connected in some way or other with the Lowther family and the Earls of Lonsdale.

Lowther New Town and Lowther Village were built by the Lowthers in the 17th and 18th centuries respectively to replace the old Lowther village, which was demolished to make way for Lowther Church.

Lowther New Town (including the present Lowther estates office) was built as an estate village in the 1680s. Lowther Village was designed by the Adam brothers in the 1780s as a model village for estate workers; it was intended to be on a circular plan, but the crescent was only half completed.

The church is a virtual monument to the Lowthers and has some lavish memorials to them. In the churchard is a great mausoleum to William, fourth Earl of Lonsdale (1757–1844) to whom Wordsworth dedicated *The Excursion*.

The most famous Earl, however, was the sporting fifth one – the 'Yellow Earl', who patronised boxing (hence the Lonsdale Belt), tennis, athletics and 'virtually anything that ran'. He was a fine horseman himself and started the Lowther Sheepdog Trials. His Yellow Rolls-Royce was a familiar sight at local and national sporting events, and he became the first President of the Automobile Association (in 1911).

Lowther Estates has converted the 150 acres of the former castle park into the Lowther Wildlife Park. Here animals and birds roam free or are housed in special enclosures. Among them are five species of deer, many types of cattle and sheep, and some exotic Oriental and European birds, as well as wolves, otters, badgers and so on. There is a special pond for ducks and waders, around which runs a little train – one of the many children's amenities. The park and café are open daily from Easter to October.

Also on the estate is the Lowther Outdoor Activity Centre and Countryside Museum. This provides opportunities for individuals and groups to study many aspects of life in the countryside, including a section on plants and animals, rocks and soil formation.

On the last complete weekend (Friday to Sunday) before 12 August, the Lowther Horse Driving Trials and Country Fair is held. One of the country's leading sporting occasions, Lowther has become a mecca for driving and country fair enthusiasts from all over the country.

Martindale

Map Ref: 80NY4319

Martindale is found south of Howtown (see page 44) in the fells on the eastern side of Ullswater.

There are some houses clustered on the south side of the hill on the road from Howtown. There is another cluster at Sandwick (pronounced 'Sannick') where the waters of Martindale enter Ullswater. Otherwise there are farms dotting the two valleys of Boredale and Howegrain (with its extension up Rampsgill and Bannerdale).

Despite being about the smallest independent parish in the Church of England, Martindale boasts two churches. About half a mile along Howegrain is the old church of St Martin, built in the 16th century on the site of an older one. By 1880 St Martin's had fallen into such a state of disrepair that St Peter's was built at the top of the pass (The Hause) from Howtown. Now St Martin's has been repaired it is worth a visit to this charming little church. During the summer months services are held there (July and August).

There is a feeling of peace and timelessness about this valley.

St Peter's Church has some good stained glass. Just below it, at the junction where the roads to Howegrain and Boredale/Sandwick divide, is a new workshop called Howegrain Studio, where craftsman Laurence Graves restores antiques and does other creative work. People can watch him at work in a room which used to be the Old Reading Room, recently renovated by Dalemain Estates.

Beyond the entrance to Boredale, another quiet valley, the road goes down to Sandwick where there is a sign saying: 'Please be careful on this road, the lambs don't know the country code'. Sandwick is a delightful spot with a bridge over the river. The road does not go down to the shore, but cars can be left at the bridge. A footpath goes to the shore, or to Howtown or Patterdale. The scenic walk from Patterdale to Howtown goes through Sandwick.

Matterdale End and Dockray

Map Ref: 80NY3923

Matterdale End is known primarily for its old and beautifully-located church.

Halfway between Matterdale End and Dockray, Matterdale Church is an excellent example of a Lakeland fell church and from it there are splendid views across the Lake to Place Fell and High Street.

The local inhabitants petitioned Bishop Best for a church of their own in 1566. The building was completed in 1573. On one of the original beams is carved that date and some initials, which have interested visitors and historians ever since.

Until recently it was not generally known whose initials they were. Now it is believed that 'LP' stands for 'Lancelot Pattinson,' the most likely builder of the church. He was one of the Windermere Pattinsons who have been building in the Lake District for over 400 years. George Pattinson has it on the authority of his grandfather that the Pattinsons built Matterdale Church.

The date '1663' can also be seen on a pew-end at the back of the church; the altar and communion rails are probably of the same period. The original font is also probably late 17th century. Other items of interest include the knob in the pulpit which was for the preacher's gown, and the wide bench by the door which was used for coffins at burials. There is a seat outside from which visitors can enjoy the splendid view.

AA recommends:
Guest Houses: Ivy House (farmhouse), tel. Glenridding 227

Millom

Map Ref: 68SD1780

Millom is a town in the south-west corner of Cumbria, overlooking the Duddon Estuary. The National Park boundary is just two miles away along the Whicham valley (see page 63).

The quiet vale of Mosedale, far from the summer crowds

Just within the Park and only four miles from Millom is Black Combe (1,970ft) from which some of the longest and widest views in Britain can be seen.

Millom developed quickly in the second half of the 19th century as the result of the growth of the iron industry. Jobs were created for local people and other workers were attracted from the surrounding rural areas.

After Millom Iron Works closed in 1968, there were very few jobs left in the town. But with the establishment of some new light industries and encouragement from Cumbria County Council, the area began to revive. Now there is a Project Officer and special committee working to encourage more industrial and tourism enterprises to come to the town. A Folk Museum has been opened which includes a full scale reconstruction of a drift in the Hodbarrow Iron Ore Mine, a replica of a miner's cottage kitchen and a blacksmith's forge. There is also a display of agricultural relics. The Tourist Information Centre is at the Folk Museum in St George's Road (tel. Millom 2555).

Many improvement schemes have been started, including a £2M reclamation scheme on the old Hodbarrow Iron Works site. This will create not only a large open parkland but will also include the development of a number of wildlife habitats for water fowl, little tern, natterjack toads and other species found in the Duddon area (see also entry for Haverigg on page 42).

About two and a half miles further north on the A5093 in the hamlet of Hallthwaites is a herb garden where old English herbs, some of them going back to the medieval period, are grown and sold. Called 'Country Matters,' the garden can be found down the lane just north of the junction with the A595.

Millom is the home town of famous modern poet Norman Nicholson OBE, who still lives in the house in which he was born in 1914. He won the Queen's Medal for Poetry in 1977 and was awarded an Hon D Litt by Liverpool University in 1980. He can be heard reading one of his poems in the recorded poetry section of the Lake District National Park Centre, Brockhole, Windermere (see page 64).

AA recommends:
Garages: Old Moor, 7–11 Palmers Lane, tel. Millom 2565.

Moresby

Map Ref: 68NY9821

Moresby, two miles north of Whitehaven, is the home of the internationally-known Rosehill Theatre, or more properly the Sir Nicholas Sekers Theatre at Rosehill, just to the south of Moresby village.

Moresby, however, was a place of importance at least 1,900 years before the theatre, for the Romans built a fort here as part of their Solway-Hadrian's Wall defences. Then, just after the Norman Conquest, one Maurice, or Morris, settled here and gave his name to the settlement. The 19th-century Church of St Bridget, which has a pleasing interior, was built on the site of an earlier church within the limits of the Roman fort to the west of the village. It therefore occupies the same commanding position overlooking the sea. Earlier this century Rose Hill was described as a 'delightfully situated residence in the township'. It later became

...the home of Sir Nicholas Sekers, one of a family who had left Hungary in 1937 and then set up a firm in Whitehaven producing high quality silk and rayon fabrics. In 1959 Sir Nicholas built a beautiful silk-lined theatre, designed by Sir Oliver Messel, on a site adjacent to his house. It quickly acquired a national and even international reputation for the quality of its presentations, which include concerts, plays and small scale but popular variety shows. An intimate theatre with its own restaurant, in a converted barn, it is popular with artists and audiences alike. For details ring Whitehaven 2422.

Mosedale

Map Ref: 7NY3532

Hotels: Roseneath Country House, Low Moresby, 2-star, Country House Hotel. tel, Whitehaven 61572

AA recommends:

Mosedale is a small, very quiet place on the road to Hesket Newmarket and Caldbeck, where the River Caldew crosses the road below Carrock Fell and Bowscale. There is an ancient Quaker Meeting House in Mosedale, built in 1702, enlarged in 1884 and restored in 1973. To help maintain it, volunteers offer light refreshments to visitors.

From here a narrow road goes along the north side of the Caldew skirting Carrock Fell to Swineside. The volcanic rock of this area contains many minerals and it is possible to pick up bits of many varieties. The original Carrock mines were closed, but a limited amount of mining takes place with a permit ensuring that any damage to the landscape will be made good.

Muncaster

Map Ref: 88SD1096

Muncaster is mainly associated with Muncaster Castle, situated on the A595 west coast road just one mile east of Ravenglass. There are superb views of Scafell and other Lakeland Fells including Black Combe to the south.

The castle has been the home of the Pennington family since the 13th century. It was enlarged in 1325 when a defensive pele tower was erected. This is incorporated in one of the towers of the later building, enlarged in the 15th and 16th centuries.

In 1464 Sir John Pennington gave shelter to King Henry VI when, during the Wars of the Roses, the monarch was found wandering by a local shepherd and taken to Muncaster. In gratitude the King presented Sir John with the famous 'Luck of Muncaster', a fragile enamelled glass dish, which so long as it remains intact ensures the succession of the Pennington family at Muncaster Castle.

This delicate dish is responsible, according to legend, for the long succession of the Penningtons at Muncaster Castle (above)

Other treasures in the house include beautiful furniture, paintings and tapestries. Among the paintings is the famous one of Thomas Skelton, the 'late fool of Muncaster', whose antics in the 17th century gave rise to the words 'tom fool' and 'tomfoolery'.

Muncaster is renowned for its magnificent rhododendron garden, through which there is a Nature Trail which also passes the fourth largest heronry in England. A bird garden, with many rare and exotic birds, a wallaby enclosure and some Himalayan bears can also be seen.

Also in Muncaster is Muncaster Mill, on the A595 less than a mile to the north of the Ravenglass turn-off. This is a reconstructed 18th-century corn mill. Restored to working order, the 13ft water wheel now turns in the millrace, and three pairs of stones husk and grind the grain, producing traditional stone ground flours which are on sale. It is served by the Ravenglass and Eskdale railway, whose trains stop at the Mill station regularly during the season.

Mungrisdale

Map Ref: 7NY3630

Mungrisdale's properties include an old village hall, the Mill Inn and the Church of St Kentigern, otherwise called St Mungo, who gave his name to the village (the 'griseDale' addition means 'pigs vale'). The present church, rebuilt in 1756, is a low whitewashed building, well cared for by the villagers. It contains a fine three-decker pulpit made in 1679 and a tablet to Raisley Calvert, whose son was nursed by Wordsworth when he was dying of consumption.

AA recommends:

Guest Houses: Mill Guest House, tel: Threlkeld 659

Wham Head (farmhouse), tel: Skelton 289

Mill (inn), tel, Threlkeld 632

Natland

Map Ref: 93SD5289

Natland is a neat and attractive village which has won the county's Best Kept Village competition. In 1983 the judge found Natland 'almost impossible to fault'. There is a cluster of old houses round the church and green whose records go back to the 13th century. Modern buildings have spread as the demand for housing has grown in this area.

Just half a mile to the east of Natland, across the A65, is The Helm, a long hill on which stood an Iron Age hill fort. It is worth the climb to enjoy the extensive views of the open countryside unfolding below.

The Lancaster to Kendal canal was opened in 1819, the route passing between Natland and the River Kent. The section of the canal between Canal Head, Kendal, and Stainton (a hamlet two miles south of Natland) has since been closed and drained. But the towpath has remained a public right of way. Plans have now been mooted to convert the towpath for use as a 'cycleway', a combined cycleway and footpath.

There is a canal bank Nature Trail along the ponded section between Stainton and Crooklands.

Hacking (experienced riders only) and riding instruction are available all the year round from Larkrigg, Natland.

Near Sawrey

Map Ref: 91SD3795

This village on the edge of Esthwaite Water has been immortalised by the fame achieved by Beatrix Potter.

The authoress first came to Near Sawrey in 1896 when her parents rented a furnished house in the village called 'Lakeland' (now 'Ees Wyke'). After describing the village 'as nearly perfect a little place as I ever lived in', she bought 'Hill Top', a 17th-century farmhouse, with the help of royalties from *The Tale of Peter Rabbit* (1900) and eventually made it her home.

Several of her subsequent tales were written while she was living at 'Hill Top', including some of the most popular ones such as *Tom Kitten* (1907), *Jemima Puddleduck* (1908) and *Samuel Whiskers* (1908). Six of her stories were specifically connected with the house.

'Hill Top' is now a museum, kept in the style in which she (and her animal friends) knew it. It contains her china, furniture, pictures and original drawings.

Owing to the small size of the house, it may be necessary to restrict numbers visiting at any one time; delays may occur at peak viewing times. There is a small layby opposite 'Hill Top', but a larger parking area past the adjacent 'Tower Bank Arms' (the inn which is pictured in *The Tale of Jemima Puddleduck* and is also owned by the National Trust).

Esthwaite Water is privately owned. The launching of rowing boats only (no sailing or powered craft) is possible from the south-western shore with permits. These may be obtained from Esthwaite Howe, Near Sawrey, where also rowing boats may be hired (Hawkshead 331).

Fishing permits, as well as launching permits, may be obtained from Hawkshead Post Office, who will also advise on rowing boats for fishing.

AA recommends:
Guest Houses: High Green Gate, *tel.* Hawkshead 296
Sawrey House Private Hotel, *tel.* Hawkshead 387

Newby Bridge

Map Ref: 91SD3686

Newby Bridge takes its name from the 16th-century five-arched bridge that spans the River Leven on its way from Windermere lake (about a mile away) to Morecambe Bay.

On the downstream side of the bridge is a long weir to control the flow of water out of Windermere, which adds to the interest of the river at that point.

Less than a mile from Newby Bridge up the east side of the lake is Fell Foot Country Park, owned and run by the National Trust. This is an attractive 18-acre estate on the lake with boat launching facilities for non-powered craft, rowing boat hire, touring caravan pitches, holiday chalets, an adventure playground, a café, and an information centre. Fishing licences are also obtainable there.

AA recommends:
Hotels: Swan, 3-star, *tel.* Newby Bridge 31681
Self Catering: Stock Park Mansion, *tel.* Newby Bridge 31549
Guest Houses: Furness Fells, *tel.* Newby Bridge 31260

Newlands

Map Ref: 77NY2420

Every valley, said Wordsworth, has its distinct and separate character. The Newlands valley is very different from the nearby Borrowdale valley. Settlement is so scattered that, apart from a few farms, there are only two small hamlets, Stair and Littletown.

Littletown, aptly named, was immortalised in Beatrix Potter's *Tale of Mrs Tiggy Winkle*, where its buildings feature in some of the drawings. The farm of Stair has the inscription TF 1647. It is said that Thomas Fairfax, commander of the Parliamentary forces in the Civil War, stayed there.

It was the Parliamentary forces who, in 1651, destroyed the forge at Brigham where all the ore from the Newlands mines

was smelted. This finally put an end to the mining industry in Newlands, although by that time it was in any case declining.

Mining had started in the valley at the time of Queen Elizabeth I. Rich veins of copper and lead, even a little gold, were found on the fells of Catbells and Maiden Moor on the east side of the valley.

The ravages of mining have now been healed by nature although one can discern grassy spoil heaps and mossy adits. The splendour of this valley makes it a favourite spot with visitors.

One very interesting natural feature on the road over to Buttermere is the Keskadale Oak Wood above Keskadale. This has considerable scientific importance because it is one of the few surviving relics of primeval forest which once covered Lake District fells.

Newton Reigny

Map Ref: 75NY4731

This attractive village is named after the de Reigny family, who owned this area in the 12th century. Both the old and new houses contribute to its pleasing appearance and character.

The Church of St John, restored in 1891, has a double bell-cote. The beam of the church is said to have the names of the two carpenters who built the roof in 1585 carved in it. This is similar to the beam at Matterdale Church where initials carved on that at the same period are now believed by many to be those of the builder and others.

Across the River Petteril is Catterlen Hall, a fine example of a fortified manor house complete with 15th-century pele tower. Now a farm, it was once the manorial residence of the De Vaux family.

Less than a mile from Newton Reigny on the road to Penrith is Newton Rigg, which since 1896 has been the home of the Cumbria College of Agriculture and Forestry. Visitors genuinely interested in agriculture and horticulture education are welcome on Friday afternoons when the gardens are open, but they should make an appointment (tel. Penrith 63791).

The gentle landscape of Newlands Valley was once the scene of extensive mining in the 17th century

Pooley Bridge

Map Ref: 75NY4724

Standing at the north end of Ullswater, where the River Eamont flows out, Pooley Bridge is a busy tourist village for much of the year. The first settlement was the Dunmallet fort on a wooded hill on the west side of the river, and the outline of this can still be seen. Below it today there is a car park with access to the river-bank, making a good picnic area. Also on that side of the river, a few hundred yards along the B5320, is the steamer pier for the Ullswater steamers for Howtown (see page 44) and Glenridding (see page 39).

In the centre of the village, east of the river, are hotels and guest houses. There is also a Tourist Information Centre (tel. Pooley Bridge 530) in the Eusemere Lodge car park from where a guided walk starts.

Pooley Bridge has a little church, but Barton Church, some one and a half miles along the B5320 towards Penrith, may be found more interesting, as it is a big 'minster' church which once served a vast area. The old mounting block can be seen next to what used to be the stables. The church stands on its own now, but is well cared for and well worth a visit. Restored in 1904, it still has splendid features including a fine Norman central tower.

Trekking facilities are available at Ellerslea Trekking Centre in Roe Head Lane (April to October). Fishing licences may be obtained (and cycles hired) from Lake Leisure, Pooley Bridge, and Tree Tops Ltd, Wood View, Pooley Bridge. Boats may be launched at Howtown, three miles south on the east side of the lake, but there is a maximum size of 20ft and since 13 July 1983 there has been a 10mph speed limit on the lake. Sailing dinghies can be hired from the Ullswater Sailing School, Glenridding, also motor boats and rowing boats in Glenridding.

AA recommends:
Hotels: Sharrow Bay, Sharrow Bay, 2-rosette, 3-red-star Country House Hotel, tel. Pooley Bridge 301
Campsites: Hillcroft Caravan and Camping site, 1-pennant, tel. Pooley Bridge 363
Guest Houses: Barton Hall (farmhouse), tel. Pooley Bridge 275

Penrith

Map Ref: 75NY5130

This is an ancient but still bustling market town, with a long history and many old Cumberland-style houses.

It was after the Scots burnt Penrith in 1345 that William Strickland, Rector of Homcastle, later Bishop of Carlisle, got permission to build the first castle in 1397–99. Of his castle, only the curtain wall remains. A brief history of the castle can be seen on a notice board at the site, which also gives a plan and explains the significance of what now remains. It is set in a public park (complete with moat) near the station, and access is free.

Penrith parish church of St Andrew was rebuilt in 1722 although the west tower survives from an earlier building. In the churchyard is the Giant's Grave, with stones 15ft apart supposed to mark the head and feet of Ewan or Owen Caesario, a hero of gigantic stature who is said to have been King of Cumbria 920–37 AD. Also in the churchyard is the grave of Wordsworth's mother, who died when he was only eight years old.

Penrith received its first market charter in 1223, and it has continued as a busy market town ever since. It is the centre of a rich agricultural area, and the annual Penrith Show is one of the finest in Cumbria. Held on a Saturday in July, it features livestock classes and trade displays, sheep dog trials, dog obedience competitions, show jumping and other main ring displays, also sidestalls (tel. Bampton 325).

In Castlegate Foundry the Penrith Steam Museum has recently been formed. This is a working museum with several steam engines and a collection of agricultural and engineering equipment. Horse riding facilities are available from Grange Stables, Cliburn; Round Thorn Riding Centre, Beacon Edge; Sockbridge Riding Centre, Sockbridge; and Glendowlin Farm, Yanwath.

There is an indoor swimming pool in Southend Road, and a Golf Club in Salkeld Road, Penrith.

Fishing permits may be obtained from John Norris, in Victoria Road, Penrith, and Charles Sykes in Great Dockray, Penrith. For details of other tourist attractions and opportunities in the area enquire from the Tourist Information Centre, Robinson's School, Middlegate (tel. Penrith 64671 ext 33).

Cycles may be hired from Harpers Cycles in Middlegate and Castlegate.

AA recommends:
Hotels: Clifton Hill, 2-star. tel. Penrith 62717
George, Devonshire Street, 2-star. tel. Penrith 62696
Strickland, Corney Square, 2-star. tel. Penrith 62262
Abbotsford, Wordsworth Street, 1-star. tel. Penrith 63940
Glen Cottage, Corney Square, 1-star. tel. Penrith 62221
Station, Castlegate, 1-star, tel. 62072
Campsites: Thacka Lea Caravan Site, Thacka Lane, 3-pennants, tel. Penrith 63319
Guest Houses: Brandelhow, 1 Portland Place, tel. Penrith 64470
Pategill Villas, Carleton Road, tel. Penrith 63153
Woodland House Hotel, Wordsworth Street, tel. Penrith 64177
Garages: County, Old London Road, tel. Penrith 64571
Ullswater Road Garages, Ullswater Road, tel. Penrith 64545
Regent, Tynefield Bridge Lane, tel. Penrith 62594

Patterdale

Map Ref: 80NY3915

Patterdale was named after St Patrick, who is said to have walked here after being shipwrecked on the Duddon Sands in AD 540. It is now a popular little tourist village. St Patrick's Church, built in 1853, is so close to footpaths to Helvellyn (3,118ft) that a notice in the porch reads: 'Helvellyn praises God, but please do not bring it into church on your boots.' There are marvellous views of the mountains from the churchyard.

This church is notable for its tapestries by Ann Macbeth, embroideress extraordinary, who lived in Patterdale from 1921 until her death in 1948 aged 73. She had a house, High Bield, built high on the rocks above Harrsop (see page 42), but she left that mainly for her nephews and nieces. She herself stayed or made her home in several houses in the dale, including Wordsworth Cottage. From there came inspiration for her two famous wall hangings, including one with the musical notes of Hubert Parry's *Jerusalem* (the WI 'hymn') embroidered on it. After this was admired by Queen Mary at a London exhibition, it was given to Patterdale Church so that it would stay in the dale which inspired it.

Dog Trials. Held on the Late Summer Bank Holiday Saturday, these brilliantly demonstrate the ability of man and dog to work together to control and manage a group of sheep.

Trekking is available from April to October at Side Farm, Patterdale.

AA recommends:
Hotels: Patterdale, 2-star.
tel. Glenridding 231

Walking sticks and shepherds' crooks on show at Patterdale's Sheep Dog Trials

Portinscale

Map Ref: 77NY2523

Portinscale is a residential village with some tourist accommodation on the north-west corner of Derwent Water.

Motor boats, rowing boats, sailing dinghies and windsurfing boards may be hired from Nichol End Marine at the south end of the village. There are also slipping, launching and mooring facilities for a wide range of craft, although visitors should bear in mind that there is a speed limit of 10mph on the lake. Sailing and windsurfing tuition are available (tel. Keswick 72742).

The public launch services operated by the Keswick Launch Company call at the landing stage at Nichol End to put down and pick up passengers. Special rates are available for party bookings.

The facilities of the Derwentwater Boat Club in Portinscale are also available to visitors from Easter to October. These include car parking, temporary membership and moorings for those bringing their own craft. There is also a windsurfing school, and some self-catering accommodation (tel. Keswick 72912). Fishing permits may be obtained from the Derwentwater Hotel.

A little further along the road around the lake is the Lingholm Estate (home of Viscount Rochdale), where the lovely formal and woodland gardens are open to the public daily (except Sunday) from April to October. They contain a one-and-a-half-mile garden walk, a variety of interesting shrubs and exceptionally good views of the lake and Borrowdale.

AA recommends:
Hotels: Derwentwater, 3-star, *tel.* Keswick 72538
Guest Houses: Derwent Lodge, *tel.* Keswick 72746
Rickerby Grange, *tel.* Keswick 72344

Ravenglass

Map Ref: 88SD0896

Ravenglass is a very attractive west coast village within the National Park.

The Romans made it their naval base for the whole of their occupation of north-west England. They built a fort there, just south of the present village, in AD 78, which accommodated 1,000 men. It remained in use for about 300 years. The Bath House, known as Walls Castle, is one of the highest standing remains of a Roman building in this country (and it can be seen on a short walk from the village).

Ravenglass was given a market charter by King John in 1208, and it continued to flourish as a port until the Industrial Revolution, when ports serving the new major industrial centres became more important.

By the 1880s Ravenglass port trade had declined and even the products of the local iron mines on the fells were transported by train instead of boat.

However, that had one valuable side-effect for which visitors to Ravenglass are very grateful today. For in 1875 the Whitehaven Iron Mines Ltd built a 3ft gauge railway from the station at Ravenglass to the Nab Gill mines at Boot about seven miles up the valley. A year later it was opened to passengers. It survived the failure of the mining company in 1882, but closed in 1913. Two years later it was reopened with a 15-inch gauge and a terminus at Dalegarth just short of Boot (see page 28). It continued to carry passengers and freight, including granite from Beckfoot quarry, off and on until 1960. Then, when it seemed the end had come, the railway was put up for auction and purchased, with the help of Colin Gilbert and Lord Wakefield of Kendal, by a Preservation Society for £14,000.

Lord Wakefield headed the company which was then formed to run it until his death in August 1983. 'La'al Ratty' now provides a daily service from the end of March to the end of October (with some trains at other times), using steam and diesel engines, to Muncaster Mill (see page 51), Irton Road and Eskdale Green (see page 38), Beckfoot and Dalegarth/Boot. (tel. Ravenglass 226)

On the edge of Ravenglass, just before the railway bridge, are the car park and platforms of the Ravenglass and Eskdale Railway. In the car park there is a Tourist Information Centre (Ravenglass 278), from where details can be obtained of a guided walk and other opportunities in the area. Next to the car park is the Ravenglass Railway Museum, with a slide presentation as well as historical details. On the platform there is a leaflet telling what of natural interest and wildlife can be seen up Eskdale and in the fields along the track during the journey along the seven-mile railway.

Fishing licences are available from the Pennington Arms Hotel.

Visitors may launch their own boats from the ramp at the end of the main street within three hours of high water. There are, however, no boat hire facilities in Ravenglass.

Ravenglass Gullery and Nature Reserve is situated on the Drigg dunes on the other side of the estuary (see page 36).

Muncaster Castle, famous for its art treasures, and especially notable for its superb gardens, is less than a mile to the east (see page 51).

AA recommends:
Hotels: Pennington Arms, 1-star, *tel.* Ravenglass 222
Campsites: Walls Caravan Park, 2-pennants, *tel.* Ravenglass 250

The Ravenglass terminus of The Ravenglass and Eskdale Railway, the departure point for an old-fashioned trip to Dalegarth

Rosthwaite

Map Ref: 77NY2514

Rosthwaite lies in the middle of the Borrowdale valley, where it broadens out south of the Jaws of Borrowdale.

There are a number of old farms and buildings in Rosthwaite. The National Trust own two of the farms and other property in the area. The Lake District Special Planning Board has opened a new car park with toilets on the north side of the village.

On the side of the road to Seatoller (see page 57) is Johnny Wood. Also owned by the National Trust, this is a fine oak woodland with interesting flora through which there is now a nature trail. Details of the two-and-a-half-mile walk, on which there are also superb views, may be obtained from the Seatoller Dalehead Information Base (Phone Borrowdale 294).

The whole area around Rosthwaite and Borrowdale is notable for broadleaved woodlands, many of which are owned by the National Trust. There are excellent examples of valley-side woods, rich in mosses and beautiful in appearance. Like all such woods, they are extremely attractive to birds of many species.

AA recommends:
Hotels: Scafell, 3-star, *tel.* Borrowdale 208

Rowrah

Map Ref: 68NY0518

At Rowrah, just a mile from the western boundary of the National Park, is one of the few purpose-built go-kart racing tracks in Britain. It is reached on the Kirkland road from Rowrah, which is on the A5086 some three miles north of Cleator Moor. Just west of Kirkland is a narrow road that leads to the old Kelton Head Quarry, which has been used for kart racing since 1963.

Rusland

Map Ref: 91SD3488

Of interest to visitors in the Rusland valley, which lies between the foot of Windermere and the foot of Coniston, is Rusland Hall.

This is a Georgian mansion, well-known for a collection of self-playing musical instruments which is one of the largest collections in Europe. It includes self-acting grand pianos, a variety of self-playing upright pianos, pianolas, and even a pneumatic orchestrelle organ. Many of them are rare items from that period in musical history which immediately preceded the gramophone. Very few of these instruments were made after that period. Also on display is vintage photographic equipment and a modern steam car.

In the gardens are many specimens of trees with pleasant views and garden walks. Beautiful peacocks strut around the lawns, including white peacocks for which Rusland is famous. The house is open daily from April to October (except Sunday) (Phone Satterthwaite 276).

On either side of the approach road to Rusland from Newby Bridge are the Rusland Woods. Some 400 acres of these

Rydal Water – evening light playing over autumn colours

Rusland Hall, built in about 1720 and extended in the 1840s, is famous for its rare white peacocks

broadleaved deciduous woodlands, which clothe the valley sides, have recently been acquired by the Lake District Special Planning Board in order to preserve their amenity value and conserve their wildlife.

Rydal

Map Ref: 85NY3606

Rydal was the home of William Wordsworth from 1813 until his death in 1850.

Up the hill from the main road in Rydal is Rydal Mount, to which Wordsworth brought his family after they had lived in Grasmere since 1799 (see page 41). He had by then written most of the poems which made him famous.

Now lived in by his great, great grand-daughter, the house contains some very fine family portraits, furniture which belonged to the poet, personal possessions and first editions. The gardens are still laid out in their original form. It is open daily from March to October, and daily except Wednesdays from November to mid-January. Next to the house is the famous 'Dora's Field', clad in spring with 'jocund daffodils'. Just below Rydal Mount is the Church of St Mary, where Wordsworth worshipped. The Wordsworth pew is in front of the pulpit.

On the other side of the hill is Rydal Hall, which was the home of the le Flemings, once one of the major families in the area. It is now owned by the Church of England as a Diocesan conference and study centre, while the grounds are partly used as a camp site for Boy Scouts and Girl Guides. It is not open to the general public, but the striking 18th-century façade can be seen from the main road approaching Rydal from Ambleside.

In the grounds of Rydal Hall, on the Ambleside side, the Rydal Sheepdog Trials are held on the second Thursday after the first Monday in August. The Ambleside Sports are also held there.

About half a mile north along the A591 is Nab Cottage, an 18th-century farmhouse where Thomas de Quincey courted Margaret Simpson, the farmer's daughter, whom he married. Hartley Coleridge lodged there later.

Further north along the A591 is White Moss Common, with a large car park which is the starting point of a three-quarters of a mile nature walk. Part of this goes over a wet shore walkway, built by the Lake District Special Planning Board so that people can enjoy the variety of flora and fauna to be found in a habitat they would not normally have access to. In May the nearby Penny Rock Woods are full of bluebells. On the opposite side of the road from the car park is a popular riverside picnic area.

Rydal Water is a beautiful little lake, owned by the National Trust, who do not permit private boating or boats for fishing, but permits for fishing from the shore may be obtained from The Cycle Shop, The Slack, Ambleside.

AA recommends:
Hotels: Glen Rothay, 2-star, *tel.* Ambleside 32524
White Moss House, 1-rosette, 1-red-star, *tel.* Grasmere 295
Guest Houses: Rydal Lodge Hotel, *tel.* Ambleside 33208

St John's-in-the-Vale

Map Ref: 78NY3122

St John's-in-the-Vale is the name given to a scattered farming community which occupies the valley on both sides of St John's Beck between Threlkeld (see page 60) and Thirlmere (see page 59).

A sign about half way along the valley points to St John's-in-the-Vale church, which is much visited, though the lane to it is narrow. Although now off the beaten track, nearly a mile west of the B5322, the church was once on an important road leading from Matterdale (see page 50) across St John's-in-the-Vale to the Naddle Valley and the road to Keswick. It occupies a 'romantic position' between the St John's and Naddle Valleys.

The name of the valley and the church is believed to come from the Knights Hospitallers of the Order of St John of Jerusalem, who are thought to have had a church on the site of the present one as early as the 13th century. However, the earliest documentary reference to a chapel is in 1554, since when there has always been a chapel or church here.

In the church yard are some beautifully lettered headstones. One of these commemorates John Richardson (1817–1886), a well known poet in the local Lakeland dialect, who helped his father build the church school and then taught there for 22 years.

AA recommends:
Guest Houses: Shundraw (farmhouse), *tel.* Threlkeld 227

Santon Bridge

Map Ref: 82NY1101

Santon Bridge is a small village built around a crossing point of the River Irt, halfway between Wast Water and the point where it flows into the sea at Drigg (see page 36).

The Bridge Inn, Santon Bridge, is one of the venues for the Biggest Liar in the World competition. The contest was instigated in 1974 in memory of Will Ritson (1808–1890), a popular publican who lived at Wasdale Head (see page 62).

He became known as the World's Biggest Liar through telling tall stories with such towering sincerity that his awe-struck patrons eventually gave him the 'biggest liar' accolade as a mark of their respect.

Now there is an annual competition to find someone worthy to follow in 'Auld Will's' footsteps. The contest is run by Copeland Borough Council as one of their official entertainments in the presence of the Mayor. One recent prize, given by an Egremont bookmaker, enabled Jos Naylor, Wasdale's champion fell-runner, who won the 'biggest liar' competition that year, to fly to the USA to take part in a contest that sounds even more bizarre – the World Cherry-pip Spitting Competition! Anyone over 18 may enter, provided they are not members of the legal profession or politicians!

There is a Craft Shop in Santon Bridge from which fishing licences may be obtained.

Satterthwaite

Map Ref: 91SD3392

Satterthwaite is in a clearing in the Grizedale Forest, midway between lakes Windermere and Coniston, surrounded by wooded hills.

In the church is kept a lovely story of how the village came into existence. Written by local children, it starts: 'The first people to settle in this valley were the Vikings. Rolf and his family sailed into Rusland Pool in his long boat. He built a farm in Rusland. During the summer when the hay was growing, they took the sheep up to the summer farm (saeter) at Satterthwaite and the pigs to Grizedale'.

Two miles south-west of the village is Graythwaite Hall, the present home of the Sandys family. It was Edwin Sandys (1519–1588), who became Archbishop of York and founded Hawkshead Grammar School (see page 42). The house is not open to the public, but the seven acres of gardens, with shrubs, rhododenrons, and azaleas, are open daily from April to June. (Phone Newby Bridge 31333).

The Forestry Commission's Bogle Crag picnic area and waymarked forest walks are north of Satterthwaite on the way to Grizedale.

Seascale

Map Ref: 68NY0301

Seascale retains its character as a seaside village despite its proximity to the Calder Hall power station and associated works of British Nuclear Fuels Ltd (BNFL) at Sellafield. The National Park is only just over two miles away at Gosforth.

A residential estate has been built on the outskirts of Seascale mainly to house workers at BNFL, but the village has remained uncommercialized. It has a sandy, boulder-strewn beach approached over shingle. To the south the beach is backed by sand dunes and can be reached by a rough track from the B5344 one mile south-east. To the north, the area behind the dunes is occupied by the Seascale Golf Club links.

Boats can be launched over a shingle beach, although in strong westerly winds boating is impossible.

Horse riding facilities are available from Fleming Hall between Seascale and Gosforth, reached from Gosforth.

BNFL have a new Exhibition Centre at Sellafield, just two miles up the coast, for those interested in the history of the plant. This includes the world's first industrialized nuclear power station at Calder Hall and the Windscale nuclear fuel re-processing plant.

The Windscale plant, built by the UK Atomic Energy Authority, was opened in 1951. Calder Hall power station with its twin cooling towers was also built by the UKAEA and opened in 1956. In 1971 they were split off from the UKAEA and since have been operated by BNFL.

At the new Exhibition Centre various displays, models, films and other informative material explains the mysteries of the nuclear world. Staff are available to answer questions about the varied aspects of the nuclear industry in general and the Sellafield works in particular (tel. Seascale 28074/27735).

AA recommends:
Hotels: Wansfell, Drigg Road, 2-star, *tel.* Seascale 28301

The scree slopes of Wanthwaite Crags dominate St John's-in-the-Vale

Countryside near Seascale, with Calder Hall looming in the distance

Seathwaite (Duddon Valley)

Map Ref: 77SD2296

The Dunnerdale Seathwaite – not to be confused with the Borrowdale Seathwaite (see Seatoller) – is about two-thirds of the way up the Duddon Valley. The village may be approached from the south along the valley road from Duddon Bridge (see page 36) and Ulpha (see page 61).

The Seathwaite Church of the Holy Trinity, built in 1874, replaced an earlier one about which Wordsworth wrote one of his 35 Duddon sonnets. In the church is a memorial plaque to Reverand Robert Walker (1709–1802) who was parson of the old church for 67 years and to whom Wordsworth refers in the sonnet as one 'whose good works formed an endless retinue'. Because of his good works, he became known as 'Wonderful Walker'. In the church is one of the chairs he made himself; outside the porch is a stone used for clipping sheep by Wonderful Walker and so inscribed. He and his wife, who made all their clothes, died in the same year, both aged nearly 93.

Seatoller

Map Ref: 77NY2413

Seatoller stands near the head of the beautiful and dramatic Borrowdale Valley (B5289 south from Keswick), where Hause Gill from the Honister Pass joins the River Derwent.

Until the opening of the quarries on Honister Pass in about 1643, there was only a farm here. Then cottages were built for quarry workers. Slates were taken by pack horse over the Sty Head Pass to Wasdale and then on to the coast at Drigg (see page 36).

The quarries still produce high quality slate, and The Buttermere and Westmorland Green Slate Company are happy for small parties, at a modest charge, to visit their roadside plant at the top of Honister Pass to see slate being dressed (cut into blocks and slabs), riven (split) and polished for use as tiles, slates, ornamental paving and monuments (tel. Borrowdale 230, giving 24 hours notice if possible).

In Seatoller itself is the Lake District National Park Dalehead Base, a converted barn housing a blend of interesting displays and study facilities related to the geography, geology and history of the area. There are frequent illustrated talks and

craft events at the centre, and guided walks from it. The centre is open daily from 30 March to 10 April and 27 May to 2 October, also at weekends between Easter and Spring Bank Holidays (tel. Borrowdale 294).

Details of a nature trail in Johnny Wood with superb views between Seatoller and Rosthwaite (see page 55) may be obtained there. The lower floor has room for rucksacks and there is drying space.

About a mile further up the Borrowdale valley itself is Seathwaite, which has the unenviable reputation of being the wettest inhabited spot in England, with 120 inches of rain a year. However, locals assure tourists that the number of rainy days is not much more than elsewhere; it is just that, when it does rain, more comes down!

AA recommends:
Self Catering: High Stile Cottage, Top Row, *tel.* Keswick 72717

Sedgwick and Sizergh

Map Ref: 93SD5187 and SD5087

Sedgwick is a large village once noted for its gunpowder works, which were established in Low Park wood in the early 19th century and continued in operation for 100 years. Along with other gunpowder works in Cumbria, it closed when most of the mining in the county ceased.

In 1923 the various buildings where gunpowder was worked were demolished – as the law requires when explosives cease to be manufactured – but the leat through which water was diverted from the River Kent to the great waterwheel, the wheel pit, a few buildings and some tramway track were left.

In 1983, at the invitation of the National Trust, who now own the site – which they lease to the Caravan Club – some Kendal schoolchildren cleared the rubble away from the site so that what remains of the old workings can be seen more clearly and their important contribution to industrial archaeology be better appreciated.

Just a mile from Sedgwick on the other side of the A591 is Sizergh Castle. A few hundred yards along the A6 from the roundabout is a sign to this castle, which is now owned by the National Trust. The castle's 14th-century pele tower rises to 60 ft, and contains some original fireplaces, floors and windows. Later additions include the Great Hall, built in 1450 but added to and decorated in later centuries. There are a number of panelled

rooms with fine carved overmantels (1536–75) and some fine adze-hewn floors. Among the contents are early English and French furniture and china, a collection of Stuart portraits and relics.

The gardens, laid out in the 18th century, contain a rock garden, rose garden and daffodils.

Horse riding facilities are available in the area at Larkrigg, just north of Sedgwick. Its address is Natland (see page 51) but it is nearer Sedgwick.

Shap

Map Ref: 81NY5615

Shap village is just a mile outside the National Park on high moorland between Penrith and Kendal at about 850ft.

The recent history of the village is related to the importance of the north to south route on which it stands. It became a stage coach route in 1763 when the turnpike road was built from Kendal to Eamont Bridge. This eventually became the A6, the main north to south route along the west of England. Then came the main railway line, which skirts the east of the village.

Now that the M6 takes the heavy traffic, Shap is a quiet village again and people are able to enjoy the drive over the moors from Kendal to Shap. Although the road ascends to 1500ft, it is wide, and was quite an engineering feat. It is now regarded as a scenic route.

Shap's main interest is its Abbey, which is west of the village along the road to Bampton and Haweswater (see page 26). The remains are by the Lowther river.

The Thunder Stone, near Shap, part of a prehistoric stone circle

Shap Abbey was founded by 'white canons' of the Premonstratensian Order. They were monastic canons who wore white clothes – hence their name. The abbey was built at the end of the 12th century and dissolved in 1540. The most impressive feature of the ruins is the west tower of the abbey church, built about 1500 and still standing to almost full height. The plan of the church can be clearly seen, and some 13th-century buildings stand to first floor height. Part of the cellarage below the refectory can also be seen, and some 14th-century vaulting.

North east of the abbey, just along the Bampton road past the abbey turn-off, are some prehistoric standing stones including the well known Thunder Stone.

AA recommends:
Hotels: Shap Wells, 2-star, *tel.* Shap 628
Guest Houses: Brookfield, *tel.* Shap 397
Green (farmhouse), *tel.* Shap 619
Southfield (farmhouse), *tel.* Shap 282
Garages: T. Simpson and Sons, The Garage, *tel.* Shap 212

Silecroft

Map Ref: 68SD1281

This is a small village on the south-west Cumbrian coast, just inside the National Park.

Silecroft was once the centre of an ancient industry involving the evaporation of sea-water in coastal pans to produce salt. The only evidence of this now is in its name, as it is with Silloth.

The long, sandy beach is good for bathing, and above the broad strip of shingle there are pleasant spots for picnics. In the shingle many different types of Lake District rock can be found. At low tide the beach is dappled with rock pools.

Where the road ends at the beach, small craft may be launched over grass and pebbles within two hours of high water (boating is not advisable in high winds).

The Isle of Man can be seen from Silecroft on clear days. Behind the village rises Black Combe, from the summit of which Scotland and Wales can also be seen (see page 28). There is a footpath up Black Combe from nearby Whicham (see page 63).

AA recommends:
Campsites: Silecroft Caravan Site, 2-pennants, *tel.* Millom 2659
Self Catering: The Cottage, Kellet Farm, *tel.* Millom 2727
Hartrees House, *tel.* Millom 2727
Garages: Valley End Filling Station, *tel.* Millom 2407

Skelton

Map Ref: 74NY4335

This is mainly an agricultural community north of Greystoke with some 18th-century houses, a small village green and a village hall. The BBC have a transmitter nearby beaming out world news.

Skelton Show is held on the third Saturday in August. This is an agricultural show with events for animals, show jumping, produce, crafts and trade stands.

Near Skelton, a mile along the B5305 towards Penrith and the M6, is Hutton-in-the-Forest, one of the area's major stately houses. This is the home of Lord Inglewood, former MP for Westmorland, whose family (the Vanes) have occupied it since the 17th century.

Originally a 14th-century pele tower, Hutton-in-the-Forest has been added to by successive generations throughout the years up to Victorian times, showing an interesting evolution of styles. The Long Gallery and the classical façade are of particular interest, and pictures, tapestries and furniture of many periods are on view in the Hall.

The gardens and terraces surrounding the house date from the late 17th century, and the Park and Woodlands contain an outstanding collection of specimen trees. There is a waymarked walk through the woods with an explanatory leaflet. The woods on the estate are among the best in the North of England and have won a number of prizes including the Royal Forestry Society Gold Medal in 1968.

Skelwith Bridge

Map Ref: 85NY3403

Where the Ambleside to Coniston road (A593) crosses the River Brathay is Skelwith Bridge. Just before the bridge, the B5343 goes off to Elterwater (see page 37) and Great Langdale.

The Kirkstone Galleries supply green slate building materials and hand-crafted articles from a workshop in Skelwith Bridge.

Guided walks start outside the Skelwith Bridge Hotel. Details are obtainable from the National Park Information Centre in Ambleside, where particulars of other activities are available. Fishing permits for the Brathay River are available from the Cycle Shop, The Slack, Ambleside.

After rain it is worth visiting Skelwith Force, where the combined waters of Langdale Beck and the River Brathay rush over a 15ft drop. It is reached by following

the Coniston road a few yards then turning right along a signposted footpath. North of Skelwith Bridge lies the charming Loughrigg Tarn.

AA recommends:
Hotels: Skelwith Bridge Hotel, 2-star, *tel.* Ambleside 32115
Campsites: Neaum Crag Camping and Caravan Site, 3-pennants, *tel.* Ambleside 33221

Staveley (near Kendal)

Map Ref: 92SD4698

This is a large village with a narrow main street often congested in summer, but plans for a bypass have been agreed (after years of local pressure) and work was due to start during the 1983/84 financial year.

The Staveley Wood Turning Company and Peter Hall Woodcraft remind us that Staveley was formerly a centre of woodland industry, particularly bobbin making. Peter Hall is a craftsman who makes traditional furniture in solid oak, ash or mahogany and restores antique furniture. Visitors are welcome to watch work in progress at his workshop, which is just off the main road at the Windermere end of the village.

There are signs of other old Staveley industries, including old mill buildings, and a former coppice drying shed with stone pillars, which has now been turned into flats. This can be seen on the main road just west of the village centre.

One and a half miles along the road towards Windermere is the hamlet of Ings. The 18th-century church here, which has a marble floor, was built by Robert Bateman. An epitaph to him written by Wordsworth can be seen on a brass plaque in the church.

Riding facilities (instruction and hacking) are available all year from Park House Riding Centre, Staveley.

AA recommends:
Campsites: Ashes Lane Caravan and Camping Park, 4-pennants, *tel.* Staveley 821119
Self Catering: Browfoot Dale and Browfoot Fell, Browfoot Farm, Kentmore Valley, *tel.* Windermere 4175
Low Brow House, Browfoot Farm, Kentmore Valley, *tel.* Malmesbury 2219

Strands (Nether Wasdale)

Map Ref: 82NY1204

Strands and Nether Wasdale are alternative names for the same small village just over a mile from the foot of Wast Water.

During the season Strands provides useful facilities for people staying in or visiting Wasdale, including two inns.

On the village green is a drinking fountain presented by Eleanor Tatom of Calder Abbey in 1880. There is a village hall next to the parish church of Nether Wasdale, which contains altar panelling and pulpit carving from York Minster.

The Nether Wasdale Nature Trail starts near Strands at the southern end of Wast Water. This is a three-and-a-half mile walk covering a variety of scenery including the lake shore, riverside, a plantation, a tarn, areas of bog and a lane with dry stone walls. There is also a shorter alternative walk. The bird and plant life typical of these habitats is explained in a

Delightful Loughrigg Tarn, beneath Loughrigg Fell, north of Skelwith Bridge

Wordsworth and Coleridge used to meet at an inn by Thirlmere, since drowned by the waters of this reservoir

leaflet available from the National Trust campsite at Wasdale Head (see page 62), the Cumbria Trust for Nature Conservation (Ambleside 2476) and National Park Information Centres.

No boating is permitted on Wast Water, which is owned by the National Trust, but permits to fish for trout, pike and perch may be obtained from the Warden of the National Trust campsite.

Thirlmere

Map Ref: 78NY3116

The Thirlmere area underwent a drastic change at the end of the 19th century when Manchester Corporation flooded the valley to form the three and three quarter-mile long reservoir (1890–92). Two small lakes, Leathe's Water and Wythburn Water, were joined up and greatly expanded. Many of the old properties that constituted the villages of Armboth (in the north) and Wythburn (in the south) were submerged.

A monkey puzzle tree on the north-west shore of Thirlmere (by the new Armboth parking area) is all that remains of old Armboth. The tree used to stand in the grounds of the now submerged Armboth House, a 'palatial Mansion' which belonged to Countess Ossalinsky and was the setting for Sir Hall Cain's novel *The Shadow of Crime*.

At the south end, only Wythburn Church (on the east side of the A591) and three houses at Steel End remain to remind people of the former village of Wythburn.

Further north still are the remains of the 'Rock of Names' containing Wordsworth's and Coleridge's initials. Many requests were made to the Waterworks Committee to remove this rock when the lake was raised. This was agreed but it was found impossible. Fragments of rock with initials on them were collected by Canon Rawnsley and his wife and built into a cairn on a solid base of stone above the A591 (the 'new' road). The church, however, did survive, and is of considerable interest. Dating from 1640, it was rebuilt in 1740 and enlarged in 1872. It is typical of the Lakeland rural churches, with thick stone walls and stone flags. By the church is a car park at the start of one of the most popular Lake District climbs, up 3,118ft Helvellyn.

Two miles north of Wythburn Church along the A591 are two more car parks, one on either side of the road. The one on the east side (which has a toilet) is at the start of the Swirls Forest Trail, which passes through coniferous woodlands of various species and ages (leaflet at start of trail).

From the car park on the west side (Station Coppice), overlooking Thirlmere, a new footpath has been created, reaching to the shore and running north along it.

In addition to the various paths in the area, there are now waymarked paths on the east side of the lake, which enable walkers to avoid the A591 between Dunmail Raise and Stanah.

Between the Swirls car parks and the junction of the A591 with the B5322 to Threlkeld are the four settlements of Thirlspot, Dale Head, Stanah and Legburthwaite that constitute the village of Thirlmere.

At Thirlspot is the King's Head Inn and the start of another footpath to Helvellyn. At Dale Head is the post office. At Legburthwaite there is a large village hall, a youth hostel and the Legburthwaite Mission. A new car park leads to a delightful picnic area by the side of St John's Beck. Nearby is the Castle Rock of Triermain, made famous by Sir Walter Scott.

Going west from the A591 at Legburthwaite is a road around the north end of Thirlmere. This leads over the dam which has a plaque commemorating the start of work on the reservoir on 22 August 1890. There is a public car park with shore access at the other side.

Thornthwaite

Map Ref: 71NY2225

Thornthwaite is a scattered village on the south-west corner of Bassenthwaite, sharing with nearby Braithwaite the Victory Memorial Hall on the other side of the road to Braithwaite village. They were joint winners of the 1982 Best Kept Village award.

Many of Thornthwaite's houses are on the hillside above the old road. Further along the road is the 17th-century Swan Hotel. From there, looking up the fellside north to Barf (1536ft) one can see The Bishop of Barf, a pinnacle of rock half way up and painted white resembling a man in a surplice.

There used to be a bobbin mill and a woollen factory in Thornthwaite, and nearby a lead mine. There is still forestry work in Thornthwaite Forest, an extensive forest on the west side of Bassenthwaite Lake, with the addition of Dodd Wood on the east side (see page 26). There are forest trails and footpaths and also a forest map, obtainable from the Forestry Commission's Whinlatter Visitor Centre on the Whinlatter Pass above Thornthwaite; this can be reached from Braithwaite by car (see page 29).

In the village are the well-known Thornthwaite Galleries, with exhibitions of paintings, sculpture, ceramics and other works of art and also light refreshments. The galleries are open (including Sunday and Bank Holidays) throughout the year.

From Thornthwaite there is easy access to the lake shore from the Powter Howe car park (near the Swan Hotel) through the wood. This car park can also be used for forest walks in the Whinlatter Forest. There is also access to the shore from Woodend car park, three quarters of a mile north of the Swan Hotel along the road. It is necessary to cross the A66 to get to the attractive, grassy promontories which provide delightful picnic places.

See also Bassenthwaite (page 26).

AA recommends:
Hotels: Swan, 2-star, *tel.* Braithwaite 256
Thwaite House, 2-star, Country House Hotel, *tel.* Braithwaite 281
Woodend Country House, 2-star, Country House Hotel, *tel.* Braithwaite 206
Guest Houses: Ladstock Country House Hotel, *tel.* Braithwaite 210
Garages: Thornthwaite Garage, *tel.* Braithwaite 238

Threlkeld

Map Ref: 72NY3125

'Thrall's well' is situated mostly north of and above the Keswick to Penrith Road (A66) and the river. It rises up the lower slopes of 2,874ft Blencathra, sometimes called Saddleback because of its shape.

In Threlkeld village, the Church of St Mary, built in 1777, was restored in 1911, when a font was made for it out of Threlkeld granite. There is also a substantial village hall built in 1901, (called a 'Public Room'), and two old inns.

Threlkeld is well known for its Sheep Dog Trials, held in August in Burns Field. The kennels of the Blencathra fell pack, Lakeland's premier fox-hunting pack (formed in 1840) are also in the village.

Granite was quarried at Threlkeld until 1980, and much evidence of the industry remains. Lead mining was also once important here.

AA recommends:
Self Catering: 3 Blencathra View, *tel.* Keswick 73216
Netherend and T'Otherend, *tel.* Threlkeld 671

Torver

Map Ref: 90SD2894

Less than a mile west of Coniston Water, Torver lies at the junction of the Coniston to Broughton Road (A593) with the road to Blawith (A5084).

Torver has a post office, a shop, an inn and a church. Before 1538 the Torver dead had to be carried through all sorts of weather to Ulverston for burial. In that year, Archbishop Cranmer granted a deed of consecration, permitting burials at the Torver chapel burial ground. The present Church of St Luke was built in 1883 on a site where there has been Christian worship since the 12th century.

Two miles south of Torver, on the lake shore, is the Planning Board's public car park and picnic area (where canoes and

sailing dinghies may be launched). From there to Coniston Hall, two miles north of Torver, there is a shore walk.

Fishing is permitted from the shore where it is owned by the National Trust, the LDSPB or the Forestry Commission; consent from the landowner is required before fishing other sections. No permit is needed, but a NWWA licence may be obtained from Lakeland House Shop, Coniston.

Visitors are welcome to see craftsmen at work at the Fell Workshop, Brocklebank, just south of Torver, where pottery, sculpture and wood products are made.

Troutbeck (near Windermere)

Map Ref: 86NY4002

Troutbeck village mainly occupies the western hillside of the Troutbeck Valley two-and-a-half-miles north of Windermere.

In the main settlement there are a number of 17th- and 18th-century farms and houses grouped around wells (piped water was installed only recently).

At the south end of the village is Townend, built in 1626 by George Browne, a yeoman farmer, and occupied by the Browne family until 1944. It is undoubtedly one of the finest examples of a yeoman farmer's house in the Lake District, and it was acquired by the National Trust in 1947.

Townend contains the original home-made carved furniture, domestic utensils and papers of the Browne family, who, along with other landowners, bred and fostered the familiar Herdwick sheep which can withstand hard winters and live in upland areas. Their wool was used mainly for rugs, but the National Trust has encouraged the spinning of it into thread suitable for knitting and for weaving into fine wool cloth.

The Queen's Head Inn, Troutbeck, is the venue for an annual mayor-making ceremony which goes back (on and off) to 1780. Each year a 'Hunting Mayor' used to

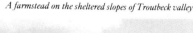

Much of the lovely furniture in Townend house is of carved oak

be elected to set off the local hunt and ensure that each person in the parish got a square meal at least once a year. Nowadays he sets off the Coniston foxhounds at the start of the season, sells tickets for a dinner, and during the evening's merrymaking nominates his own successor in the 'Mayor's Parlour' at the inn. This keeps alive an ancient tradition once more widespread in Cumbria.

With over 12 houses predating Townend and many other buildings of character in the village, the Lake District Special Planning Board decided in 1981 to make the whole village a Conservation Area. 'Troutbeck is a settlement of outstanding character and value and worthy of conservation,' they said. The area includes the old village school and Troutbeck Church east of the main village by the river and the A592. An interesting feature of the church is the 1873 east window, the combined work of Edward Burne-Jones, William Morris and Ford Maddox Brown, the latter two helping when on holiday in the area.

Further along the A592 (outside the Conservation Area) is Limefitt Park camping and caravan site. Its facilities include an International Grass Ski Centre, providing ski equipment and boot hire, instruction, a ski lift and nursery.

Horse riding facilities (trekking) are also available at Limefitt Park from Easter to the end of October.

AA recommends:
Hotels: Mortal Man, 2-star, *tel.* Ambleside 33193
Self Catering: Birkhead Cottages, *tel.* Ambleside 32288

Uldale

Map Ref: 71NY2436

Uldale is on the lower slopes of the north-facing Uldale Fells on the northern fringe of the National Park. Most of the buildings in the village, which is just above the River Ellen, are 18th and 19th century.

Mary White, daughter of a prosperous Uldale farmer from Ruthwaite (three-quarters of a mile to the west), married the famous huntsman John Peel in 1797 at the age of 18. Mary's mother objected to the marriage and forbade the banns. So 20-year-old John carried Mary off one night and they eloped to Gretna Green, where they were married by the blacksmith. Some months later they were married again in Caldbeck Church.

A farmstead on the sheltered slopes of Troutbeck valley

One mile south of Uldale is Over Water, a small lake less than a quarter mile long, and Little Tarn, even smaller, which feed into the River Ellen.

Over Water is a starting point for one of the Lake District's marathon fell runs that takes in all 27 lakes, meres and waters in the area. The runner has to touch each stretch of water as he passes it, right round to the last lake, Loweswater. In June 1983, champion fell runner Jos Naylor MBE, of Wasdale Head, set a new record for the 106-mile round, which involves 18,000ft of ascent, in 19hrs 14mins 25secs.

Craftswoman Anne Utting weaves rugs at Greenrigg Cottage on Caldbeck Common between Uldale and Caldbeck, and welcomes visitors.

AA recommends:
Hotels: Overwater Hall, 2-star, Country House Hotel, tel. Bassenthwaite Lake 234

Ulpha

Map Ref: 89SD1993

Ulf, son of Evard, was granted this manor just after the Norman Conquest – hence its name. It is set amidst the romantic scenery of the Duddon Valley.

On the hills around Ulpha are many remains of ancient British settlements, including cairns and sepulchral mounds. Some of these have been excavated and found to contain rough chambers with calcified human remains, stag horns and other animal remains.

The stone-built church of St John the Baptist is delightfully placed on high ground. This is the famous church about which Wordsworth wrote one of his Duddon sonnets:

The Kirk of Ulpha to the pilgrim's eye
Is welcome as a star, that doth present
Its shining forehead through the
peaceful rent
Of a black cloud diffused o'er half the
sky . . .
How sweet were leisure! could it yield no
more
Than 'mid that wave-washed
churchyard to recline,
From pastoral graves extracting
thoughts divine; . . .'

There was a church in Ulpha in the reign of Henry III; it was restored in 1882 and again in 1934. The font is pre-Reformation. The altar is made from a fruit tree, and is regarded as unique. The pitch-pipe used to give a note for singing before an organ was installed (towards the end of the 19th century) is preserved.

The road to Ulpha from Eskdale Green, over Birker Fell, has marvellous views.

AA recommends:
Self Catering: Miterdale, tel. Broughton-in-Furness 203

Ulverston

Map Ref: 68SD2878

The Saxon Ulph gave his name to this town. But later, under Henry I, it came under the ownership of Stephen, the King's nephew, who gave it to Furness Abbey. Granted a market charter in the 13th century, Ulverston continued to grow, despite being sacked and burned by the Scots in 1316 and 1322.

The parish church of St Mary was founded in the reign of Henry I in 1111,

(called the 'Four Ones Church'). But it was soon appropriated by the Conishead Priory, which had quickly developed out of a hospital for the poor. However, after the priory was dismantled, the parishioners of Ulverston used the priory stones (and some from Furness Abbey) to restore their own church, probably completing the work in the reign of Elizabeth I. The tower they built from priory stones, with 6ft thick walls, is still there today. Almost all the rest was rebuilt in 1866.

The church has a very special north-west window made of early 19th-century painted glass (1805). There is only one other like it in the country (in Salisbury Cathedral).

Conishead Priory, one and a half miles out of Ulverston on the Bardsea road, has recently returned to religious use. After the Dissolution, various familes had built there including the Braddylls (who built a huge Gothic mansion on the 70-acre estate). In the 1970s the badly neglected house was taken over by the Buddhist Manjushri Institute of Tibetan Studies, who are gradually restoring it with the help of grants and subscriptions. Visitors are welcome.

Another religious building, of international importance, is Swarthmoor Hall, just outside Ulverston on the Barrow Road. It was the home of Judge Fell (later Chancellor of the Duchy of Lancaster), who allowed George Fox, the Founder of the Society of Friends, to live there when he visited Ulverston in the 1650s. Although George Fox was ejected from Ulverston Church on two of the three times he went to speak there – once being set upon by the mob – Judge Fell and his wife Margaret always made him and his friends welcome at Swarthmoor Hall. Eleven years after Judge Fell died, George Fox married his widow, whom he had converted to Quakerism, in 1669. The Hall then became the base for Quaker operations throughout Britain, even though both George Fox and his wife spent time in prison for their beliefs. It is still owned by the Society of Friends, who welcome visitors.

Ulverston (the second largest town in the

South Lakeland District after Kendal) is a lively mixture of old and new, with narrow, shop-lined streets radiating from the market square. The market is held every Thursday and Saturday. During the Spring Bank Holiday the Hiring Fair is still held at the Gill, continuing an old tradition.

Another tradition is maintained at Cumbria Crystal, in Lightburn Road, where, in the old cattle market, glassblowers display their skill (including cutting and engraving) to the public during working hours (from Monday to Friday). At Studio Galleries in Theatre Street, other craftsmen are engaged in producing stained, painted and engraved glass, and welcome visitors from Tuesday to Saturday.

At Wendy Todd Textiles, in the Corn Mill Galleries, screen printing of textiles is carried out on Tuesday to Saturday; visitors will also enjoy the 17th-century restored mill with its working waterwheel, milling museum and family garden.

A recently opened attraction in Stan Laurel's hometown is the world's only Laurel and Hardy museum – in King Street, a fascinating place including films and tapes, Hollywood props and personal items belonging to the Kings of Comedy.

Also in Ulverston is the Renaissance Arts Centre, 17 Fountain Street, which acts as a Tourist Information Centre for the Ulverston area (tel. Ulverston 52299).

Riding facilities are available all year from Ghyll Farm Riding Stables, Pennington. There is an indoor swimming pool in Priory Road. The Ulverston Golf Club course is in Bardsea Park. Ulverston is on the Cumbria Cycle Way and spares and repairs are obtainable from Harvey Jackson, Market Place. Fishing permits are available from Fishing Tackle in Market Street.

AA recommends:
Hotels: Lonsdale House, Daltongate, 2-star, tel. Ulverston 52598
Sefton House, Queen Street, 2-star, tel. Ulverston 52190
Railway, Princes Street, 1-star, tel. Ulverston 52208

Ulverston – a happy blend of old and new centred on the market square

Underbarrow

Map Ref: 92SD4692

Underbarrow is at the foot of Helsington Barrow, a 700ft limestone ridge west of Kendal. The village is at the crossroads of routes from Kendal to Crosthwaite, Newby Bridge and Ulverston and from Crook to Levens. It is not a distinct crossroads but a network of roads. The village is therefore rather scattered, but nonetheless it does have a nucleus of old houses and farms and a character which merits attention. In 1983 Underbarrow won the title of 'Best Kept Small Village of South Lakeland'.

The church of All Saints, at the north end of the village, is in a beautiful setting above Chapel Beck. The present building was erected in 1869, but there has been a church on the site for nearly 1,000 years. The church is proud of its chalice, made in 1609, and of its old oil lamps, still hanging from the roof.

There is only one inn now, the Punch Bowl, but there used to be three, serving the needs of travellers and coaches using the Kendal to Ulverston road. There are delightful views along it, especially on top of the Barrow towards Kendal.

AA recommends:
Restaurants: Greenriggs Country House Hotel, 2-forks, *tel.* Crosthwaite 387

Waberthwaite

Map Ref: 88SD1194

Waberthwaite lies in an attractive position between the River Esk and the western fells south of Muncaster (see page 51), just inside the National Park. Most of the village is strung out along or near to the main road (A595), but part of it, Hall Waberthwaite, lies by the 'wath' or ford, three-quarters of a mile west of the road, from which the village takes its name.

Linking Waberthwaite with Muncaster on the other side of the Esk, the ford is passable at low tides and at one time traffic used it. The church of St John's at Hall Waberthwaite served as a chapel for Muncaster Castle and the vicar, who had charge of Muncaster also, timed the services to suit the tides. The interior has hardly changed since 1807 when the box pews were put in, and the church is now included in the Cumbria Tourist Board's Christian Heritage Trail.

Waberthwaite is noted as one of the places specialising in making Cumberland sausage. Sold in one long strip, rather than in links, this sausage is made from pork and herbs. As it contains no 'filling', it is usually more expensive than ordinary sausage. Traditionally, a sauce made from Bramley apples, brown sugar and a pinch of mace is served as an accompaniment to it.

Wasdale Head (and West Water)

Map Ref: 82NY1808

The parish of Wasdale Head, at the head of West Water, is said to contain England's highest mountain, deepest lake, smallest church and biggest liar.

The mountain is Scafell Pike at 3,206ft high and the lake is Wast Water at 250ft deep. Their right to those records is undisputed.

The claim that the Wasdale Head Church of St Olaf is England's smallest church is less easy to corroborate, but in a study recently of the six smallest churches in England, Reverand Raymond Bowers, Rector of Gosforth, Nether Wasdale and Wasdale Head, discovered that Wasdale Head definitely had the smallest cubic capacity of any used church in England, being only 35ft 9in × 14ft 2in in area with walls just 6ft 6in high.

The forbidding grey wall of the Screes drops sheer into Wast Water, England's deepest lake

The 400-year-old church must also be one of the most visited churches in England. During a service there are often rows of boots and rucksacks outside. Its normal seating capacity is 39, but it has held 70. It has many links with climbers and the first climbing association of Great Britain was founded here. In the graveyard are a number of memorials to people who have been killed in climbing accidents overseas, as well as some in the Lake District. Inside the church are three ancient beams said to have been constructed of timber from Viking wrecks.

It was a publican at the hotel who was given the accolade of 'The World's Biggest Liar' in the 19th century. Will Ritson (1808–1890) earned the title by telling the most amazing tall tales in such a convincing way that they sounded believable. He claimed, for instance, that the turnips in Wasdale were so big that after the dalesfolk had 'quarried' them for their Sunday lunch the remainder could be used as sheds for Herdwick sheep.

Today, 'Ritson's Bar' at the inn serves as a memorial to 'Auld Will'. Another is the annual 'Biggest Liar in the World' competition, instituted in 1974 by Copeland Borough council to find a person worthy to hold the title for a year. One of the venues is the Bridge Inn, Santon Bridge (see page 56).

The Wasdale Show is held at Wasdale Head on the second Saturday in October. This is one of the premier sheep shows in Cumbria with many different classes for both sheep and shepherd's dogs, as well as competitions for shepherd's crooks and boots, fell races, hound trails and wrestling.

Also at the lake head is the National Trust campsite. A nature trail which starts at the southern end of Wast Water takes in part of the lake shore and riverside; the bird and plant life is explained in a leaflet obtainable from the National Trust campsite.

No private craft are allowed on three-

mile long Wast Water, which is owned by
the National Trust. But fishing (for trout,
pike and perch) is allowed by permit from
the warden of the NT campsite.

There are small parking spaces along the
north side of the lake where the shore is
ideal for picnics. On the opposite side of
the lake screes come right down to the
water. The view from the north shore
towards the head of the lake, dominated by
Great Gable, is one of the grandest in the
country and is used as the official emblem
of the National Park.

AA recommends:
Hotels: Wasdale Head Inn, 2-star,
tel. Wasdale 229
Self Catering: Andrew House,
tel. Wasdale 243

Watendlath

Map Ref: 78NY2716

The Watendlath valley, south-east of
Derwent Water, is reached from a minor
road turning off from the B5289 two miles
south of Keswick.

About half a mile up the narrow, twisting
road along this 'hanging valley' is Ashness
Bridge. This is probably the best-known
and most photographed bridge in the Lake
District with a splendid view of woods, lake
and Skiddaw in the distance. Higher up
there is another viewpoint, called 'Surprise
View', of lake and mountains.

The hamlet of Watendlath, which only
recently had mains electricity, consists of a
number of old farm houses. The National
Trust own all the buildings so that their
traditional character will be preserved.

Watendlath today is not much different
from the description of it by Sir Hugh
Walpole (1884–1941) in his novel *Judith
Paris*. He lived across Borrowdale at
Manesty, and set the whole of his *Rogue
Herries* series in the Borrowdale area.
Judith Paris was based in Watendlath,
which he described in the book as being 'an
exceedingly remote little valley lying
among the higher hills above Borrowdale'
with 'a dark tarn and Watendlath beck that
ran down the strath until it tumbled over
the hill at Lodore'.

There is now a car park and teas are
served at the farmhouse featured as Judith
Paris' home.

Waterhead (on Windermere)

Map Ref: 85NY3703

Waterhead is that part of Ambleside which
has grown up round the north-east corner
of Windermere lake. It has developed as a
popular lakeside holiday and residential
area south of the main village.

Today, Waterhead has a number of fine
hotels, as well as a host of guest houses and
other types of accommodation. The
Ambleside Motor Launch Company has
motor boats and rowing boats for hire,
operates regular launch services to
Bowness and cruises round the head of the
lake. British Rail Sealink steamers have
regular sailings to Bowness and Lakeside
during the season. Other companies offer
sailing dinghy and motor boat hire. Some
boat launching is permitted from the beach
on payment of a charge to the boating
company. Waterhead Marine have some
launching and full marina facilities. About
a mile south of Waterhead along the A591,
the Low Wood Hotel offers launching

Ancient Ashness Bridge with the towering bulk of Skiddaw in the distance

facilities. An annual Power Boat Records
Attempts Week, is held during October.

There is a purpose-built National Park
Information Centre in the public car park
at Waterhead where information about
most of the facilities and opportunities in
the area may be obtained. One of the
guided walks starts from the Waterhead
Information Centre; fishing permits may
also be obtained there.

One of the big properties in Waterhead,
Stagshaw, has marvellous gardens, mainly
shrubs, trees and bulbs, with many azaleas
and rhododendrons. There are good views
also from these gardens, which are now
owned by the National Trust.

A new facility in the Waterhead area
which opened in the summer of 1983 is the
Low Wood Water Ski Centre by the Low
Wood Hotel. The Low Wood Ski Club
have operated there for some years, but
now the new centre, built with the help of
the Sports Council and Tourist Board
grants, also provides water ski facilities and
instruction for the public on Monday to
Friday. For details phone Ambleside
33773.

AA recommends:
Hotels: Waterhead, Lake Road, 3-star,
tel. Ambleside 32566
Regent, 2-star, *tel.* Ambleside 32254
Wateredge, Borrans Road, 2-star,
tel. Ambleside 32332
Low Wood, 3-star, *tel.* Ambleside 3338
Guest Houses: Romney Hotel,
tel. Ambleside 32219

Watermillock (on Ullswater)

Map Ref: 80NY4422

Watermillock is a scattered village
including the properties on the north-west
shore of Ullswater and the hamlet of Cove
a mile from the lake up the fells.

The church of All Saints, opened in
1882, is south of Cove, just before the
junction of the two roads that lead to the
lake. West of the church is Priest's Crag.
This got its name, so the story goes, from a
17th-century bishop who did not like the
noise people made when hunting in the

woods near the church; he said it disturbed
the congregation. He therefore had the
wood cut down – and that is why there is no
wood there today.

Near Rampsbeck is a marina where
motor boats, rowing boats and wind-
surfers can be hired, and boats launched;
there is also a picnic area. Next to it is a
boat park operated by Ullswater Marine.

AA recommends:
Hotels: Leeming House, 3-star, Country
House Hotel, *tel.* Pooley Bridge 444
Old Church, 1-star, Country House Hotel,
tel. Pooley Bridge 204
Campsites: Quiet Site, 3-pennants,
tel. Pooley Bridge 337
Ullswater Caravan and Camping Site,
3-pennants, *tel.* Pooley Bridge 666
Guest Houses: Knotts Mill Country
House, *tel.* Pooley Bridge 472

Whicham

Map Ref: 88SD1382

Whicham is a small village in the south-
west corner of the National Park.

The slopes of Black Combe (see page
28) rise up to the north, and Whicham is
the nearest village to its 1,970ft summit.
There is a footpath from Whicham to the
top.

The village itself is scattered, with some
recent bungalows and houses, but the
Church of St Mary is of ancient
foundation, restored in 1858 and 1901.
This is an attractive building with a bell-
cote with two bells surmounted by a stone
cross.

Whicham Hall, now a farm, is to the east
of the A595 along a lane to oddly-named
Po House (signposted). From Po House
there is a footpath leading to the remains of
the Stone Circle which lies between the
Whicham Valley and Kirksanton on the
A5093.

Very near Whicham village are the
splendid beaches and shore car park of
Silecroft (see page 58).

AA recommends:
Self Catering: Brockwood Park,
tel. Lowestoft 62292

Windermere

Map Ref: 92SD4198

The small town of Windermere, on the A591, is one mile from Lake Windermere. It developed out of the hamlet of Birthwaite after the railway reached Birthwaite in 1847. This area was quite distinct from Bowness which had developed earlier near the lake.

The new branch line to 'Windermere Station', immediately brought more of the world's goods – and a lot more of the world – to Windermere.

Rigg's Windermere Hotel was also opened in 1847 and Rigg's coaches took visitors to many other parts of the Lake

The gardens of Windermere's Lake District Cheshire Home

Lake Windermere – a lovely stretch of water which is excellent for sailing

District. Windermere village, as it then became known, began to expand very quickly as the popularity of the area grew. The wealthy began to build some fine mansions, especially along the road to Ambleside.

Many of the big houses have since been turned into hotels or guest houses. One of them, Brockhole, half way between Windermere and Ambleside along the A591, is now the Lake District National Park Visitor Centre. It was built by Manchester businessman William Henry Gaddum in 1899, with landscaped gardens. The property later became a nursing home for a while. Then in 1969 the Lake District Planning Board bought it and converted it into England's first National Park Visitor Centre. It has proved a great success. Some 150,000 visitors come each year to see the 'Living Lakeland' exhibition on the evolution and development of the National Park, to watch films and slideshows on the Lake District, to enjoy the 30 acre gardens and to see the Beatrix Potter grotto. Brockhole has its own nature trail along the lake shore and through a woodland with globe flowers and red squirrels and splendid views of the hills. This trail starts at the Brockhole jetty where a launch service calls. All the facilities (including café, reference library, putting green, and picnic areas) are open from late March to early November.

In the grounds of another fine house (now the Lake District Cheshire Home) on the Patterdale road (A592) are the gardens of the Lakeland Horticultural Society. These contain a splendid collection of rhododendrons, azaleas, conifers, ornamental and flowering trees and shrubs, also many alpines and heathers. The gardens are open at all reasonable times. South of Windermere town, reached off the Crook road (B5284), are the gardens of Matson Ground House, with flowering shrubs and rock and water gardens. These are open daily, except Sundays, from April to September.

At a house called Wynlass Beck, on the corner of the Patterdale road, are stables

where instruction, trekking and hacking are available all year round. Riding facilities are also available at the Craig Level Riding School along Lake Road leading to Bowness and at Limefitt Park, Troutbeck, further along the road to Patterdale. There is a tourist information centre near the station.

AA recommends:
Hotels: Langdale Chase, 3-star, Country House Hotel, *tel.* Ambleside 32201
Low Wood, 3-star, *tel.* Ambleside 33338
Priory, Rayrigg Road, 3-star, *tel.* Windermere 4377
Miller Howe, Rayrigg Road, 2-rosette, 2-red-star, *tel.* Windermere 2536
Applegarth, College Road, 2-star, *tel.* Windermere 3206
Ellerthwaite Lodge, New Road, 2-star, *tel.* Windermere 5115
Grey Walls, Elleray Road, 2-star, *tel.* Windermere 3741
Hideaway, Phoenix Way, 2-star, *tel.* Windermere 3070
Holbeck Ghyll, Holbeck Lane, 2-star, Country House Hotel, *tel.* Ambleside 32375
Sun, Troutbeck Bridge, 2-star, *tel.* Windermere 3274
Ravensworth, Ambleside Road, 1-star, *tel.* Windermere 3747
Willowsmere, Ambleside Road, 1-star, *tel.* Windermere 3575
Restaurants: Rogers, 4 High Street, 1-fork, *tel.* Windermere 4954
Campsites: White Cross Bay Caravan Park, Troutbeck Bridge, 4-pennants, *tel.* Windermere 3937
Self Catering: Abbotsgarth, *tel.* Windermere 5144
Applethwaite Holiday Flats, The Heaning, *tel.* Windermere 3453
Beaumont Flats 3–6, Thornbarrow Road, *tel.* Windermere 5144
Guest Houses: Archway, College Road, *tel.* Windermere 5613
Clifton House, Ellerthwaite Road, *tel.* Windermere 4968
Glenville Hotel, Lake Road, *tel.* Windermere 3371

Greenriggs, 8 Upper Oak Street,
tel. Windermere 2265
Hairsthorpe, Holly Road, *tel.* Windermere
3445
Hawksmoor, Lake Road, *tel.* Windermere
2110
Hilton House Hotel, New Road,
tel. Windermere 3934
Hollythwaite, Holly Road,
tel. Windermere 2219
Kenilworth, Holly Road, *tel.* Windermere
4004
Lone Ash, 7 Upper Oak Street,
tel. Windermere 4727
Mylne Bridge Private Hotel, Brookside,
Lake Road, *tel.* Windermere 3314
Oakfield, 46 Oak Street, *tel.* Windermere
5692
Orrest Head House, Kendal Road,
tel. Windermere 4315
Rosemount, Lake Road, *tel.* Windermere
3739
St. John's Lodge, Lake Road,
tel. Windermere 3078
Tudor, 60 Main Street, *tel.* Windermere
2363
Waverley Hotel, College Road,
tel. Windermere 5026
Westlake, Lake Road, *tel.* Windermere
3020
White Rose, Broad Street,
tel. Windermere 5180

Winster

Map Ref: 92SD4193

This picturesque village lies at the head of
the Winster valley 2 miles from Bowness-
on-Windermere on the A5074 road to the
Lyth Valley.

A whitewashed cottage, dated 1600,
used to house the post office. Down the
road opposite the inn, is Holy Trinity
Church in a very fine setting, built in 1875.

One and a half miles south of Winster,
on the road to Cartmel Fell (see page 32) is
Ludderburn Moss, a quiet access area
owned by the Lake District Special
Planning Board. This provides some
pleasant picnic spots with a panoramic
view from the highest point, which is easily
reached.

Witherslack

Map Ref: 92SD4383

Situated a mile north of the A590 and
about four miles west of Levens Bridge,
Witherslack has a post office, a store and
village hall.

The Church of St Paul was built under
the terms of the will of John Barwick
(1618–1669), an ardent Royalist who was
committed at one time to the Tower of
London. After the restoration of the
Monarchy, he was offered the Bishopric of
Carlisle, but declined this. However, he
became Dean of St Paul's in 1644, where
he was buried. A sundial was erected to his
memory in the Witherslack churchyard
and this can still be seen, with the date
1671 and the initials 'JB' on the dial.

His younger brother Peter was a
physician to Charles II; he refused to leave
London during the Plague, staying to help
those suffering. Both men were born in
Witherslack and panels bearing their arms

Yanwath Hall – originally built in 1322 as a defensive tower

are in the church. Restored in 1861, the
church is a pleasant place with four pillars
and some fine 17th-century woodwork.

There are some magnificent stretches of
broadleaved woodland around
Witherslack, with public footpaths through
them.

Whitbarrow Scar, north-east of
Witherslack, is a long prominent limestone
scar, with a steep west-facing rock face of
great interest to naturalists as limestone is
rare in the National Park.

The Lake District Special Planning
Board has established a nature reserve at
Chapel Head Scar so that the area can be
managed for people to use it for recreation
without damaging the important areas for
rare plants.

Wray

Map Ref: 85SD3799

Wray consists of the two hamlets of High
Wray and Low Wray and a number of
scattered properties occupying the north-
west shore of Windermere. It lies east of
the B5286 road to Hawkshead from
Ambleside.

Low Wray contains Wray Castle and the
church. The castle, which looks imposing
and very impressive from the front, was
built between 1840 and 1847 by Dr James
Dawson, a Liverpool surgeon. It is now
owned by the National Trust and occupied
by the Marine Radio and Radar College
RMS Wray Castle. There is public access to
the grounds and woodland. The lake shore
is also open to the public. There is a path
all along the shore from the Castle to the
Sawrey landing of the Windermere Ferry
at Ferry House. For this the National
Trust, who own the shore there, have
produced a Claife Shore Nature Trail
leaflet giving information about the woods,
the flora and fauna and also about the
freshwater life.

The NT allow non-powered craft to be
launched from this shore at Harrowslack
(half a mile north of Ferry House) and at
some other points on payment of fees to
Mr Alan Langstaff, Harrowslack Cottage,
Far Sawrey or a NT warden (against an
official receipt). Fishing (for trout, char,
perch and pike) is free and no permit is
required.

In High Wray are the village hall and
club. There are footpaths over Claife to
Near Sawrey and Far Sawrey.

At Belle Grange, a house near the shore,
south of High Wray, Sir Henry Segrave
died on 13 June 1930 after his speedboat,
Miss England II, crashed earlier that day on
Windermere. He was attempting to
improve on a world water speed record he
had broken five minutes before when he
took it from the Americans with an average
speed of 98.76mph. One of his two
mechanics was also killed when the boat
'flipped'.

AA recommends:
Campsites: Low Wray National Trust
Campsite, 2-pennants, *tel.* Ambleside
32810

Yanwath

Map Ref: 75NY5127

Yanwath is a small village on the B5320
between the National Park boundary and
the A6 at Eamont Bridge (see page 36).
Both the M6 and the main north-south
railway line are close by, passing under the
B5320.

The village is noted for Yanwath Hall,
regarded as possibly the best example of a
manorial hall in England. Sited on the
bank of the River Eamont, it has a big
well-preserved pele tower built by John de
Sutton in 1322. In 1671 the Hall passed to
the Lowther estate and it has stayed with
them ever since.

The Hall, now a farmhouse, can be seen
from the approach lane which leads north
from the village just beside the railway.
Glendowlin Farm provides horse-riding
facilities from March to October.

A great friend of William Wordsworth,
the Quaker Thomas Wilkinson (1751–
1836), lived in Yanwath. In 1791 he
walked to London in eight days to attend a
Quaker Meeting. In 1806 he was asked by
Wordsworth to arrange the purchase of
Broad How cottage in Patterdale for him.
When he learned that he had to pay £1,000
for it, instead of the £800 Wordsworth
thought it was worth or was prepared to
pay, Thomas asked the Earl of Lonsdale to
put up the difference, which he did. This
was the start of Lord Lonsdale's patronage
of the poet, although Wordsworth was
somewhat embarrassed that Lord
Lonsdale had been approached behind his
back. He never lived in the cottage, but let
it to a local farmer. The cottage, now called
Wordsworth Cottage, still exists.

Lake District Legend

GRID REFERENCE SYSTEM

The map references used in this book are based on the Ordnance Survey National Grid, correct to within 1000 metres. They comprise two letters and four figures, and are preceded by the atlas page number.

Thus the reference for Coniston appears **90 SD 3097**

90 is the atlas page number

SD identifies the major (100km) grid square concerned (see diag)

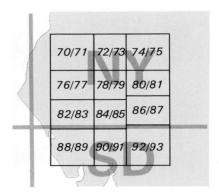

70/71	72/73	74/75
76/77	78/79	80/81
82/83	84/85	86/87
88/89	90/91	92/93

NY
SD

TOURIST INFORMATION (All Scales)

- Camp Site
- Caravan Site
- Information Centre
- Parking Facilities
- Viewpoint
- Picnic site
- Golf course or links
- Castle
- Cave
- Country park
- Garden
- Historic house
- Nature reserve
- Other tourist feature
- Preserved railway
- Racecourse
- Wildlife park
- Museum
- Nature or forest trail
- Ancient monument or Historic building
- Places of interest
- Telephones
- PC Public Convenience
- ▲ Youth Hostel

Mountain Rescue Post with telephone and supervisor

Mountain Rescue Kit Equipment only

ORIENTATION

1°10′E   0°33′E

Grid North / Magnetic North / True North

1°09′E   0°32′E

True North
Difference from Grid North at sheet corners is shown on left.

Magnetic North
About 6½° W of Grid North in 1984 decreasing by about ½° in three years.

3097 locates the lower left-hand corner of the kilometre grid square in which Coniston appears.

30 can be found along the bottom edge of the page, reading W to E

97 can be found along the right hand side of the page, reading S to N

○ Coniston

98
97
96
29   30   31

1:63,360 or 1 INCH to 1 MILE

ROADS & PATHS Not necessarily rights of way

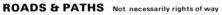

- M6 Motorway
- A 6 (T) Trunk Road
- A 592 Main Road } Single & Dual Carriageway
- B 5289 Secondary Road
- A 886 Narrow Trunk or Main Road with passing places
- 14ft of metalling or over (not included above)
- Under 14ft of metalling tarred and untarred
- Minor Road in towns, Drive or Track (unmetalled) (Unfenced roads are shown by short pecks)
- Path
- Gradients: 1 in 5 and Steeper 1 in 7 to 1 in 5

MISCELLANEOUS

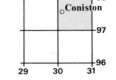

- Church or Chapel { with Tower / with Spire / without Tower or Spire
- △ Triangulation Pillar
- Intersection, Lat & Long at 5′ intervals (not shown where it confuses important detail)
- Electricity Transmission Line (with pylons spaced conventionally)
- Bus or Coach Station
- Wind Pump
- Radio or TV Mast
- Wood   Orchard
- Park or Ornamental Grounds
- Bracken, Heath and Rough Grassland
- Quarry   Open Pit

RAILWAYS

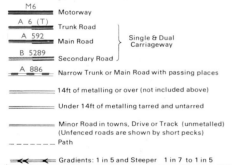

- Viaduct
- Principal Station
- Bridge
- Cutting
- Multiple
- Foot Bridge
- Station
- Bridge
- Tunnel
- Station (closed to passengers)
- Level Crossing
- Embankment
- Single
- Mineral Line, Siding or Tramway
- Narrow Gauge Track

ABBREVIATIONS

P	Post Office	.T		PO
PH	Public House	.A	Telephone	AA
CH	Club House	.R	Call Box	RAC
.MP	Mile Post			
.MS	Mile Stone			
TH	Town Hall, Guildhall or equivalent			
PC	Public Convenience (in rural areas)			

WATER FEATURES

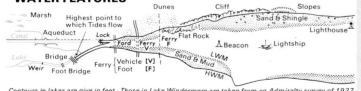

- Marsh
- Dunes
- Cliff
- Slopes
- Highest point to which Tides flow
- Sand & Shingle
- Aqueduct
- Canal
- Lock
- Flat Rock
- Lighthouse
- Lake
- Ford Ferry F
- ▲ Beacon
- Lightship
- Bridge
- Ferry { Vehicle [V] / Foot [F]
- Sand & Mud
- LWM
- Weir Foot Bridge
- HWM

Contours in lakes are give in feet. Those in Lake Windermere are taken from an Admiralty survey of 1937, those in other lakes are taken from soundings by Hugh Robert Mill, D. Sc., and Edward Heawood, M. A.

ANTIQUITIES

- VILLA Roman Antiquity (AD 43 to AD 420)
- Castle Other Antiquities
- ✝ Site of Antiquity
- ⚔ 1066 Site of Battle (with date)

RELIEF

Heights in feet above Mean Sea Level

- ·275 surveyed by levelling
- ·1091 not surveyed by levelling
- Contours at 50ft intervals

To convert feet to metres multiply by 0.3048

BOUNDARIES

- National Park
- — — County
- — · — · — County Borough or County with Civil Parish
- .... Civil Parish
- NT } National Trust { always open / opening restricted
- FC Forestry Commission Access Land

PUBLIC RIGHTS OF WAY

- ....Footpath } Public Paths
- — — — — — Bridleway
- ＋ ＋ ＋ ＋ Road used as a Public Path

Danger Area MOD Ranges in the area. Danger! Observe warning notices

Public rights of way indicated by these symbols have been derived from Definitive Maps as amended by later enactments or instruments held by Ordnance Survey on 1st October 1983 and are shown subject to the limitations imposed by the scale of mapping.

The representation in this atlas of any other road track or path is no evidence of the existence of a right of way

1:250,000 or ¼ INCH to 1 MILE

ROADS   Not necessarily rights of way

Motorway with service area and junction with junction number

A 6 (T) Dual carriageway — Trunk road

A 52 Dual carriageway — Main road

A 52 Dual carriageway — Roundabout or multiple level junction

B 5289 Dual carriageway — Secondary road

Other tarred road

Other minor road

Gradient 1 in 7 and steeper

RAILWAYS

Road crossing under or over standard gauge track

Level crossing

Station

Narrow gauge track

WATER FEATURES

Cliff
Slopes
Flat rock
Short ferry routes for vehicles
Lake   Transport — (lift on)
Bridge   Ferry   for vehicles — (drive on)
Low water mark
Foreshore
High water mark
Canal   Dunes

ANTIQUITIES

☼ Native fortress

...... Roman road (course of)

Castle • Other antiquities

CANOVIVM • Roman antiquity

GENERAL FEATURES

Buildings

Wood

⊕ Civil aerodrome (with custom facilities)

⅄ Radio or TV mast

⅄ Lighthouse

.T
.A } Telephone call box
.R

PO
AA
RAC

RELIEF

Feet	Metres	
		.274
		Heights in feet above mean sea Level
3000	914	
2000	610	
1400	427	
1000	305	Contours at 200 ft intervals
600	183	
200	61	
0	0	To convert feet to metres multiply by 0.3048

1:25,000 or 2½ INCHES to 1 MILE

ROADS AND PATHS Not necessarily rights of way

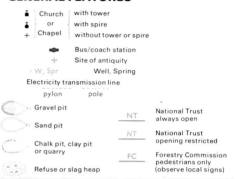

A 31(T) Trunk road

A 35 Main road

B 3074 Secondary road

A 35 Dual carriageway

Road generally over 4m wide

Road generally under 4m wide

.... Path

- - - - - Permitted path

— — — Permitted bridleway

Paths and bridleways along which landowners have permitted public use but which are not public rights of way. The agreement may be withdrawn.

GENERAL FEATURES

Church } with tower
or } with spire
Chapel } without tower or spire

⛟ Bus/coach station

✢ Site of antiquity

W, Spr   Well, Spring

Electricity transmission line
pylon   pole

Gravel pit

Sand pit

Chalk pit, clay pit or quarry

Refuse or slag heap

NT National Trust always open

NT National Trust opening restricted

FC Forestry Commission pedestrians only (observe local signs)

HEIGHTS AND ROCK FEATURES

Contours are at 10 metres vertical interval

50   Determined   ground survey
285 •   by   air survey

Surface heights are to the nearest metre above mean sea level Heights shown close to a triangulation pillar refer to the station height at ground level and not necessarily to the summit

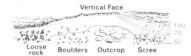

Vertical Face
100
70
50
Loose rock   Boulders   Outcrop   Scree

PUBLIC RIGHTS OF WAY

Public rights of way shown on this Atlas may not be evident on the ground

- - - - - } Public Paths { Footpath
— — — { Bridleway

+ + + + + By-way open to all traffic

⊢ ⊣ ⊢ ⊣ Road used as a public path

Where rights of way are co–incident with walks they have been omitted

Public rights of way indicated have been derived from Definitive Maps as amended by later enactments or instruments held by Ordnance Survey between 1st November 1981 and 1st February 1982 and are shown subject to the limitations imposed by the scale of mapping.

The representation on this map of any other road, track or path is no evidence of the existence of a right of way.

WALKS AND DRIVES (All Scales)

18 👣 Start point of walk

→ Route of walk

— Line of Walk

- - - - Alternative route

— — — Ferry route

5 🚗 Start point of drive

→ Route of drive

⌐ Featured Drive

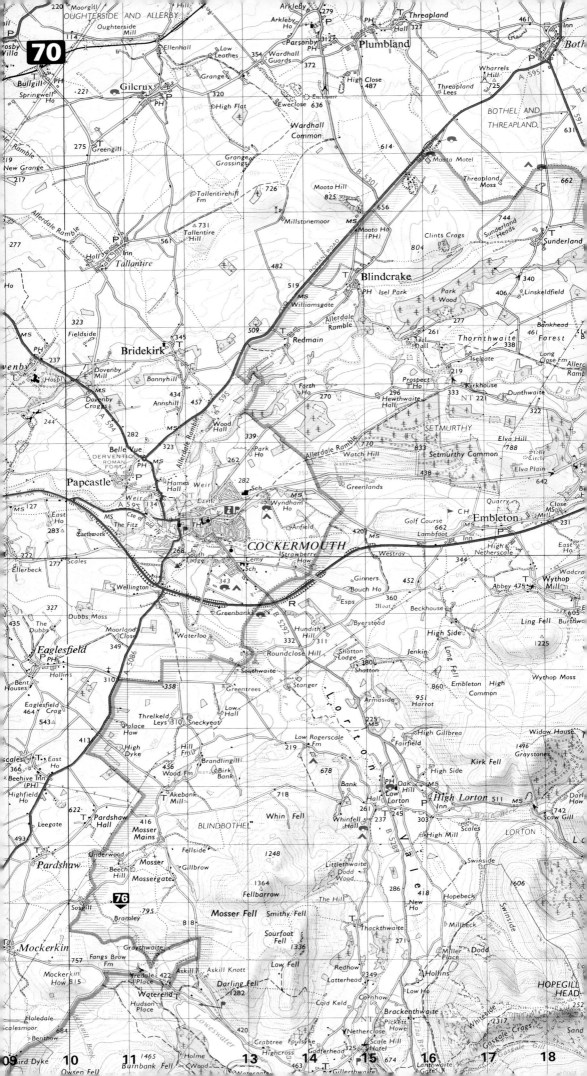

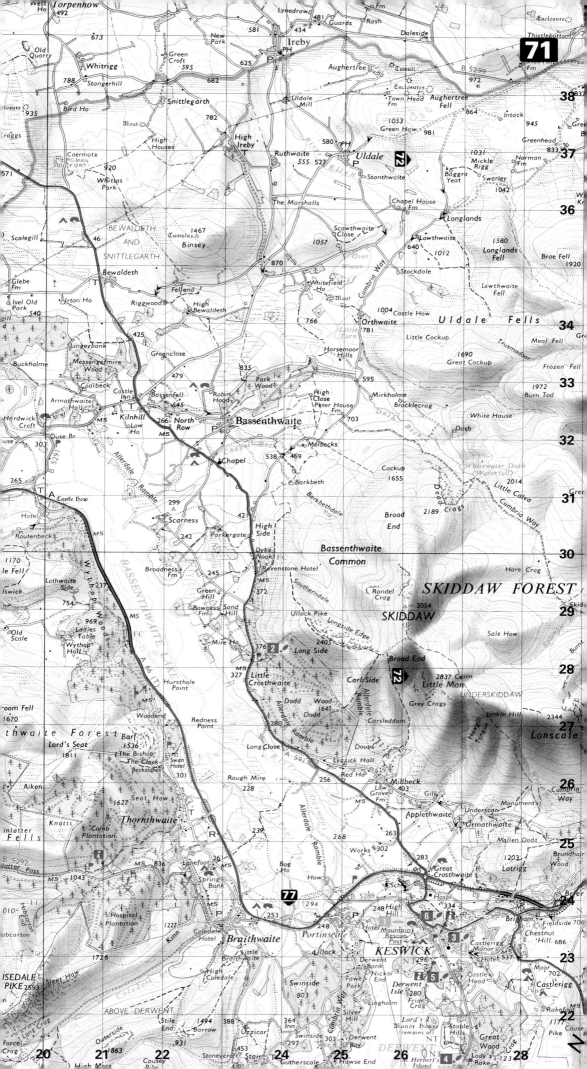

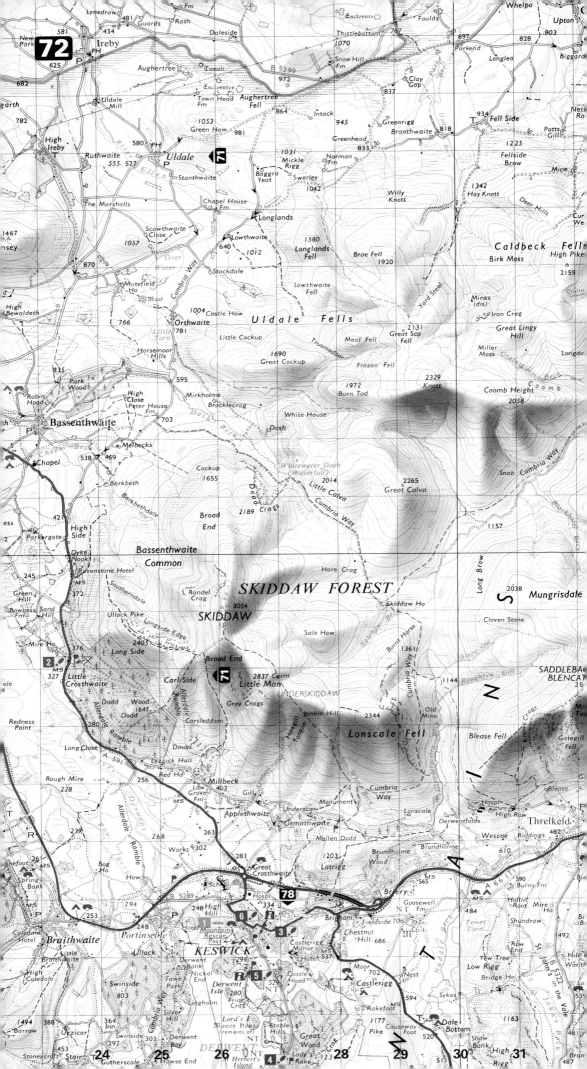

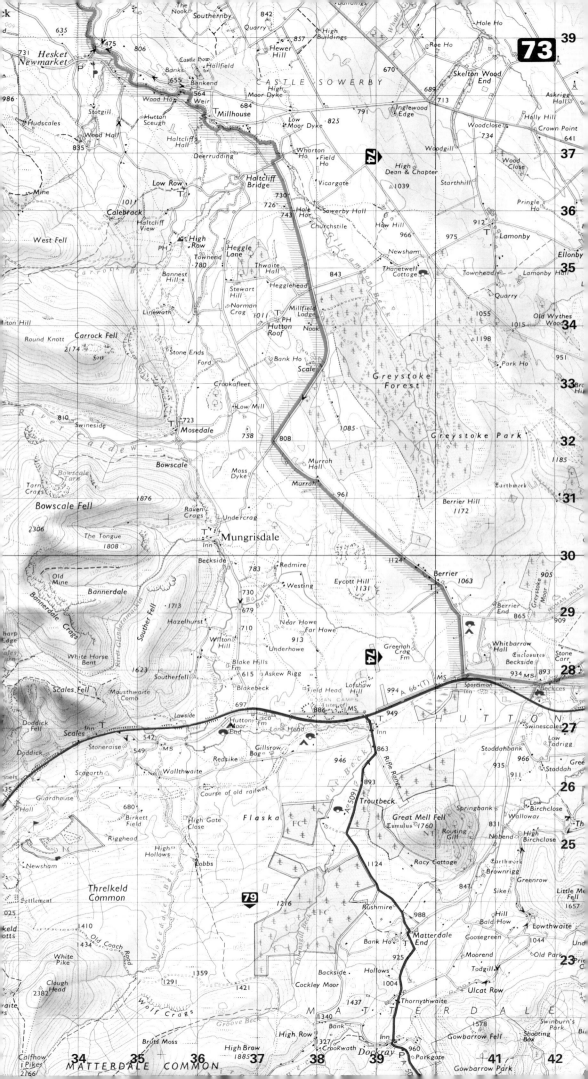

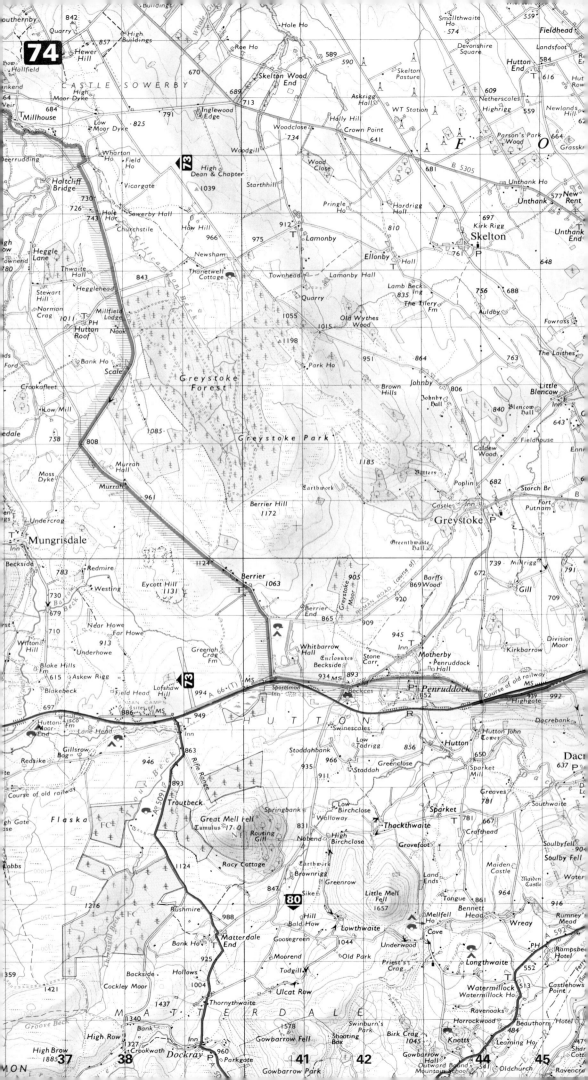

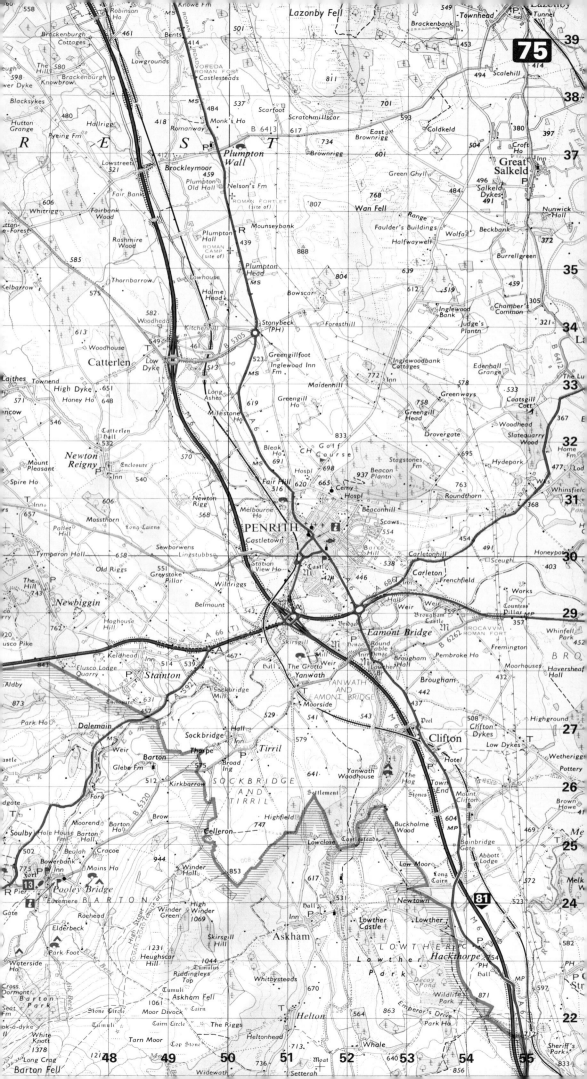

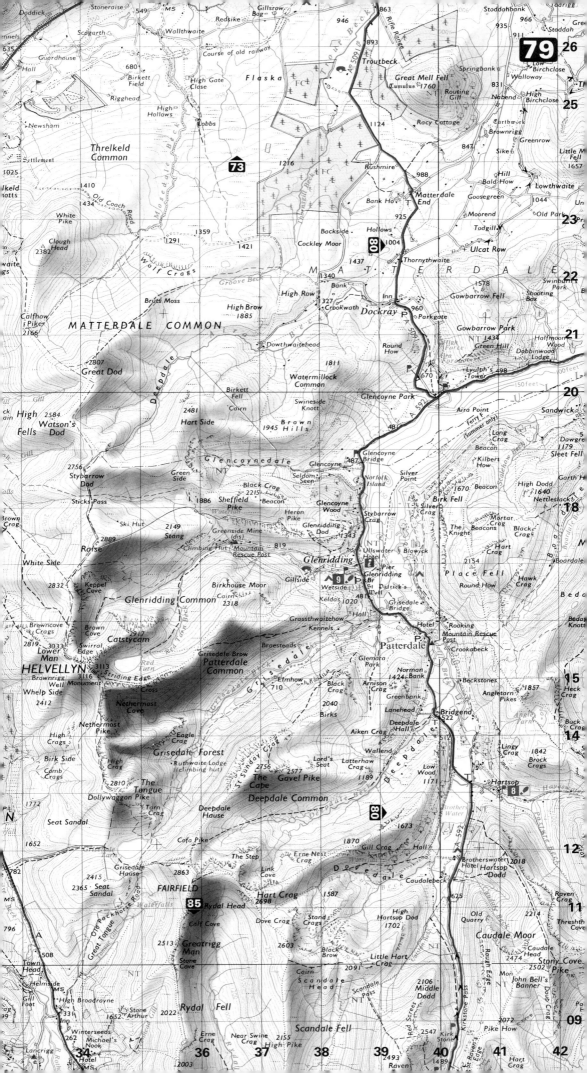

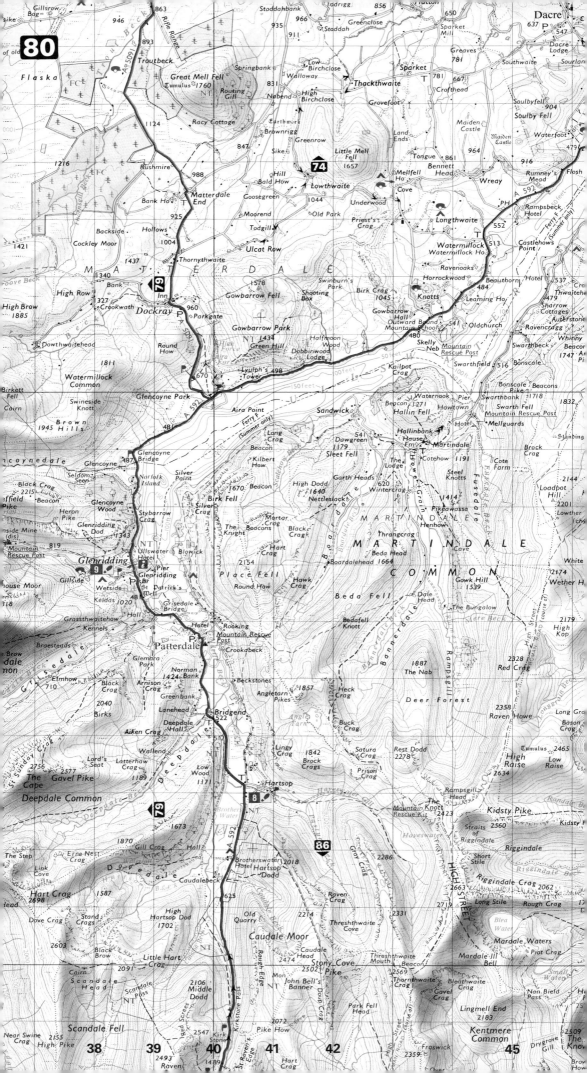

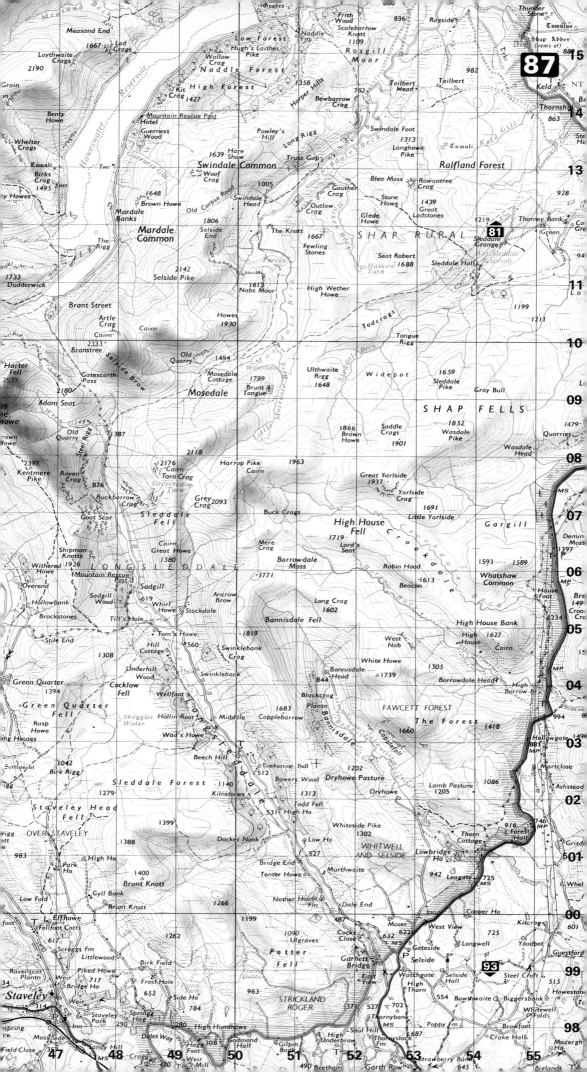

TOUR 1
60 MILES
Northern Lakeland

From Keswick this tour quickly passes into enchanting countryside. First visiting Derwent Water and dark Barrowdale, it ascends Honister Pass to dramatic mountain scenery before dropping to Buttermere.
Another high pass is taken to Bassenthwaite Lake and to quiet open moorland roads before the return to Keswick

The Buzzard
There are few areas of the Lake District that are not regularly patrolled by the handsome buzzard

Leave Keswick *(see page 46) by the Borrowdale road, B5289.* The drive soon follows the eastern shores of Derwent Water, with steep wooded slopes to the left. Farther on, the cliffs of Falcon Crag tower above the road and there are more excellent views over the lake. The road then enters the attractive valley of Borrowdale, keeping to the east bank of the River Derwent. Later the conical, tree covered summit of Castle Crag is prominent to the right, and as Borrowdale widens out there are panoramic views of the numerous peaks ahead.

Continue through Rosthwaite (see page 55) and Seatoller (see page 57), then begin the ascent of Honister Pass (1 in 4). The pass, which rises to 1,176ft, offers superb mountain scenery and on the descent there is a spectacular view down into Buttermere, with steep scree-covered slopes sweeping down to the road on either side.

After the descent, follow the waters of Buttermere and remain on the B5289 through the hamlet of Buttermere (see page 30). The drive then follows the shore of Crummock Water, with more high peaks on either side of the road.

Almost 2 miles beyond the lake turn right (signed Lorton, Cockermouth), then in another 2 miles turn right on to an unclassified road and shortly go over the crossroads for High Lorton. At the end of the village turn right, signed Keswick, then at the T-junction turn right again on to the B5292. An ascent is then made over the Whinlatter Pass (1,043ft) and on the wooded descent there are views to the left overlooking Bassenthwaite Lake.

Continue the descent into Braithwaite village (see page 29). Here turn left (signed Cockermouth A66), then turn left again to join the A66. Later the drive runs alongside Bassenthwaite Lake with views of Skiddaw (3,054ft) across the water.

After 3½ miles, at the far end of the lake, turn right onto the B5291 (signed Castle Inn) then turn right again. In ¾ mile turn right and cross the river bridge. At the Castle Inn turn right then left over the main road to join the unclassified Uldale road. In 2¼ miles bear right and continue to Uldale (see page 60). The rugged peaks of the Lakeland Fells now give way to gentler, undulating moorland scenery in the vicinity of Uldale.

At Uldale go over the crossroads with the Caldbeck road and ascend, then in 2¼ miles join the B5299. After another 1½ miles bear left and continue to Caldbeck (see page 31). Here branch right on to an unclassified road, signed Hesket Newmarket. At Hesket Newmarket (see page 43) bear left, then ½ mile farther bear right, signed Mungrisdale. In 2½ miles pass the Horse and Farrier PH, then cross the river bridge and turn right. The drive now follows a moorland road to skirt the eastern flank of the 'Skiddaw massif', passing below the sheer rock

Blencathra, or Saddleback as it is also known, a prominent peak to the north-east of Keswick

face of Carrock Fell (2,174ft). Beyond the hamlet of Mungrisdale (see page 51) there are fine views ahead of Matterdale Common, with Souther Fell to the right.

Later, at the junction with the A66, turn right (signed Keswick). The peak of Saddleback (2,847ft) is now prominent to the right, and at the edge of Threlkeld the road passes directly below it.

Nearly 3 miles after the turning to Threlkeld branch left on to the A591 for the return to Keswick.

Central Mountains

A drive through the heart of Lakeland from the shores of Windermere, over the Kirkstone Pass to Ullswater and with superb views of the central mountains. Before the return to Ambleside Thirlmere's forest-cloaked shoreline and the gentler lakes of Grasmere and Rydal Water are visited, favourite haunts of the poet Wordsworth.

Rydal Water, one of the smallest lakes, and also one of the prettiest

Leave Ambleside *(see page 24) on the Kendal road, A591.* The early part of the drive winds along the shoreline of Lake Windermere and after 2½ miles passes the entrance to the Lake District National Park Centre at Brockhole.

One mile beyond the centre turn left on to an unclassified road, signed Troutbeck. A winding valley route following the Trout Beck is taken to reach the hillside village of Troutbeck (see page 60).

Keep forward through Troutbeck and in 1 mile turn left onto the A592, signed Kirkstone. An ascent is then made of the Kirkstone Pass over wild and exposed mountain scenery.

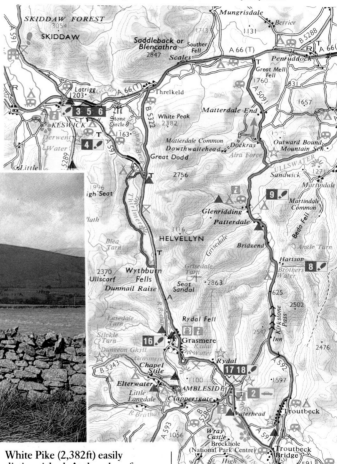

Continue through Patterdale (see page 53) and Glenridding (see page 39). The drive now follows the wooded shore of Ullswater with the huge mass of Martindale Common towering above the lake to the right, and the rugged peaks of Matterdale Common to the left.

Two and a quarter miles beyond Glenridding turn left on to the A5091 (signed Dockray, Keswick) and then ascend. Continue through Dockray and Matterdale End (see page 50). Great Mell Fell (1,760ft) can then be seen on the right and on the descent there is an excellent view ahead of Saddleback (2,847ft).

On reaching the junction with the A66 turn left, signed Keswick. There are more panoramic views ahead of the central Lake District mountains with, on the left, the conical shape of White Pike (2,382ft) easily distinguished. At the edge of Threlkeld (see page 60) the road passes beneath Saddleback.

After passing the turning to Threlkeld turn left on to the B5322 (signed Windermere A591). The drive now proceeds along St John's Vale and as the valley narrows the road follows close to the banks of St John's Beck which is flanked by rocky crags and thick woodland.

After 4 miles turn right on to the A591 (no sign), then turn left on to an unclassified road (signed Public Road Round Lake). In ¾ mile keep left. This winding road follows the western bank of the Thirlmere Reservoir. Thick woodland stands above the road to the right, and to the left, beyond the far shore, is the massive bulk of Helvellyn (3,116ft).

At the far end of Thirlmere turn right onto the A591 (no sign). An ascent is then made over Dunmail Raise, with fine mountain scenery all around, before the gradual descent into the valley of the River Rothay.

Pass the turning to Grasmere village and continue along the A591 through Rydal (see page 55) for the return to Ambleside. The final part of the drive passes by the two smaller lakes of Grasmere and Rydal Water. The villages of Grasmere and Rydal have strong associations with the poet William Wordsworth.

TOUR 3
62 MILES

The Eastern Fells

The cheerful, busy town of Windermere beside its lake
is the start point for a tour which passes through
Kendal, famous for its mint cake, and Penrith, the
ancient capital of old Cumbria.
The ruins of Shap Abbey and the animals
of Lowther Wildlife Park can both be seen
along the way.

Leave Windermere *(see page 64) by
the Kendal road, A591.* A pleasant
valley route, with Hugill Fell to the
left, is taken to reach Staveley (see
page 58).

*Three miles beyond Staveley take the
left-hand lane to join the A5284 and
enter Kendal (see page 44). Leave the
town by following the Penrith signs along
the A6.* The drive now begins the
ascent over Shap Fell and on the
approach to the road's summit
(1,397ft) there are excellent views of
the Lakeland fells to the left and the
distant Pennines to the right. After
the summit there is a gradual descent
for 5 miles to the moorland village of
Shap (see page 57).

*At the end of Shap turn left on to an
unclassified road, signed Bampton. In ¾
mile bear right (note the road to Shap
Abbey, on left) then continue to Bampton
Grange. Here cross the river bridge and
bear right, signed Askham (alternatively
turn left to visit Haweswater). At
Bampton (see page 26) bear right again.*
The drive now follows the attractive
valley of the River Lowther to the
village of Askham (see page 25).

*Here turn right (signed Lowther).
Descend the main street and cross the
river bridge, then bear left.* A pretty
stretch of river bank is followed
before the drive passes through the
attractive grounds of Lowther Park
(see page 49).

Eagle Owl
*This is the largest of Europe's many
species of owl. It can be seen at
Lowther Wildlife Park*

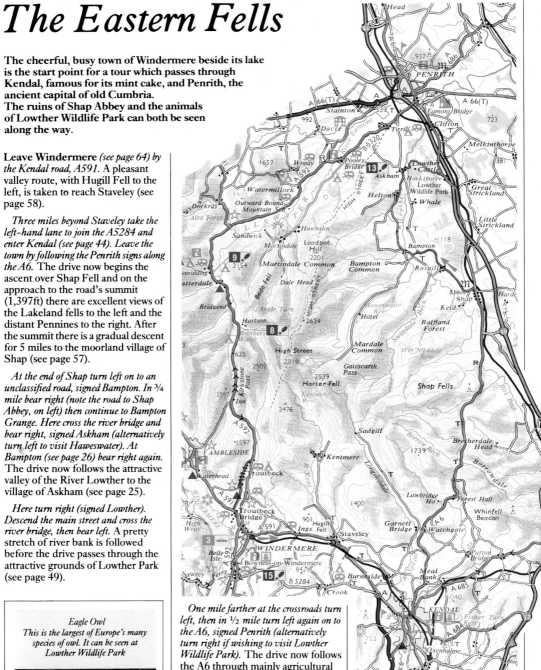

*One mile farther at the crossroads turn
left, then in ½ mile turn left again on to
the A6, signed Penrith (alternatively
turn right if wishing to visit Lowther
Wildlife Park).* The drive now follows
the A6 through mainly agricultural
countryside and passes the village of
Clifton (see page 33) to reach
Eamont Bridge.

*At Eamont Bridge (see page 36) turn
left on to the B5320, signed Ullswater.*
As the road heads westwards the
Lakeland peaks become prominent
again on the approach to the lakeside
village of Pooley Bridge.

*Cross the River Eamont at Pooley
Bridge (see page 53) and in ½ mile join
the Windermere road, A592.* Continue
down the western shore of Ullswater,
with views of Martindale Common,
whose peaks tower above the far
shore.

*At the southern end of the lake pass
through Glenridding (see page 39) and
Patterdale (see page 53).* The drive
then enters a narrow valley and skirts
the small lake of Brothers Water to

begin the long ascent of the
Kirkstone Pass. Steep scree-covered
fells tower above the road on either
side and more rocky crags can be
seen on the approach to the summit.
At 1,489ft, this is the highest road in
the Lake District. The winding
descent is through wild scenery,
following the edge of a deep valley.

*Three miles after the summit branch
right on to an unclassified road (signed
Ambleside) and pass through Troutbeck
(see page 60).* From this hillside village
there are views ahead over Lake
Windermere to the fells beyond.

*At the end of the village branch left
(signed Windermere) and in 1½ miles
turn left on to the A591 for the return to
Windermere.*

The Southern Lakes

From Coniston *follow signs Broughton to leave by the A593.* To the right of the road is the massive bulk of the Old Man of Coniston.

In 2½ miles, at Torver (see page 60), turn left on to the Lancaster road, A5084. After another 1½ miles the road runs alongside Coniston Water and then passes a car park with a lakeside picnic area. Continuing southwards the drive leaves Coniston Water and enters the pleasant valley of the River Crake. The wooded Furness Fells rise to the left.

At the edge of Lowick Green turn left on to the A5092, then in just over ¼ mile turn left on to an unclassified road, signed Spark Bridge. At Spark Bridge cross the river and turn right, signed Newby Bridge. In ½ mile go over the crossroads and in another ½ mile bear right. At the next T-junction turn left on to the A590, signed Lancaster. To the right of this level main road there are occasional glimpses of the head of Morecambe Bay.

In 1¾ miles pass the southern terminus of the Lakeside and Haverthwaite Railway. The drive then follows the valley of the River Lune to reach Newby Bridge.

Here turn left onto an unclassified road (signed Lakeside, Hawkshead) and cross the bridge. On the far side turn left, then bear right. (The turning on the left leads to Rusland Hall.) Continue to Lakeside and in ¾ mile bear right, passing a restored bobbin mill. This winding road heads northwards through more thickly wooded countryside alongside the western shore of Lake Windermere.

In 2¼ miles pass Graythwaite Hall Gardens (on left) then branch right, signed Far Sawrey. Later descend (1 in 6) then in 1¾ miles turn left and continue to Far Sawrey. Here bear left, then turn left on to the B5285, signed Hawkshead, to reach Near Sawrey (see

Coniston Water and Lake Windermere are visited by this tour, which for much of its length skirts the huge Grizedale Forest. A highlight of the drive is a detour to The Tarns, arguably the finest of many lakeland beauty spots. Visits to Beatrix Potter's house and to Brantwood, the home of Victorian writer John Ruskin, give the tour a literary flavour.

Tarn Hows – one of Lakeland's best-loved beauty spots

page 52). The drive then follows the northern shoreline of Esthwaite Water with fine mountain views ahead, including the peak of the Old Man of Coniston (2,631ft).

At the edge of Hawkshead (see page 42) turn right, signed Coniston. Skirt the village and in ½ mile turn left. *After ¾ mile, at the top of the ascent, branch right on to an unclassified road, signed Tarn Hows.* Another ascent is made to Tarn Hows, situated in woodland overlooking The Tarns – a tree-lined lake considered to be the prettiest beauty spot in the Lake District.

Beyond the car park join the one-way system and in 1 mile turn right on to the B5285, signed Coniston. Almost half a mile farther an unclassified road on the left leads along the eastern side of Coniston Water to car park for lake steamers. The main drive returns to Coniston.

*A head of steam
Travelling on the Lakeside and Haverthwaite Railway is a lovely way to see the Lake District*

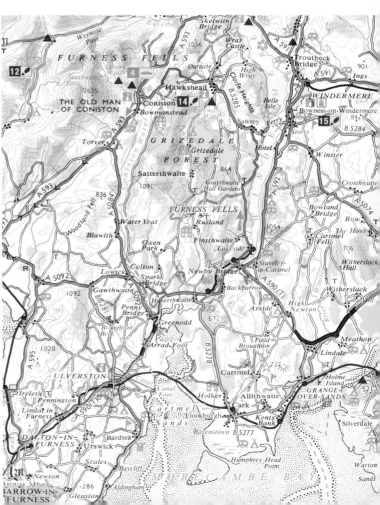

TOUR 5
Wordsworth Country

Impressive fell and dale scenery provides the backcloth for this delightful drive through countryside where Wordsworth spent most of his life. From the gentler Lakeland the poet so loved the route takes in the most dramatic scenery of the Langdale Pikes and the Wrynose Pass, where the views can be breathtaking and where some of the summits are truly hair-raising. In contrast is the pastoral scenery of the Duddon Valley.

The drive starts from Ambleside (see page 24). Follow signs Keswick to leave by the A591. The early part of the tour is through pleasant woodland and mountain scenery, passing through Rydal village (see page 55) and along the shores of Rydal Water and Grasmere.

Two and a quarter miles beyond Rydal turn left on to the B5287 and enter the village of Grasmere (see page 41). Here, cross the river bridge and turn left to leave by the unclassified Langdale road. A winding road along the west side of Grasmere is then followed before making the steep ascent of Red Bank (1 in 4), passing through thick woodland.

At the top of the ascent turn right. This picturesque moorland road soon offers fine views down into the valley of the Great Langdale Beck, and of the surrounding hills.

At the hamlet of Chapel Stile (see page 32) pass the church and keep left, then turn right on to the B5343 (no sign). The drive continues through Great Langdale with magnificent mountain scenery, especially ahead towards the end of the valley where the great jagged peaks of the Langdale Pikes are prominent. Later, Dungeon Ghyll, a spectacular waterfall over rocky outcrops, can be seen to the right.

Mountain pass
Some of the Lake District's high passes are very dramatic – Wrynose Pass is one of the best

Pass the New Dungeon Ghyll Hotel and in ¾ mile turn left on to a narrow unclassified road (no sign). A steep winding ascent is then made over a pass (722ft) with several hairpin bends. From the summit the lovely waters of Blea Tarn can be seen on the right, and on the descent there are excellent views of the green valley of Little Langdale.

At the foot of the descent turn sharp right and begin the ascent of Wrynose Pass (1 in 3). This road, which rises to 1,281ft, is enclosed by steep sloping peaks and just before the summit (on the right) is the Three Shires Stone where the old counties of Cumberland, Lancashire and Westmorland used to meet. On the descent there are fine views ahead into the valley of Wrynose Bottom and beyond to Hardknott Pass where the road can be seen winding its way over the ridges.

Two miles after the summit turn left, signed Broughton via Duddon Valley. An attractive run is then made following the banks of the River Duddon along Dunnerdale.

Pass through Seathwaite (see page 57) to Hall Dunnerdale. Here bear right then left over the river bridge and continue to Ulpha (see page 61). In 1¼ mile keep left and cross the river bridge. The drive now follows the southern part of

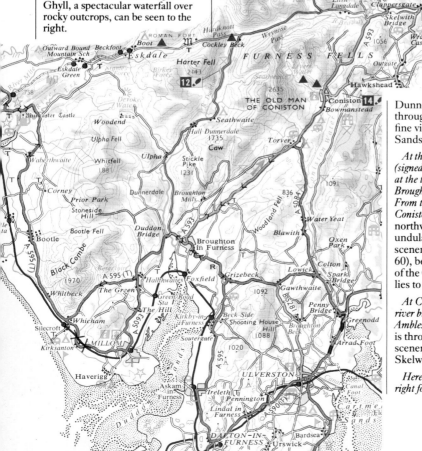

Dunnerdale and later descends through thick woodland with fine views ahead over Duddon Sands.

At the junction with the A595 turn left (signed Lancaster) and ½ mile farther, at the top of the ascent, bear left to enter Broughton-in-Furness (see page 30). From the square turn left, A593, signed Coniston. The tour now heads northwards along a sharply undulating road, with good fell scenery, to reach Torver (see page 60), beyond which the massive bulk of the Old Man of Coniston (2,631ft) lies to the left.

At Coniston (see page 34) cross the river bridge and turn left, signed Ambleside. The final part of the drive is through more fell and mountain scenery before the long descent to Skelwith Bridge (see page 58).

Here cross the river bridge and bear right for the return to Ambleside.

Between Lake and Sea

A visit to the seaside may not sound like a tour of the Lakes, but this drive also visits Wast Water, the deepest English lake; beautiful Dunnerdale, immortalised by Wordsworth; and climbs the heights of Hardknott Pass by way of numerous hairpin bends. Muncaster Castle and the Ravenglass and Eskdale Railway are among the places of interest this tour offers.

Steam engine at Dalegarth Station

The drive starts at Broughton-in-Furness *(see page 30). Leave by the Workington road, A595. After the ascent* turn right, then descend to Duddon Bridge *(see page 36). By the nearside of the river bridge turn right on to an unclassified road, signed Ulpha and Seathwaite.* The drive now heads northwards along a hilly road through Dunnerdale.

After 3 miles cross a river bridge and turn right for Ulpha. Here keep forward, signed Seathwaite. Continue up Dunnerdale through woodland and fell scenery to Hall Dunnerdale.

Bear right then left across the River Duddon and later pass through Seathwaite (see page 57). Proceeding northwards, the road skirts Dunnerdale Forest with Harter Fell (2,129ft) prominent to the left.

One and three quarter miles beyond the Dunnerdale Forest Picnic Area turn left across the river bridge, signed Hardknott Pass. An ascent is then made of the notorious Hardknott Pass. This narrow road has several hairpin bends and a gradient of 1 in 3. Although the scenery is magnificent it is possibly the most difficult pass in the Lake District. After the summit at 1,291ft there are good views on the descent down into Eskdale. The drive continues through picturesque Eskdale, passing the edge of Boot village (see page 28) and Dalegarth Station – the terminus of the Ravenglass and Eskdale Railway, with its steam engines and delightful old-fashioned rolling stock.

In 1¾ miles, at the George IV PH, turn right (signed Whitehaven) to reach Eskdale Green (see page 38). More high ground is then crossed, with the forested slopes of Irton Fell on the right, to reach Stanton Bridge.

On the nearside of the river bridge turn right, signed Wasdale. Almost 2 miles farther cross the River Irt and turn right, signed Wasdale Head, then turn right again. Shortly this road runs along the shore of Wast Water – perhaps the wildest of all the lakes. There is a magnificent view across the lake; with The Screes sloping steeply down towards the water, backed by Sca Fell.

Two miles after joining the lakeside turn left, signed Gosforth. (Alternatively keep forward to visit Wadale Head.) The final part of the drive heads westwards and passes under the high crags of Buckbarrow before entering gentler countryside.

At Gosforth (see page 40) turn right, signed Seascale. In ¼ mile turn left then shortly cross the main road and join the B5344 to reach Seascale (see page 56).

Follow the B5344 southwards and pass through Drigg (see page 36) to reach Holmrook (see page 44). Here turn right onto the A595. The early part of the drive is mainly through agricultural countryside just inland from the west Cumbrian coast.

Ascend onto higher ground and pass the turning (on the right) to Ravenglass. The main drive keeps left with the Barrow road and in ½ mile passes the entrance to Muncaster Castle. *Shortly descend, then in 1¾ miles branch left on to an unclassified road, signed Broughton-in-Furness, Scenic Route.* An ascent is then made along a moorland road to cross Corney Fell where there are good views at over 1,300ft.

Later bear left down the long descent and in 2¼ miles turn left on to the A595 (signed Barrow). Cross Duddon Bridge and ascend for the return to Broughton-in-Furness.

Coastal dunes
The extensive sand dunes at Drigg are one of the strongholds of the natterjack toad

WALK 1
A stroll round Buttermere

Allow 2 hours

This is a delightful walk round the shores of one of the Lake District's most beautiful lakes. It is a walk to savour, and with a picnic meal could last most of the day.

Start at Buttermere village (NY175170). Follow the track starting to the left of the Fish Hotel, and keep left, ignoring a right branch for Scale Force. The long strands of falling water ahead form Sourmilk Gill, spilling from Bleaberry Tarn.

In ¼ mile go over bridges and keep left following the lakeshore path. Buttermere was probably ancient

'Buthar's Mere', Buthar being a Norse settler. The area bristles with Norse names. The mountains are 'fells' from Norse 'fjall', streams are 'becks' (bekr), ravines are 'gills', small lakes 'tarns' (tjorn), waterfalls 'forces' (foss). The Vikings settled here in large numbers in the 9th and 10th centuries, it is presumed peacefully. Some were Christians, and they came as agriculturists and sheep farmers. The clear lake is over 90ft deep and contains trout, and the deep-water fish of the trout family, 'char', a species left from the Ice Age.

At the head of the lake turn left over the bridge and follow the path to Gatesgarth Farm and a metalled road. Turn left on to the road, follow it for ½ mile and then turn left again between gateposts on to the lakeshore path. The path goes by Shingle Point under pine trees. From here are classic Lakeland views no photographer can resist. Left and above the head of the lake is Fleetwith Pike. To the right of that is Haystacks and the sweep of fell side called Warnscale (Norse 'Skali', summer pasture) and the peaks of High Crag, High Stile, and Red Pike. The two great hollows, or 'combes', were scooped out by retreating ice in the Ice Age. Down by the lakeside the path continues along a delightful terrace before unexpectedly disappearing into a tunnel through a wall of solid rock. Story has it that the one-time landowner hated to see his gardeners idle on wet days, and so he put them to the task of tunnelling to keep them occupied. The path emerges to meander through lakeside trees, which charmingly frame and reframe the delightful scene as you pass them by.

Follow the path beyond the end of the lake. Go through a farmyard back to the start.

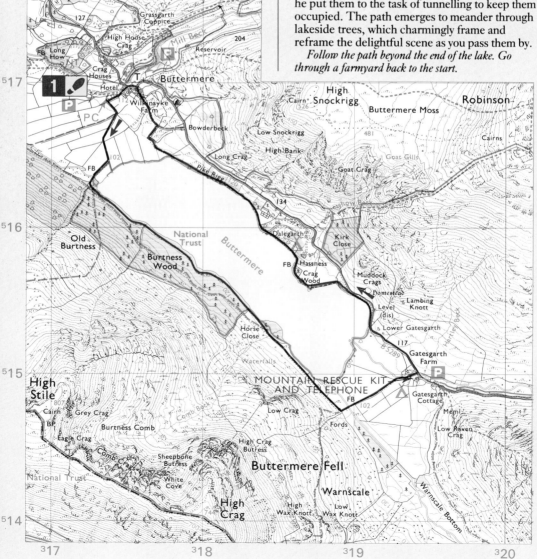

In the high forest

Allow 2½ hours, or 3½ with a detour to the summit

This walk is a steep climb on mainly good paths and tracks, through forest with occasional 'surprise' viewpoints over Bassenthwaite Lake to Derwent Water. An optional detour takes in Dodd summit (1,660ft).

The walk starts at Mirehouse car park (NY235282) which is four miles from Keswick on the Carlisle (A591) road, and on the right just inside the forest. Care is needed on the approach. The Mirehouse estate belongs to the Spedding family. The house, between the road and the lake, has strong literary connections. In the 19th century literary lions such as Wordsworth, Southey, Francis Bacon, Thomas Carlyle, Tennyson and Fitzgerald, all personal friends of the Speddings, were in varying degrees frequent visitors to the house. By the car park is the old estate sawmill, now used as a refreshment room.

Cross the footbridge by the sawmill and climb some steps and follow the path until it joins a forest road. Turn right along this road. The forest is a mixture of planted conifers and native broadleaved trees, some of which have grown naturally from self-sown seeds. The rock here is Skiddaw Slate, for Dodd is a spur from Skiddaw.

Keep on climbing, keeping to the road, which will eventually become a track. There is an optional detour along this stretch, to the summit of the Dodd. It is by a signposted path which leads off to the right of the main

The red squirrel is still found in many Lakeland woods

path. There could be some wet rock and possibly some mud to cope with. The view from the summit is exceptional, with views over the central fells from south to west. Bassenthwaite Lake is seen in full, and northwards, if it is clear, Scottish hills are visible beyond the Solway. The return to the main path is by the same route.

Continue on the forest road, descending. When it is joined by a road from the left, continue right. There are views down to Keswick through fire-breaks, and later, views over Bassenthwaite Lake. Derwent Water and Bassenthwaite were obviously one large lake following the Ice Age, but were split by silt washed from the hills during the catastrophic storms which came later, before vegetation and trees became established to stabilise the mountain slopes.

A road joins the track from the right, but continue descending. When the track bends very sharply to the left, look for and take an old track on the right which ascends a little, levels and becomes a footpath. As the ravine of Skill Beck is approached, go left to descend a footpath by its side. There is then a choice of a direct steep descent to the car park, or a longer but easier route down to the left.

WALK 3
Views from the fells

Allow at least 3½ hours

Latrigg is the nearest fell to Keswick. It rises steeply to 950ft and looks formidable. A zig-zag track leads to the summit and is easily accomplished by the reasonably healthy of all ages. The views are superb; but the weather must be clear.

The walk starts in Keswick (NY268235). Walk up Station Street by Fitz Park, round the front of the Keswick Hotel, and then round behind to go by a housing estate. Watch for a lane on the right which runs in a straight line between hedges and fences to cross the A66 by a bridge. Follow this. Go on beyond a cottage and pick up the path round the west side of Latrigg. There is a view left to Bassenthwaite Lake. After leaving the trees a good view towards Skiddaw opens up.

After a further ¾ mile the path begins to level and the Latrigg route leaves sharply to the right and zig-zags. One can rest occasionally on the way up to admire views over Keswick, but the view from the summit reveals a vast area and is breathtaking. All of Derwent Water is there in its glory, and beyond it the tree-clad crags of Borrowdale. Newlands valley is to the right of it. The high fells are in full view including Great Gable and leftwards past Scafell Pike, Bow Fell, part of the Coniston Old Man range, and mighty Helvellyn. To the right of centre are the Buttermere and Grasmoor ranges. To the north-west is Bassenthwaite Lake backed by Thornthwaite Forest. Skiddaw blocks the northern view. Its neighbour, Blencathra (Saddleback) is to its right, in the north-east.

Follow the path on towards Blencathra. After 300yds cross a stile and go left by a fence, then follow the path right towards the fringe of a wood. Here a track is reached. Follow this for about ½ mile to a metalled road and turn right. The way goes through woodland. No wood survives from the ancient forest, all has been planted, but this is what one would expect here if natural regeneration was allowed: oak and birch with an undercover of hazel. Unlike conifer woods, broadleaved woodlands allow a flora to thrive, including, in season, bluebells, anemones, foxgloves, wood sorrel, St John's worts and several species of fern. Below is the River Greta. The single track railway which once followed the river is no more.

An alternative route to the metalled road is by a footpath in the wood below. It rejoins the road 1¼ miles later. Cross the bridge over the A66. Continue for ½ mile to a T-junction. Turn left for the return to the starting point.

WALK 4
Airy Views

Allow 3½ hours

Although this walk involves a fairly steep ascent it is within the capabilities of any able-bodied person provided this route is followed. The less agile will take a little longer to complete it. Given a fine day the rewards are pure gold. Some will say that you have not seen the Lake District until you have seen the view over Ashness Bridge, and the airy view over Derwent Water and Bassenthwaite Lake from Walla Crag.

The walk starts from Great Wood car park (NY271212) which is on the east of the Borrowdale road (B5289) just over a mile from Keswick. At the back of the car park at its farther end a footpath starts left by a gate for Ashness. Follow this path up and then right along the hillside. The views over Derwent Water on the right are splendid. *The footpath finishes after about 1 mile at a minor road (Watendlath road). Go left a little way and walk above the bridge for a classic view with the bridge in the foreground and lakes and hills behind.*

Now go back to the path and after crossing the stile this time bear right and go up the hillside. Do not hurry this bit! *Follow the path upwards steadily until the summit cairn is reached.* The view is superb. Derwent Water is far below. To the south-west (left) can be seen Bow Fell, then Scafell Pike, Scafell, and Great Gable. Opposite is Catbells and behind is Eel Crag and Grisedale Pike. Northwards are Skiddaw and Blencathra, and to the south-east is the Helvellyn range. Down the crags to the left is the oddly named Lady's Rake. The story is that the Earl of Derwentwater supported the Jacobite rising of 1715 and in spite of influence in high places, was beheaded. His young wife avoided capture when she fled Lord's Island, by climbing the crag by this 'rake' (a gully).

The path continues on by a fence. Take care in steep places, otherwise there is no difficulty, and eventually a track is joined and a metalled road at Rakefoot Farm. In 200yds cross the footbridge soon seen on the left and bear right. Soon the path goes sharp left into Great Wood. Follow the path straight down to the car park.

Crossbills – highly specialised feeders of the conifer forests

Underscar · FBs · 189 · Water Works
Applethwaite · FBs
Ormathwaite
Ormathwaite Hall · Ford · Birkett Wood Farm · Mallen Dodd · Lonscale · FB
Round How · Gale Gill · P · Brundholme Wood · Ford
Ewe How · Cumbria Way · Latrigg · 368 · Cattle Grid · Dismantled Railway · Storms · MS 168
Whinny Brow · River Greta · Weir · Resrs
Sheep Pen · Briar Rigg · Greta Bank Farm · Ponto Brow · Briery · W
84 · Hospital · 109 · Windebrowe · Wk · A 591 · P · Goosewell Farm
Wks · Weir · Calvert's Bridge · Sch · High Fieldside · Stone Circle
Greta Hamlet · Fitz Parks · Mus · Hotel · Low Brigham · Brigham · 112 · Nether Place · Chestnut Hill · Fieldside · NT
Offices · Pol Sta · PO · KESWICK · C P · Sch · Fenton · Lonsties · Castle Lane
FB · Hotel · Hotel · MS · 127 · Resr · A 591 · Moor · 196

4

Cockshot Wood · Springs Wood · Castlerigg Hall Farm · Low Nest
Friar's Crag · FBs · FB · Borrowdale Road · 85 · Castlerigg · Mast · Castlerigg Farm · Nest Brow · MS · 172 · FB
Strandshag Bay · The Ings · 88 · Watson's Park · Ford · FB Ford · Rakefoot · Causeway Foot · T
Manor House (rems of) · The Butts · Lord's Island (NT) · Stable Hills · Deerclose Cottage · Pike
Rampsholme Island (NT) · Calfclose Bay · Great Wood · Snipes How
Scarf Stones · Wala Crag · 379 · Lady's Rake · Snipeshow Tarn
Derwent Water · Sheepfold · 355 · Low Moss · Bracken Riggs
Falls · Falcon Crag · National Trust · Sheepfold · Castlerigg Fell · Dodd Crag · Goat Crag
Landing Stage · Barrow Bay · 77 · Sheepfold · Bield · Sheepfolds · Sheepfolds
Barrow House · 85 · Brown Knotts · Sheepfold · Cairns · 590
Low Strutta · 55 · Ashness Bridge · High Strutta · Barrow Beck · Bleaberry Fell
P · Strutta Wood · 78 · FB · Lowcrag Wood · Cattle Grid

0 200 400 600 800 1 Kilometres
0 200 400 600 800 1000 1 2 Miles

SCALE 1:25 000

WALK 5
The Derwent Water ferry

Allow 2 hours

Derwent Water has the advantage of a boat service from Keswick working to a timetable and circling the lake in both directions. This gives easy access for walking to half the west shore and the lake head.

Take the anti-clockwise boat service from Keswick boat landings to disembark at Hawes End (NY264227). Go south along the lake shore. Nearest island is St Herbert's. Tradition has it that here was the 7th-century hermitage of the saint who was friend and disciple of St Cuthbert of Lindisfarne. Both saints are said to have died on the same day, in answer to a prayer of St Herbert's, in AD 687. Friar's Crag, at Keswick's shore, was where visiting friars embarked to visit the hermitage to receive the saint's blessing.

The path leaves the lake shore to go round a swamp and then rejoins it. Derwent Water is a shallow lake largely due to the vast amounts of silt washed into it over many centuries by seasonal floods. It means that it is the first of the large lakes to freeze in winter. The deepest part is almost opposite and two-thirds of the way across, at 72ft. The waters contain trout, perch and pike.

Keep to lakeshore path. Soon the old waste heaps of a mine are reached at Brandlehow. Vegetation and trees cover all, but the unnatural contours show that it is man made. Just above here was a profitable lead and silver mine which was worked for centuries.

The path leaves the shore at Brandlehow Bay (the point is in private ownership) and meets the shore again at Manesty Park. This land was one of the National Trust's earliest acquisitions. *The path takes a sweep round a wet area then returns, then later goes along walkways and bridges.* From the walkways is a view of some Borrowdale crags including Shepherd's, one of the most popular rock climbing crags in the country.

Join the road and in 200yds go left to landing stage after the Lodore Swiss Hotel to catch the boat back.

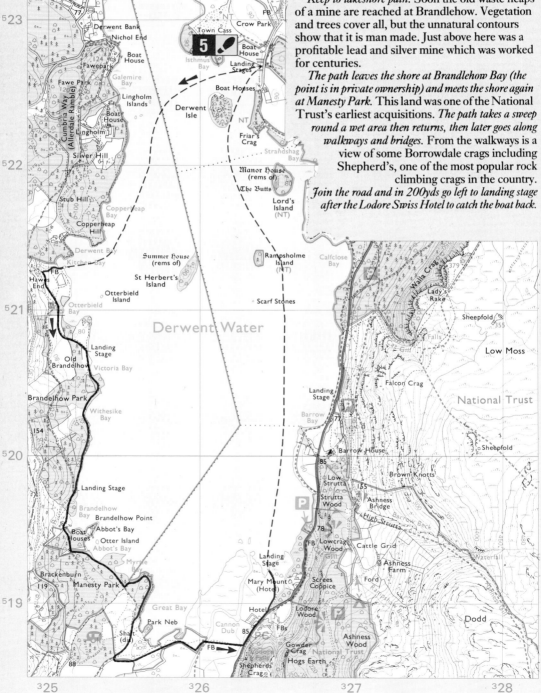

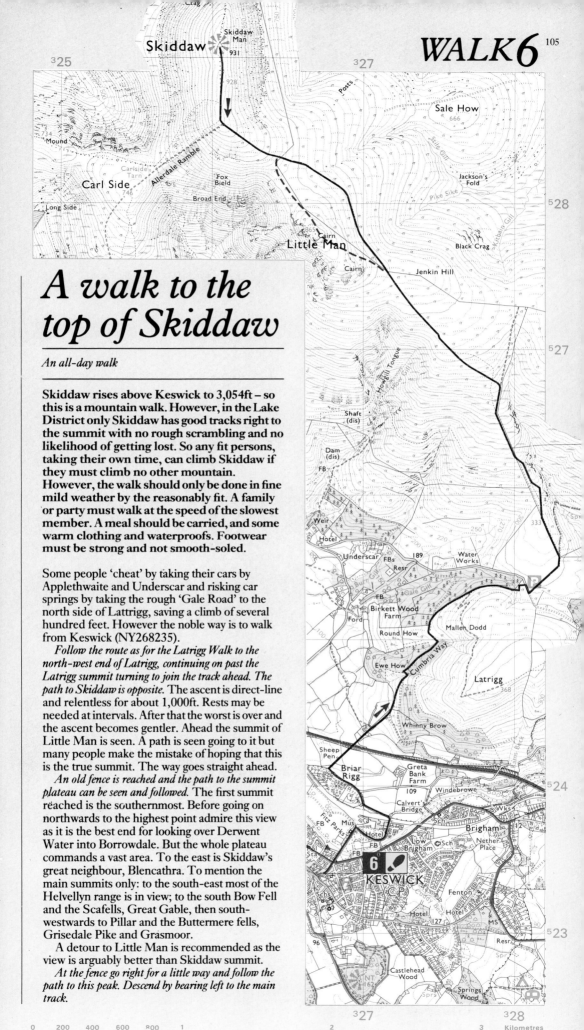

A walk to the top of Skiddaw

An all-day walk

Skiddaw rises above Keswick to 3,054ft – so this is a mountain walk. However, in the Lake District only Skiddaw has good tracks right to the summit with no rough scrambling and no likelihood of getting lost. So any fit persons, taking their own time, can climb Skiddaw if they must climb no other mountain.
However, the walk should only be done in fine mild weather by the reasonably fit. A family or party must walk at the speed of the slowest member. A meal should be carried, and some warm clothing and waterproofs. Footwear must be strong and not smooth-soled.

Some people 'cheat' by taking their cars by Applethwaite and Underscar and risking car springs by taking the rough 'Gale Road' to the north side of Lattrigg, saving a climb of several hundred feet. However the noble way is to walk from Keswick (NY268235).
Follow the route as for the Latrigg Walk to the north-west end of Latrigg, continuing on past the Latrigg summit turning to join the track ahead. The path to Skiddaw is opposite. The ascent is direct-line and relentless for about 1,000ft. Rests may be needed at intervals. After that the worst is over and the ascent becomes gentler. Ahead the summit of Little Man is seen. A path is seen going to it but many people make the mistake of hoping that this is the true summit. The way goes straight ahead.
An old fence is reached and the path to the summit plateau can be seen and followed. The first summit reached is the southernmost. Before going on northwards to the highest point admire this view as it is the best end for looking over Derwent Water into Borrowdale. But the whole plateau commands a vast area. To the east is Skiddaw's great neighbour, Blencathra. To mention the main summits only: to the south-east most of the Helvellyn range is in view; to the south Bow Fell and the Scafells, Great Gable, then south-westwards to Pillar and the Buttermere fells, Grisedale Pike and Grasmoor.
A detour to Little Man is recommended as the view is arguably better than Skiddaw summit.
At the fence go right for a little way and follow the path to this peak. Descend by bearing left to the main track.

The house of Judith Paris

Allow 2 hours 10 minutes (shorter route)
3 hours (longer route)

This walk follows a rough bridleway and involves a climb of 1,000ft. But it is by no means formidable. The reward is an excellent view over Borrowdale, and a visit to the pretty hamlet of Watendlath sitting by its own tarn in its private little valley. This is a photographer's dream. The return is by the same route, but the best views are on the return descent. There is the option of lengthening the walk to take in the idyllic heights of Brund Fell, which offers even wider prospects given clear conditions, and this is recommended with the warning that the route contends with some wet sections.

The walk starts at Rosthwaite in Borrowdale. There is a car park (NY258147) by the Institute on the Keswick side of the village. Leave the lane from the Institute, go left and cross the road then almost immediately go right over the bridge to pick up the clear bridle track to the left of Hazel Bank. Follow it all the way.

This was a packhorse route from Borrowdale by Watendlath to Wythburn at Thirlmere. Times have changed. Wythburn was drowned under an enlarged Thirlmere in 1894 to supply water to

Manchester. The need to maintain the track diminished, and the means – cheap and abundant labour – were lost during the Industrial Revolution. *The track descends to the tarn and Watendlath.* Readers of the lastingly popular Hugh Walpole novels will seek out the house by the tarn where Judith Paris – heroine of the book of the same name – lived.

Retrace steps for the return journey. The wall on the right side of the track soon leaves and climbs the fell. The diversion to Brund Fell follows it on the left-hand side. The path is at first sketchy as it crosses wet ground (if this is found to be too unpleasant, return to bridletrack and continue the return journey along it; wet ground here is a sure sign of more to follow later). Note the shattered crag on the left. *The wall is followed all the way.* There are a number of paths as walkers have hopefully tried to avoid wetness, but all follow that wall.

The wall meets a corner after ½ mile. Do not cross the stiles here but go left to follow the wall on and round an elbow. Cross the stile found here and follow the path on up to the high points ahead. Brund Fell consists of a series of craggy peaks. The appearance is novel and fascinating. No rock climb is required for the highest point (1,363ft) which offers exhilarating views northwards across Derwentwater, and southwards to the highest land in England. Nearly all of the main Lake District peaks are seen.

Retrace steps back to that last stile. Having crossed it, go right and follow the wall down for about ½ mile all the way to the bridletrack, going right for Rosthwaite. On the descent admire the views left up to the dale head. Nearest fell is Rosthwaite Fell and behind is Great End, the northern extremity of the Scafell range. To the right, across the valley, is the bulk of Great Gable.

Hayeswater – a glaciated lake

Allow 2 hours or 2½ hours

Hayeswater sits in a north-facing corrie below the mountain ridge of High Street. Twelve thousand years ago the Lake District came out of a 'mini ice age' after about five centuries of snow and ice had accumulated in large quantities in the north- and east-facing hollows, where the sun and thawing westerly winds could not reach. Small glaciers had clawed out the rock from the High Street crags, and the debris remained fast in the ice until it thawed. This debris, dropped by the melting ice, lies in 'moraine heaps', forming a natural dam to the lake. There is an option of lengthening the walk to encircle the lake, but this means crossing very wet areas.

Park in the small car park (NY410130) just beyond the village of Hartsop. This is reached by a minor road from the bend in the A592 north-east of Brothers Water. Walk straight ahead from the car park up the track. The track reaches the side of Hayeswater Gill. Away on the right is Threshthwaite Mouth. The waste heaps of old lead mines can be seen. There are a number in this area. James Clarke,

writing of Patterdale in 1787, blamed mining for the local 'decay of rural society'; miners to him were 'abandoned, wicked and profligate', seducing the innocent inhabitants into their wicked ways. But fell farming was ever precarious and any industry which brought a little wealth into the valleys was welcome.

Cross the beck by the bridge and continue up 1¼ miles with the walls to the tarn. Go right, to the lakeside, and follow the lakeshore anti-clockwise. Strictly speaking this is a tarn: a mountain lake. The difference between tarn and lake is in the edge vegetation. A lake characteristically is fringed by the common reed, while the tarn is typically fringed with the bottle sedge *Carex rostrata.*

The descent should be by the same route but can be varied by crossing the bridge over the gill by the waterworks and joining the track on the north side.

Bottle sedge is found in shallow peaty pools and other wet places

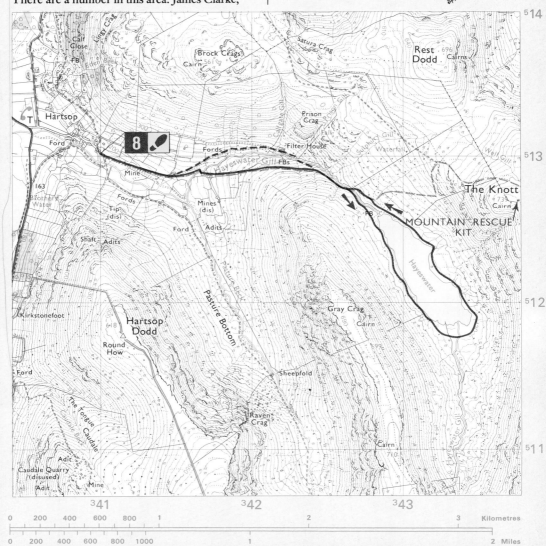

SCALE 1:25 000

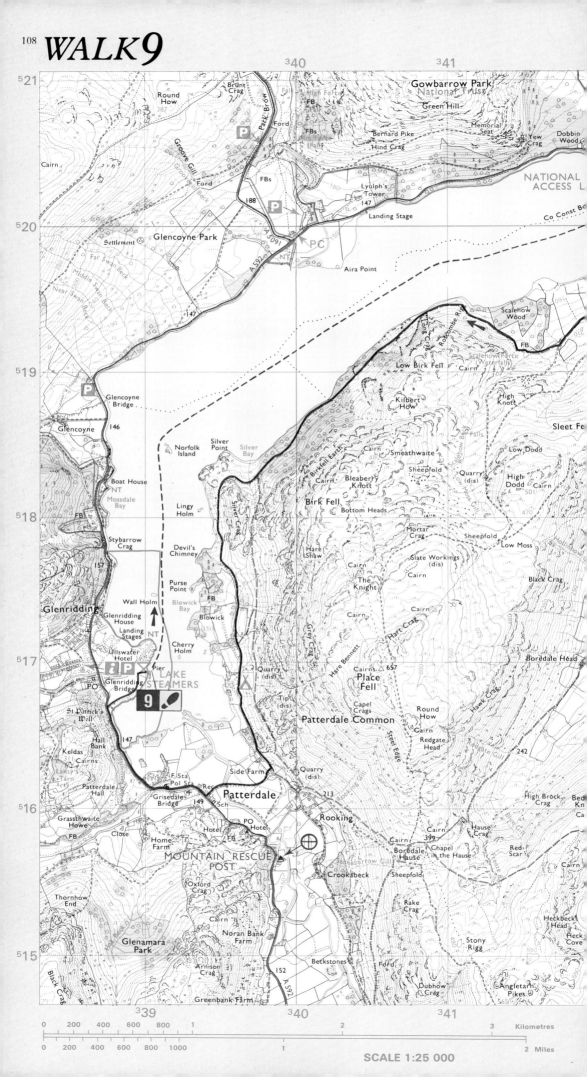

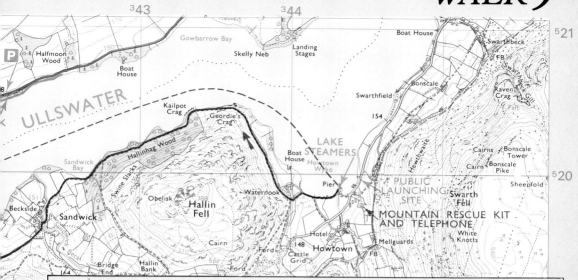

Ullswater's east shores

Allow 3 hours

This shore line and terrace walk is deservedly one of the most popular, with exhilarating views framed by lakeside trees. It is uniquely beautiful and typically Lakeland. It starts at Glenridding with a trip on the lake 'steamer' service to Howtown. Consult the Ullswater Navigation Company's timetable first. If a morning boat is caught a good idea is to take a packed lunch and enjoy a lakeshore picnic on the walk. Out of season, when the boat is not running, a car driver is needed for the trip round the lake to Howtown.

Leaving Howtown pier (NY443198) go right, along a shore path which shortly rises above the lake. After ¾ mile Geordie's Crag is reached. Just by here, across to Skelly Neb opposite, is the lake's narrowest part. At one time nets were stretched across here to catch 'schelly', a rare freshwater whitefish found only in Ullswater.

The path goes through some lovely lakeside woodland and then through a meadow, leaving the shore to join a minor road at Sandwick. Go left up the road for a few yards, then right to follow a clear path to the left of a wall. Keep right at a bridge. For a while the lake is out of view but bursts impressively into view again as the shore is neared. *The path then turns parallel to the shore on a terrace. At an open area when there is a fork keep right with the shore.* As the path rounds a crag, Helvellyn occupies much of the view. It can be seen how the retreating glaciers of the Ice Age scooped out the east-facing side of the mountain. Glencoynedale is immediately opposite. Another valley is above Glenridding where Greenside Mine at one time provided most of the jobs for the valley's workpeople. It was profitable for 200 years, producing high-quality lead before closing in 1962.

The path eventually leaves the shore and goes above a wood to follow a wall. It emerges at Side Farm and a track is taken right to Patterdale. If you have time a look into Patterdale church is recommended. Inside there are two fine tapestries depicting the Nativity and 'The Good Shepherd' set against a background of the local scenery which has just been enjoyed.

Continue northwards to Glenridding. When the pavement ends, to avoid walking in the road, take the footpath on the bank above to the left. When this finishes cross the road to a public access area, then left to the village.

A 1935 photograph of the lake steamers Raven *and* Lady of the Lake. *The inset is of a schelly, a fish unique to Ullswater*

WALK 10
The Wast Water screes

Allow 2 hours 15 minutes

Much has been made by writers of the fierce drama of Wasdale; 'horrifying', 'over-powering', is how some have described it. Indeed the view from the Gosforth road of the great mass of Wasdale Screes, 1,700ft high and apparently sliding loose into the deepest lake in England, is certainly dramatic. But Wast Water also holds its delights, and one of them is a classic view from the lake foot. This walk takes in the delight and the drama.

The char – a fish of cold, clear waters

The walk starts at Nether Wasdale (SD126040). Walk eastwards for ¼ mile to the road junction, go right and over the bridge, then immediately left along the track to Easthwaite Farm. Go left at the farm buildings. In ¼ mile at a junction in the path bear left to cross the bridge then turn right to follow the path to the lakeshore. This is National Trust land, and soon the view up the lake, framed in trees, is before you. Behind the lake are the humps of Yewbarrow, Kirkfell and Great Gable, with Lingmell, a spur of Scafell, on the right. This is a place to linger and to take photographs.

Go along the shore and in front of Wasdale Hall. The hall was built in 1826. In its early occupancy the child of the house was accidentally drowned in the lake and the area is said to be haunted by the mother and child, sometimes seen in broad daylight. The hall is now a Youth Hostel.

Emerge onto the road and walk right alongside the road for about ½ mile to the first junction. This is the often pictured scene with the Screes behind. Wast Water is about 258ft deep and was scooped out by the moving, grinding ice at the end of the Ice Age. In this action the fell opposite was undercut and it has remained at its present unstable angle for 12,000 years. Sometimes a huge mass thunders down. But local people can point out some massive boulders which have been seemingly poised precariously as far back as can be remembered. The water is very clear indeed and because it is not rich in nutrients can only be tolerated by trout and char.

Turn left and follow the roadside and in ½ mile cross the bridge at Greendale, then turn left on to a signposted footpath. Follow the path straight through until it goes between walls and emerges after 1¼ miles on to a minor road. Turn right to return to the starting point.

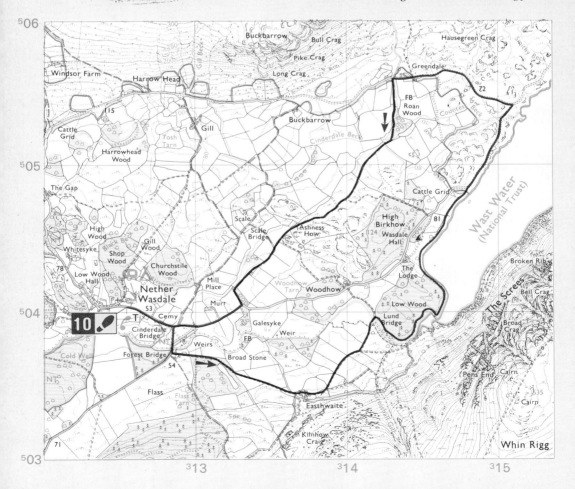

In search of solitude

Allow 3 hours

This walk demands a certain amount of stamina and a tolerance of wet ground. The return route is the most demanding. The less energetic can avoid the difficulties by returning by the outward route. Strong footwear is needed and the walk should only be done in fine weather. *Warning* – as a safety precaution lone walkers should leave details of this route with someone before setting out.

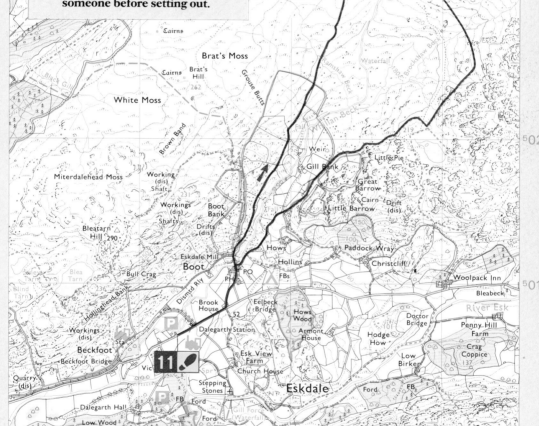

The walk starts at Dalegarth, Boot, Eskdale (NY173007). There is a car park by the terminus of the narrow-gauge railway (Ravenglass and Eskdale Railway). Walk eastwards to Boot and go left up the hamlet's one street, over the bridge and past the working water mill and up the track bearing right ahead. This was once a main communication route and you should see traces of cobbles and paved surfaces. After nearly 2½ miles the track arrives at Burnmoor Tarn past Burnmoor Lodge.

Return by the same track until a point is reached when it rises and begins to fall again. (Burnmoor Lodge is still seen on the right but might disappear beyond a rise if you go further.) Here there is a cairn and the beginning of a path which goes off through the grass to

the left. Follow this. At one point it goes across a wet section on stepping stones. It continues from there above Whillan Beck, but eventually a wooden bridge should be seen below. The approach down to it is nasty and wet. Beyond the bridge go left along the bank for a short way following the route as it climbs to a large boulder. The route is marked from this point on by white crosses on boulders. The path climbs the bank and up on to high ground to the right. It is sometimes obscure in wet places. In 1¼ miles is Eel Tarn, beautiful in high summer, when it is covered in white water lilies.

Here the path takes a sharp turn right and joins a better track going on down the valley. At crosspaths (signposted) go right to join a metalled lane which leads back to Boot.

WALK 12
Wordsworth's 'guide'

Allow 3 hours

The Duddon River valley (or 'Dunnerdale') is ten miles long from fell to sea and in that area packs a lot of varied and beautiful scenery. Wordsworth wrote fondly of the river as 'my partner and my guide' in the philosophical poem called *The River Duddon*. The poet also dedicated a remarkable series of 35 sonnets to the river. All in all, a walk with a tremendous amount to see and enjoy.

Start near the valley head from a car park (SD235995) made by the Forestry Commission by Hinning House Close. Walk along the road southwards for a short distance to a bridge on the right. This is Birks Bridge and famous for the deep clear rock pools below it, hollowed and smoothed by abrasive pebbles swept through the narrows when the river is in flood. Sometimes the floods can rise swiftly to sweep above the bridge itself.

Cross the bridge and follow the path ahead, then in 200yds fork left for Birks. Follow a forest track, bearing left for Grassguards. Go through the yard and follow the path between two typical Cumbrian stone-built walls. Leaving the forest, head for Stoneythwaite

Farm, but in ¾ mile fork left just before to descend to High Wallowbarrow. Turn left here and follow the path along a grass terrace. Go over an arch bridge. Follow the path over more small bridges to emerge at Seathwaite. Visit the church here to pay tribute to 'Wonderful Walker', mentioned by Wordsworth and others. Walker was curate here for 66 years, earning the princely sum of £50 per annum. He was farm labourer, teacher and doctor. He and his wife spun and wove their own wool to make their own clothes. He was generous to the poor and needy, yet when he died at the age of 92 in 1802 he left £200. His grave is in the churchyard and there is a memorial plaque in the church.

Go left up the road for ¼ mile then turn right between walls; keep left. In ¼ mile join a road and turn left then immediately right for Long House. Cross a bridge then go left between walls. Go on to Tongue House farmyard. From Tongue House go left along the lane for a short distance then turn right across a footbridge, past the front of the house, cross the stile and climb through the woodland. Walk on in the direction of the head of Dunnerdale and in ½ mile join the road. Turn right on to the road to return to the starting point.

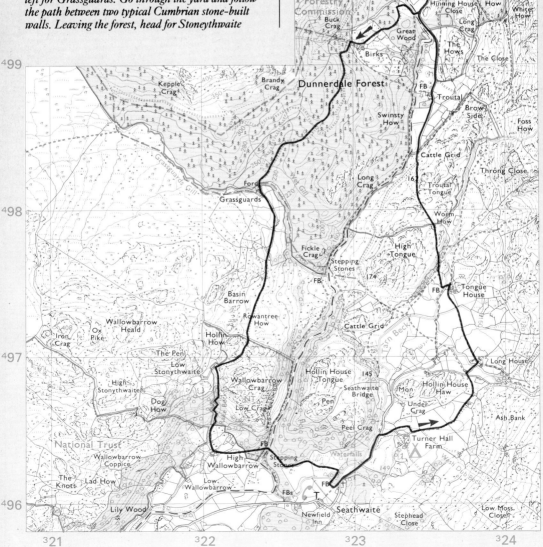

Visible history

Allow at least 3 hours

This is a fairly testing walk for those not accustomed to walking – but there are no great obstacles. Rubber boots are a good idea after wet weather. The walk visits historic Barton church before joining a Roman road with spectacular views over Ullswater.

The walk starts at Pooley Bridge (NY469244). Follow a good track (beginning just by the east wall of the Sun Inn) which travels parallel with the river for a little way before meeting it by a weir. From here the path goes through Hole House farmyard, and beyond. On reaching two gates and a kissing-gate go through the latter and follow the fence. A stile and then a gate is reached. Go left, along a short overgrown path between hedges. The path continues, bending round to the right, to cross-paths near barns (signpost). Turn left, and in 200yds cross a bridge, then turn right on to a good track towards Barton Church. First reach Barton Hall, an imposing 18th-century building. Go left through archway. Barton church, St Michael's, is well worth an inspection. The tower and the nave were built around 1150, but in 1330, when the church was in the care of Augustinian priors, the chancel was extended and wide arches were cut into the tower to allow sight and access. This gives the church a uniquely attractive feature. William Wordsworth's father is buried in the chancel.

From the church continue for ¼ mile to a T-junction, cross the road and turn right and then almost immediately turn left along a path to Celleron. The track here shortly becomes a path. There is an old lime-kiln up on the left.

There is a stile after the quarry. After climbing it go slightly left round a fence to join the road. In 50yds turn right towards a junction, then left up a minor road for 300yds before turning right up the track past Winder Hall. Note another old lime-kiln on the left.

Go through the gate after Winder Hall and bear left a little to pick up a track going south-west. This is 'Brettestrete', a road used by Iron Age man and 'improved' by the Romans. The high level was necessary to avoid the swamps and thick forests which were below. The road continues at high level for 18 miles. A detour left on to the crag, Heugh Scar, offers good views.

Ignore paths leaving to the right and continue straight on for about 1½ miles until cross tracks with a cairn and route signs is reached. Go right for Pooley Bridge. From here there are excellent views over the lower reaches of Ullswater.

0	200	400	600	800	1		2		3	Kilometres

0	200	400	600	800	1000		1			2 Miles

SCALE 1:25 000

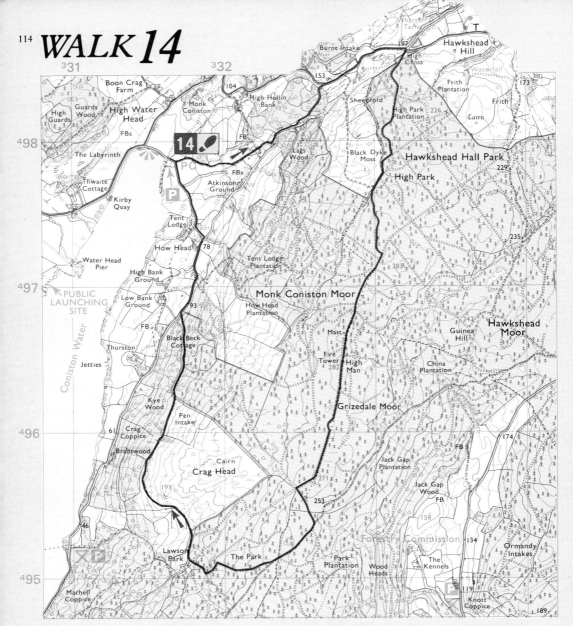

Coniston Water woodlands

Allow 2¾ hours

This is a woodland walk for most of its length, with tracks and footpaths to follow, a few wet areas to cross, and some steady climbing. The name suggests what this was: the moor of the Coniston monks. The Coniston Water area was in the ownership of Furness Abbey for four centuries and prospered from its fishing, hunting, mining and woodland industries. The moor in the abbey's days was probably open woodland inhabited by red deer – then a valuable source of meat. Descendants of those deer herds may be glimpsed during the course of the walk, especially in the early morning and the late evening.

The walk starts at Monk Coniston car park (SD316978) at the north-eastern end of Coniston Water. Walk eastwards for about 30yds then go left on a footpath between fences. At the end of the path go through a gate into a field. Cross the field, climbing to a step gate. Walk straight ahead, skirting a farmhouse and on to a minor road. Go left at the minor road to the junction with a B road and turn right. In ¼ mile, at High Cross, turn right on to a forest road. Follow this to the first junction then bear right. Continue past an open area. Here there are views over Coniston to the Coniston Old Man range.

At the next junction go left (be careful not to miss this, it appears on the left-hand side shortly before the trees again close in) and climb to a T-junction and go right. In 200yds there is a crossroads. Go straight ahead. When a forest road is reached go across it to follow a path along a fire-break between the trees. The fire-tower is passed. This is manned by foresters during fire risk periods.

In 1 mile the path finishes at a junction with a forest road. Turn left. Two junctions follow; bear right at each. The road rises, and just as it falls, look for a path going down to the right. Follow this. The path wanders down to Lawson Park. Here there is a good view over to Coniston.

Walk past the buildings on your left and bear right on to the path which leads to Coniston. This goes on through pasture above Brantwood, the home of John Ruskin from 1872 to 1900.

The way goes through a wood and joins a road. Turn right along it and in about ½ mile at the next junction turn left back to the starting point.

Ghostly quarry

Allow 4½ hours

This is a varied walk from Bowness-on-Windermere along lake shore lanes, rough tracks, hill and woodland paths.

From Bowness Pier (SD401968) walk south-west past the Information Centre and the shoreside business premises. At the far end an iron gate leads on to a footpath which goes round the lakeshore and joins the road to the ferry. Cross the lake by the ferry, disembark and walk by the buildings of Ferry House to pick up a footpath going right, by the lakeshore side of some fish tanks. This joins a lakeside road. Turn right on to this road. The metalled road finishes and becomes a track through woodland. There are fine trees here of all kinds but look especially for some very large sweet chestnuts.

The track leaves the shore as it goes round Strawberry Gardens, but continues on the other side. A shore path goes parallel with the track if preferred. After 1 mile the wall of another property is reached. This is Belle Grange. The rough track going upwards on the left was a cart road.

This is the rough track to be taken. In under ¼ mile, near the top of the hill, a path is seen joining from the left across a stream. Take this route. This climbs for a while then levels out on to a terrace walk. Shortly the path passes a hidden quarry called 'Crier of Claife' for it was here in the 18th century that a fearsome ghost which terrorised the area with its chilling screams was finally put to rest by an exorcising priest! There are one or two good viewpoints from this path.

The path comes to some rocky knolls and to a T-junction. Descend here on a path which leaves the wood to follow a woodland boundary on its left. After some wet sections the track is joined by another from the right. Continue for a further ¼ mile to a T-junction, and go left. Continue without deviation. The path dives down through a wood. After ⅓ mile watch for and take a path turning sharp right down to the shore road hiding behind buildings below. Descend and in ¼ mile join the shore road, cross by the ferry, turn left by the car park and continue by footpath and minor road past the cemetery to the pier and the starting point.

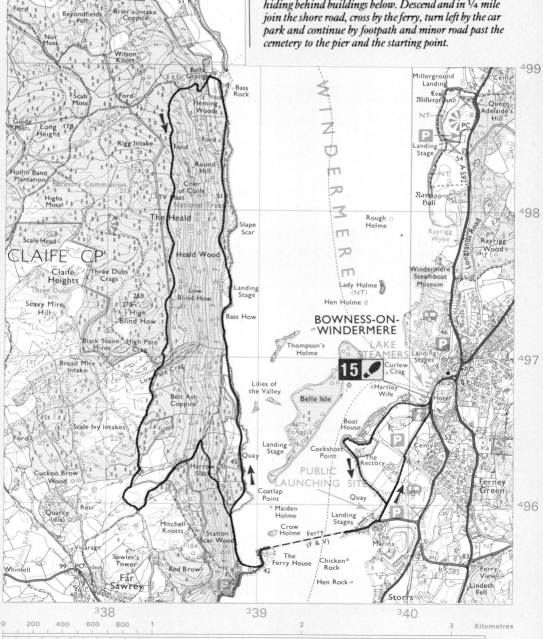

WALK 16
Wordsworth's footsteps

Allow 2 hours

The walk around Grasmere should be obligatory for all who wish to savour the true essence of Wordsworth's Lake District. It could be combined with a visit to Dove Cottage, Wordsworth's home, and the museum, which the walk passes.

From Grasmere (NY336065) take the minor road south-west for Langdale. After climbing for a mile, pass the Hunting Stile junction then watch for and go left down a path to the lakeshore. The worst part of the walk is now over. There is a pleasant walk by the waterside (National Trust land).

The walk rounds the end of the lake past a weir. Cross the footbridge into the wood opposite and bear right up a stepped footpath. After 300yds this emerges on to a field; walk on beside the river to White Moss Common. Walk up to the left and cross the main road with care. Take the minor road a little way to the left up the hill opposite. In ¼ mile, at the top of the hill, leave the road and go right on a footpath through the bracken to a viewpoint, the rocky knoll which can be seen. The prospect revealed over Rydal Water is one to linger at.

Go back to the road and continue. The wood on the right was John Wordsworth's favourite place to visit when he stayed with his brother William. John was a sea captain, who was tragically drowned at sea – the wood subsequently became known as 'John's Wood'.

At the first junction turn left. By the foot of the hill is Dove Cottage (open to the public). Here William and his sister Dorothy settled in 1799. Later William married and brought his bride here. The house got too small for a growing family and they left in 1808. However, during his time at Dove Cottage the poet wrote some of his greatest works, including the *Ode: Intimations of Immortality*, *The Prelude* and many shorter works. Next to Dove Cottage is an excellent museum and gallery. This, and the extensive library of documents and manuscripts, brings thousands of students of English Literature here from all over the world. Mention must also be made of the author Thomas de Quincey, who married a local girl and took the tenancy of Dove Cottage after the Wordsworths left.

Cross the road with care and walk back into Grasmere village. Go into St Oswald's churchyard and turn right – towards the back is the grave of the poet. William was not a modest man but he chose a modest resting place. His wife Mary is buried with him. Dora, their daughter, is in the next grave.

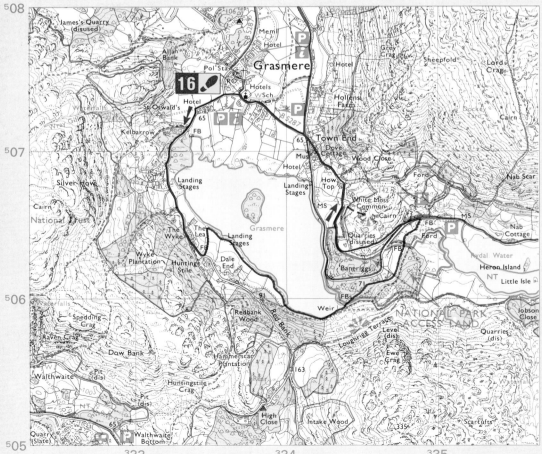

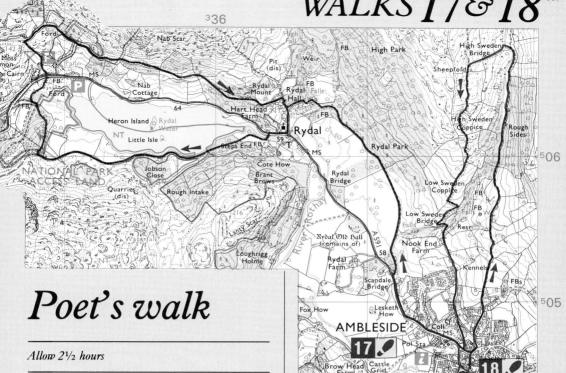

Poet's walk

Allow 2½ hours

This walk from Ambleside goes by Rydal Mount, Wordsworth's home for the last 37 years of his life; Dora's Field, where Wordsworth planted daffodils for his daughter's pleasure; and by Rydal Water, the poet's favourite lake.

Start at Ambleside (NY377046) and walk by the main road, A591, west towards Grasmere. After half a mile take the track to the right which starts beyond iron gates. This is a public path through Rydal Hall estate. Rydal Hall was the home of the land-owning Le Fleming family which made much of its fortune from the copper mines of Coniston Old Man. Sheep dog trials and the Ambleside Sports are held here.

The track goes to the right, round the hall and between buildings to emerge on to a lane. Opposite is Rydal Mount (open to the public), Wordsworth's house when he was at the height of his popularity.

Walk down the lane to the church. Wordsworth chose this site for the church but was not too happy with the result. Behind is Dora's Field – (National Trust) which is seen at its glowing best at daffodil time.

Go down to the main road, cross with care and go right. Shortly turn left down a path to a bridge. Cross the bridge and bear right through the wood towards Rydal Water. Walk along the track by the lake. Across the lake is old Nab Cottage. Here lodged De Quincey, man of letters, author of *Confessions of an Opium Eater.*

The track leaves the lake and climbs. Watch for the path going down through the wood to the right. (Before taking this path, a short diversion straight on gives a superb view over Grasmere.) *Go down the path, cross the footbridge, and go right over White Moss Common by the River Rothay. Go up and cross the road with care.* To the right of the car park opposite, a track will be seen going up the hill. *Take this for 200yds to a T-junction at the top. Turn right.* This is now the old road made long before the road in the valley bottom, and was a favourite walking route for Wordsworth.

This finishes after 1 mile at Rydal Mount. Walk back through Rydal Park.

Sweden Bridge

Allow 2½ hours

An away-from-it-all from Ambleside up tracks overhung by trees, with wide views, picturesque old arched bridges and cascading waterfalls. A steady ascent and descent of 550ft. Not for anyone in a hurry.

Start from Ambleside market cross (NY377046). Go up North Road to Kirkstone Road and after about 200yds turn left down Sweden Bridge Lane. At the next junction bear right. At the following junction turn left by Sweden Bridge Lane for High Sweden Bridge.

This was once a busy pack-pony and cart track from Ambleside to Hartsop and Patterdale. In the stone walls to the right of the path is Mountain Parsley fern, an alpine common in the Lake District and very choosy in its habitat. The wayside trees include thickets of blackthorn (sloe), hazel, rowan, and hawthorn trees. Flowers include foxglove, meadowsweet in the wetter areas, and in 'heath' type banks the harebell and the tiny yellow four-petalled flower, the tormentil (once a herb used to cure 'the torments').

In 1¼ miles cross High Sweden Bridge. A beautiful old arched bridge. Notice the water-worn rocks below.

Immediately after crossing the stream go left and then right, following an ascending path to the left of a wall. Cross the stile at the top of the rise and bear left to follow the path to a sheep fold (a small area enclosed by stone walls). Go right round a sheep pen, over a stile on the left and descend track. (Dogs on leads.) Here from the sheep pasture is a view over Ambleside and the upper part of the lake.

In ¾ mile cross Low Sweden Bridge. A larger but also beautiful bridge and waterfalls.

Follow lane down into Ambleside centre.

SCALE 1:25 000

Index

Principal entries are shown in bold type. Map references are given for each place. The National Grid referencing system is explained on page 66.

Acknowledgements

The publishers would like to thank the many individuals and organisations who helped in the preparation of this book. Special thanks are due to Cumbria County Council Archives and Planning Departments, the Lake District Special Planning Board, the South Lakeland, Allerdale and Copeland District Councils, the Cumbria and Lancashire Archaeological Unit at Lancaster University, the Cumbria Tourist Board, the National Trust, the Nature Conservancy Council and the Cumbria Trust for Nature Conservation.

The publishers also gratefully acknowledge the following for the use of their photographs and illustrations:

Abbott Hall Museum of Lakeland Life & Industry, Kendal

Ardea London (R.F. Porter, R.J.C. Blewitt, J.B. & S. Bottomley)

Martyn J. Adelman

E.A. Bowness

Heather Angel

Cumbria Tourist Board

Rick Czaja

Mary Evans Picture Library

Freshwater Biological Association

The Mansell Collection

Richard Surman

G. Wood

Fotobank

George Romney Ltd Kendal

Grasmere Gingerbread Shop

AA Publications Division Photographic Library

Other Ordnance Survey Maps of the Lake District

How to get there with the Routemaster and Tourist Series
Reach the Lake District from Manchester, Leeds or Carlisle and other parts of Northern England with Sheet 5 NORTHERN ENGLAND of the ROUTEMASTER SERIES.
Access from Penrith, Kendal, Cockermouth or Broughton-in-Furness is shown on the LAKE DISTRICT TOURIST MAP.

Exploring with the Landranger and Outdoor Leisure Maps

Landranger Series
1¼ inches to one mile or 1 : 50000 scale

These maps cover the whole of Britain and are good for local motoring and walking. Each contains tourist information such as parking, picnic places, viewpoints and rights of way. Sheets covering the Lake District are:

89   West Cumbria
90   Penrith and Keswick
96   South Lakeland
97   Kendal and Morecambe

Outdoor Leisure Series
2½ inches to one mile or 1 : 25000 scale

These maps for walkers show the countryside of Britain in great detail, including field boundaries and rights of way in England and Wales.
The maps with the walks in this book are extracted from the Outdoor Leisure Maps of the Lake District. There are four sheets in the series:

The English Lakes   NW Sheet
The English Lakes   NE Sheet
The English Lakes   SW Sheet
The English Lakes   SE Sheet